CAMBRIDGE LIBRARY COLLECTION

Books of enduring scholarly value

Literary Studies

This series provides a high-quality selection of early printings of literary works, textual editions, anthologies and literary criticism which are of lasting scholarly interest. Ranging from Old English to Shakespeare to early twentieth-century work from around the world, these books offer a valuable resource for scholars in reception history, textual editing, and literary studies.

The Life of Sir John Falstaff

Remembered for both his satirical and serious work, Robert Barnabas Brough (1828–60) was a playwright, journalist, poet and founder member of the Savage Club. Built around a series of inspired etchings by the celebrated artist George Cruikshank (1792–1878), this is a delightful fictional biography, 'from authentic sources', of that most colourful of Shakespeare's characters. We hear how our hero was descended from the great Saxon leader Hundwulf Falstaff, how the name is a corruption of 'False-thief', of his adventures with his beloved Prince Hal, and of Christmas 1412 with the Whittington family. Henry V's terrible rejection of him – 'I know thee not, old man' – is touchingly depicted, as are the episode of the laundry basket and other misadventures at Windsor, along with his sad death at the Boar's Head in 1415. First published in 1858, this book is a must-read for every lover of this larger-than-life figure.

Cambridge University Press has long been a pioneer in the reissuing of out-of-print titles from its own backlist, producing digital reprints of books that are still sought after by scholars and students but could not be reprinted economically using traditional technology. The Cambridge Library Collection extends this activity to a wider range of books which are still of importance to researchers and professionals, either for the source material they contain, or as landmarks in the history of their academic discipline.

Drawing from the world-renowned collections in the Cambridge University Library and other partner libraries, and guided by the advice of experts in each subject area, Cambridge University Press is using state-of-the-art scanning machines in its own Printing House to capture the content of each book selected for inclusion. The files are processed to give a consistently clear, crisp image, and the books finished to the high quality standard for which the Press is recognised around the world. The latest print-on-demand technology ensures that the books will remain available indefinitely, and that orders for single or multiple copies can quickly be supplied.

The Cambridge Library Collection brings back to life books of enduring scholarly value (including out-of-copyright works originally issued by other publishers) across a wide range of disciplines in the humanities and social sciences and in science and technology.

The Life of Sir John Falstaff

*With a Biography of the Knight
from Authentic Sources*

ROBERT BARNABAS BROUGH
ILLUSTRATED BY GEORGE CRUIKSHANK

CAMBRIDGE
UNIVERSITY PRESS

CAMBRIDGE UNIVERSITY PRESS

Cambridge, New York, Melbourne, Madrid, Cape Town,
Singapore, São Paolo, Delhi, Mexico City

Published in the United States of America by Cambridge University Press, New York

www.cambridge.org
Information on this title: www.cambridge.org/9781108057332

This edition first published 1858
This digitally printed version 2013

ISBN 978-1-108-05733-2 Paperback

THE

LIFE

OF

SIR JOHN FALSTAFF.

LONDON
PRINTED BY SPOTTISWOODE AND CO,
NEW-STREET SQUARE.

Sir John ffalstaff Knight

Drawn by

Wm Shakspere

Etched by

Geo. Cruikshank

London

Published by Messrs Longman, Brown, Green, Longmans and Roberts. 1857

THE

LIFE

OF

SIR JOHN FALSTAFF.

ILLUSTRATED BY

GEORGE CRUIKSHANK.

WITH

A BIOGRAPHY OF THE KNIGHT FROM AUTHENTIC SOURCES

BY

ROBERT B. BROUGH.

LONDON:

LONGMAN, BROWN, GREEN, LONGMANS, AND ROBERTS.

1858.

"Men of all sorts take a pride to gird at me: The brain of this foolish-compounded clay, man, is not able to vent anything that tends to laughter, more than I invent, or is invented on me: I am not only witty in myself, but the cause that wit is in other men."

KING HENRY IV. Part 2.

The Writer's Dedication

TO MARY E. C. BROUGH.

———+———

My dearest Sister,

The following pages represent (if nothing else) a considerable amount of labour—achieved, as you know, under the most trying circumstances—which I am mainly indebted to your sisterly care and devotion for having been able to accomplish at all.

Accept their dedication, not for their intrinsic worth, but as the only kind of testimonial of love and gratitude just now available to

Your affectionate Brother,

ROBERT B. BROUGH.

March 27, 1858.

PREFACE.

THE nature and objects of the present work require little, if any, explanation. The whole range of imaginative literature affords no instance of a fictitious personage, ranking, almost inseparably, in the public faith with the characters of actual history, parallel to that of the inimitable Falstaff of Shakspeare. Other creations of the world's greatest dramatist may be as *vraisemblable* and as vividly drawn. But the peculiar association of Falstaff with events that are known to have occurred, and personages who are known to have lived,—added to the fact that his character has been developed to greater length and with more apparent fondness than the poet was wont to indulge in,—make it a matter of positive difficulty to disbelieve that Falstaff actually lived and influenced the age he is assumed to have belonged to,—as much as to doubt that Henry the Fifth conquered at Agincourt, that Hotspur was irascible, and Glendower conceited.

It was a natural thought, then, for a modern humorist,—using the pencil and etching point as his means of expression,—a man whose competence to appreciate and illustrate the arch-humorist, Shakspeare, will scarcely be disputed — to propose to himself a series of pictures embodying the most prominent events in the imaginary career of Shakspeare's most humorous character — in which the illusion intended by the dramatist should be carried out by an attention to chronological and archæological probability of detail, in a pictorial sense, corresponding to the marvellous fidelity of historic local colour, which, surrounding the movements of Sir John Falstaff in the Shakspearian dramas, will continue (in spite of all material proof whatever) to bring the veracious records of English history during the fifteenth century into disrepute and suspicion—from the fact of their omitting all mention of Sir John Falstaff's name and achievements.

This design Mr. George Cruikshank has carried out in a series of etchings which forms the essential part of the volume now offered to the public,—with what success, it would not become the present writer— his friend and colleague—to dilate upon. It may be stated, fairly, that no pains have been spared by the artist to make his work conscientiously complete. Every locality indicated by the poet has been carefully studied either from personal observation or reference to the most authentic records—(take, for example, the views of Shrewsbury and Coventry as they appeared in the fifteenth century and the tall spire of "Paul's" before it was struck by lightning). The costumes, weapons, furniture, &c., are from the best available authorities. Had Sir John Falstaff really lived (as it must remain a matter of impossibility to persuade the majority of mankind he did not), and gone through the various experiences imagined for him by Shakspeare, it may be very safely assumed that an eye-witness of all or any of them would have observed a series of scenes very closely resembling the designs which accompany these pages.

The writer of the letter-press—in no spirit of false modesty, but in one of pure business-like candour—disclaims any share in whatever public approval the work may attract. The design was not his but the artist's;

and he has simply fulfilled, to the best of his powers, a contract, cheerfully accepted, but not drawn up by him. An imaginary biography of Falstaff, away from the scenes described by Shakspeare—supposing the kind of life that must have led up to the marvellous development of an individuality with which the poet has made us all familiar — might have been a work worthy an ambitious man's undertaking. The ambitious man would, probably, have failed to satisfy either his readers or himself,—but that is neither here nor there. The plan of this work—namely, to illustrate the life of Sir John Falstaff exclusively from the most striking passages in his career, as invented by Shakspeare — was completed by the artist ere his literary colleague was applied to for his willingly-rendered assistance. The latter claims no higher place in the transaction, than one proportionate to that of the fiddler who amuses the audience between the acts of a play, or the lecturer who talks unheeded nonsense while a panorama is unrolling.

The author may be permitted one little word of apology, and, perhaps, self-justification, for frequent breaches of punctuality in the periodical issue of the work, for which he, alone, is responsible. The concluding portion of his labours has been achieved under acute and prolonged physical suffering. This may be no excuse for loose or indifferent writing; but, in the memorable words of Ben Jonson to John Sylvester —*it is true.*

March 27, 1858

CONTENTS.

BOOK THE FIRST.

1352—1365.

BOOK THE SECOND.

1381.

BOOK THE THIRD.

1410.

CHAPTER I.

CHAP. II.

CHAP. III.

CHAP. IV.

CHAP. V.

CHAP. VI.

BOOK THE FOURTH.

1410—1413.

CHAPTER I.

CHAP. II.

CHAP. III.

CHAP. IV.

CHAP. V.

CHAP. VI.

CHAP. VII.

CHAP. VIII.

CHAP. IX.

CHAP. X.

BOOK THE FIFTH.

1413—1415.

LIST OF PLATES.

SIR JOHN FALSTAFF:

A Biography.

———◦◦◦———

BOOK THE FIRST.

1352—1365.

I.

INTRODUCTORY CHAPTER.

THE early lives of heroic personages, born at a date anterior to the invention of parish registers, police sheets, and such vehicles of subordinate renown, are usually enveloped in mystery. This remark (which is not offered merely as a specimen of the writer's originality) does not, of course, apply to that highly favoured class of heroes who may be said to be born to the business, and to note down whose earliest heroic throes and struggles official chroniclers have been retained in all ages; but exclusively to the work-a-day or journeyman hero, who has had to establish himself in the heroic line from small beginnings — who has had, as it were, to build his own pedestal in the Temple of Fame, finding his own bricks, mortar, and wheelbarrows. This kind of construction, in all ages, necessitating an immense deal of labour and application, we generally find that by the time the pedestal is finished and the hero ready to mount it, his condition of wind and limb is no longer such as to enable him to do so with any remarkable degree of alacrity; and that he has but little time and eyesight left to enjoy the prospect afforded by his eminent position. In other words, by the time a great man has acquired such dimensions as to make him an object of public attention, it is generally at the moment when—like an over-blown soap-bubble—he is about to collapse into nothing. And what man who has travelled to distinction on foot cares—when he has changed his boots—to talk or be reminded of the mud he has walked through?

These reflections are peculiarly applicable to the case of SIR JOHN
FALSTAFF, — the individual hero whose career it will be the business of these
pages to trace. That great man, at the date of those sayings and achievements which have gained him a world-wide celebrity, was — in spite of his
pardonable reluctance to admit the fact — already advanced in years. His
own accounts of his early life are meagre in the extreme, and, justice compels
us to add, by no means authentic. They are, in fact, confined to a rather
vague statement, that he was "born at three o'clock in the afternoon, with
a white head," and other physical peculiarities, which would lead to a suspicion that the knight was not wholly free from a weakness common to great
men of his epoch, namely, an ambition for the doubtful honours of a prodi-
gious birth. A further assertion of early injuries, received through too assi-
duous application to certain ecclesiastical duties, must be regarded as equally
apocryphal. Of the place of his birth, he makes no mention whatever;
nor do we find, in his admirable conversations immortalised by the historian
Shakspeare — to whose dramatic chronicles we shall frequently have to
confess our obligations in the course of this history — any allusion to the
character and circumstances of his parents.

But should the Biographer recoil before this merely negative obstacle of
barrenness, at the outset of his researches — as though a traveller, with his
mountain goal in sight, should sit down and despair because he sees the plain
beneath obscured by intervening mists ? Has not the difficulty of finding a
needle in a bottle of hay (which, by the way, has always appeared to us a
remarkable article to be kept in bottle) been greatly exaggerated ? All you
have to do, is to make sure that the needle is really in the bottle. Patience
and a microscope will lead you to its discovery. It may be stated that
between Sir John Falstaff and a needle there is not much resemblance, and
that an allusion to anything microscopic in his case is inappropriate. We
merely anticipate the objection that we may pass it over. The fact that
our knight lived to the age of threescore odd is a proof (by induction) that
he must have been born somewhere, and at a date anticipatory by some
sixty odd years of that of his death. That he had the usual number of
parents is at least probable. That he had received a good education, for his
time, we have ample proof. These are great data to go upon. The needle
is in the bottle. All we have to do, is to separate carefully the musty hay of
antiquity, aided by the glass of investigation ; to plunge boldly into the
mists of contradictory evidence, and push our way patiently till we get to the
mountain, — which, with the full length and breadth of Mr. George Cruikshank's faithful historical portrait on our opening page before us, is perhaps
a better image than the needle.

Reader! think not that we are going to trouble you to hunt with us. Deem not that we should have presumed to appear before you till we had found the needle, and cleared it from the last hayseed. Like Mohammed, of the Arabian desert, — or Mr. Albert Smith, of the Egyptian Hall, — we have been to the mountain; and, imitating the more modern popular leader, appear before you, wand in hand, ready to describe the particulars of our ascent, with illustrations. The amplest materials for the Life of Sir John Falstaff are in our possession—from his birth, even to the date of that morning when, at three of the clock, a small white head (we reject the accompanying phenomena) made its first appearance in the world; to his boyhood, —where the moving panorama will pause awhile, at the court gate, to show you Thomas Mowbray's page breaking Skogan's head, on that doubly memorable day that also witnessed an encounter between Master William Shallow and Sampson Stockfish, a fruiterer; on, past his summer of manhood, to his glorious autumn, when our knight reaped sheaves of golden renown at Gadshill and at Shrewsbury; to that second Indian summer, when Sir John Falstaff, round and glorious as the harvest moon, could still attract the gilding rays of sunny Mistress Page's view; down to that cold winter night, between twelve and one—e'en at the turning of the tide! —when those fingers that of old had grasped the hilt and managed the target, fumbled with the sheets and played with flowers—when that voice that had been the mouthpiece of Wit itself, the igniting spark of wit in others, could only babble of green fields—till Sir John Falstaff's feet grew cold as any stone, and so upward and upward till all was as cold as any stone, even as that which careless, laughing workmen fell to hewing and chipping on the following day!

And where found we all this knowledge? It is no matter. In the pursuit of our task, we shall reject the pitiful, inartistic plan of modern historians, who are ever in such trepidation to stop you with their authorities, (as though a man should wear his tailor's receipt pinned to the collar of his coat, to show that the garment has been honestly come by!) but will rather imitate the independent manly fashion of the old chroniclers, who told their stories in a simple, straightforward manner, never caring to say whence they had them, but throwing them down in the world's face, like the gages of honest, chivalrous gentlemen, whose word might not be questioned. This rule we intend observing scrupulously; except, indeed, on occasions of necessity, when we may think proper to deviate from it.

Our edifice once raised, we have removed the scaffolding. The public is invited to enter.

II.

BIRTH AND GENEALOGY OF SIR JOHN FALSTAFF.

John Falstaff was born in the city of London, at the Old Swan Tavern, near the Ebgate Stairs, at the north end of London Bridge, on the 23rd of January, 1352. It is to be regretted that the place of his birth, which, though much decayed, and frequently altered, retained its ancient name and usage for more than three centuries after the event which shed such lustre on its humble walls, should have been destroyed in the great fire of London ; whereby, as is well known to antiquarians, the wharves and buildings in that part of the town were burnt down to the water's edge. By those who believe in idle presages, this circumstance of birth in a tavern will be deemed prophetic of a life foredoomed to be for the most part spent in such places, and, indeed, to end in one. But such vain speculations are as unworthy the historian's attention as their conclusion is anticipatory of his object.

For the extreme minuteness of the details we have been so fortunate as to acquire on this important event,—even to a special mention of the very room in which our hero's first cry was heard,—we are indebted to the accidental preservation of a family letter. The publication of this document entire, with necessary orthographical and idiomatic modifications, will not merely simplify this portion of our biographical studies, but will also afford the biographer an early opportunity of asserting the independent course he means to pursue, by setting at glorious defiance the rule laid down by himself for his own observance in the closing remarks of the foregoing chapter.

𝔗𝔬 𝔪𝔶 𝔟𝔢𝔯𝔶 𝔡𝔢𝔞𝔯 𝔰𝔴𝔢𝔢𝔱 𝔚𝔦𝔣𝔢, 𝔱𝔥𝔢 𝔏𝔞𝔡𝔶 𝔄𝔩𝔦𝔠𝔢 𝔉𝔞𝔩𝔰𝔱𝔞𝔣𝔣, 𝔬𝔣 𝔉𝔞𝔩𝔰𝔱𝔞𝔣𝔣 𝔦𝔫 𝔎𝔢𝔫𝔱.
𝔗𝔥𝔦𝔰 𝔴𝔦𝔱𝔥 𝔥𝔞𝔰𝔱𝔢.

"Written at the Gate-house, in Westminster, Jan. 24. 1353.

" My dear Sweet,—I think I am the most wretched man in all England, I and no other am he. I must fain tell you the truth, which, in my great love and care for thy sweet peace, I have hitherto kept back, and would have done, cost me what might, had it been longer possible. I lie here at the suit of one Bruno, a Longobard, for a pitiful sum I was constrained to borrow of him, and for which he exacts fifty in the hundred usury. And for a miserable debt like this*, am I to be made wretched, and kept from my dear wife and child ? Did I not say I was the most unhappy wretch in England ? Oh ! pity me, my dear wife ; I am here in a foul room, with greasy rogues and villains. If I send out for civet to sweeten the

---

* It is worthy of remark that Sir Gilbert does not admit his lady so far into his confidence as to mention the amount.

air, the knaves rob me in my exchange, and bring me in foul stuff. Truly I am in the hands of thieves and robbers; for they charge me sixpence the quart for thin drugged wine, when the best Gascon wine is but fourpence the gallon in the Vintry. Thou seest how impossible it is for me to send thee the money thou dost require. Already have I shortened my gold chain by four links, for meat and drink. I may not part with more, for there be here confined certain gentlemen of the court, before whom I am fain to keep up my estate. But for all their gentility, I suspect some of their number to be no better than false knaves and coggers. For last night, they decoyed me, through my distraction and unbearable misery on thy account, into play, and stripped me of my last gold Florence, as I do think by foul means. Oh, my dear wife! how thankful thou shouldst be to be spared the sharing in my troubles! Do not grieve nor fret at the thought that they were brought on by my great love for thee, as indeed they were; for was it not my zeal to have thee make a figure at court that first got me in such debt? But have I not cheerfully borne all for thee, — as thy love hath indeed well merited? Did I consider my rank and ancestry when thou didst witch me with thy rosy cheeks and blue eyes, though but the daughter of a low-born trader? Nay! I must dwell on it, for methinks thou dost sometimes rate my love too low. Did I not bear with thine ignoble kinsmen, till they took to reviling and slighting me? I believe thou art a changeling, thou pretty rogue! and none of their blood. I meant not to tell thee of this, but I am on the matter, and it must needs out. Yesterday, on my arrest, being at the end of my wits what to do, I sent a boy to thine uncle Simpkin the Tanner, saying, that in time of suffering, ill blood should cease, and I would be willing to forget all past differences so that he would come and release me with his surety. I shame to write his answer; but that thou shouldst know, for once and all, from what a churlish stock thy good fortune hath rescued thee, it must needs be told. He sent back word, that he had thought Sir Gilbert Falstaff had forgotten all past differences long ago, including a difference of a hundred and fifty golden marks; meaning the paltry sum I had of him on my receiving the grant of arms from the King's Majesty, whom heaven preserve! I could have wept for shame and vexation.

"And yesterday, our dear little Jack was a twelvemonth old! Pretty fellow, and I not near him, to load him with sweets and knick-knacks! He should go ever in Italian velvet and Flanders lace, had I my will. Thou shouldst know this, wife, without telling; and I own (though 'tis rarely I have to chide thee) there seemed lack of love and thoughtfulness in thy vexing me about trifling things amid all my troubles. With a heart breaking for lack of kindliness and sympathy, I get a letter tormenting me about such petty grievances as hose and blankets. This was selfish, wife! The worst part of the winter is past, and the boy's homespun coat will serve well with a little piecing and darning; and for nether stocks, there is nothing like knitted wool. I must indeed urge thee to thrift, wife. It doth not behove a fallen house like ours, to waste in outward vanities; except, indeed, the wretched master, who is compelled to keep up a show in courts and cities. Thou knowest well the shifts I have been put to, to pass for a man of a hundred pounds a year, and avoid the sumptuary law. But these things are riddles to thee. I believe thou wouldst submit to see me forbidden the use of silk, gold, and silver, in my garments. Thou wouldst be content to see a man of my standing restricted to two courses of three dishes each. Well, it is not thy fault, but that of thy training.

"I would forgive thee in a greater matter than this, my sweeting, for the great love I bear thee; but I am nigh distracted with my sorrows, and know not what I write. Had it not been for those gentlemen knaves, who carried me to play with them last night (may the foul fiend seize them!), I should have gone mad. I thought of that time twelvemonth. The whole matter stood, as it were, on a picture before me. I remembered our landing at the Ebgate stairs, from the boat we took at Deptford, when thou wast taken ill. Say what thou wilt, thou shalt never persuade me but it was thy violence of temper hastened thy trouble. Thou wast well enough till it proved that I had brought thee to London without money, or preparation for thy condition. I acted (as I always do) for the best. Were there not brave rejoicings at Court, in honour of the new-founded order of knighthood, that I wished thee to see? and how could I get the money I wanted, from the churl, thy brother, which he refused, without thy presence ? Thou dost not know, and never wilt know, what I suffered for thee at that time. I was too much moved to lend a hand, as they bore thee from the boat into the Old Swan. When they had taken thee up stairs, the hostess had to ply me with strong waters, in her little room, for more than an hour. They told me afterwards, I did nothing but exclaim, many times, ' The Flagon, — where the Flemish bed is ! ' which I had heard them name as the chamber thou wast to be carried to, and wherein our dear little Jack was soon afterwards born. (I pray you send down to Dame Cackle's orchard, and beg two of her finest last year's pears, the which present to master Jack as the gift of his good father.) How I rushed out of the house when I heard thy cries ! I know not where I went, nor what company I fell into. I was as one possessed. And oh ! what agonies I endured during the five days afterwards, when I was kept from visiting or having news of thee, through a rumour of the great pestilence breaking out again near London Bridge, for fear of bringing contagion in with me, which in thy weak state would have been fatal. Well ! we shall all have our reward. But when I reflect that, during that trying time, none of thy heartless kinsfolk came near thee, I could even—— but 'tis no matter.

" But first to get me out of this accursed place. If I have not fifty silver marks by Wednesday, I am a dead man. I cannot longer endure the knowledge of thine unprotected state. Thou hast no great need of thy cramoisy velvet gown in thy secluded life. Lambert can dispose of it secretly in Sandwich, where we are not known. (Thou seest I am thoughtful to spare thee shame.) Let him also ride to Canterbury, with thy golden bracelets, and little Jack's baptism cup and trencher. They will fetch together some ten silver marks. Thou canst borrow twenty marks from Dame Adlyn, the yeoman's wife. In times like these, we must not be over nice ; and I withdraw the prohibition I have laid on this good woman's visits to Falstaff. Thou mayest even call her gossip at a pinch. Make up the rest as thou canst. Lambert himself must have saved money in our service. Promise him increase of wage (though, indeed, the last three years have been indifferently paid), and dwell upon a vassal's duty to his lord. At any rate, I *must have the money*. When thou hast raised it, let Lambert gallop post to London, and spare no expense, in order that he may arrive not later than Wednesday, for the river is already frozen over, and if the frost holds, there are to be sports on the ice, with the king and all the princes present, which I would not miss for a barony.

" I would answer thine inquiries about the blankets and under-clothing, but it is so cold in this detestable place, that I can no longer hold a pen. Happily thou art spared this.

" I commend thee to the care of Heaven, my beloved wife.

" GILBERT FALSTAFF,
" *Eques et armig.*" *

This Gilbert Falstaff was the tenth in lineal descent from Hundwulf Falstaff, the great Saxon leader who performed such signal service to William Duke of Normandy, on that prince's memorable invasion of England, and of whose exploits and succession it behoves us here to speak.

A numerous and well-armed troop of patriotic English noblemen had been enrolled some weeks for the purpose of resisting the invaders, but had been detained, debating, in a truly English manner, as to the constitutional means

---

* This remarkable epistle (which is justly esteemed the gem of the Strongate Collection) appears rather to have owed its preservation to the fact of its being scrawled on the backs of leaves torn out of a costly illuminated chronicle of the period — the authorship of which is apocryphal, — than to any intrinsic merit of composition. This fact may be accepted as significant of the hereditary Falstaff character. — ED.

of choosing a leader, till news reached them of the landing of the Norman, at a distance of a hundred and fifty miles from their camp. They were about to disperse in a panic, when Hundwulf Falstaff appeared suddenly amongst them, and, by dint of much eloquence,—also, it must be added, of some secret influences in the camp, wherein he had skilfully introduced his agents,—succeeded in rallying these disheartened warriors, and inducing them to accept him as their leader. He led them by forced marches to the Isle of Thanet, where they bivouacked in a chalk pit; expecting to come up with the main Saxon army encamped near Hastings, under prince Harold, who was notoriously in want of soldiers, on the following day. Here, while divested of their armour—as had been preconcerted between Falstaff and Duke William—they were fallen upon by a superior body of Normans and cut to pieces.

For this admirable piece of generalship and loyalty, whereby the victorious Normans were spared the opposition of some hundreds of warriors, the flower of English chivalry, Hundwulf Falstaff—contrary to the general treatment of the Saxon proprietors—was allowed not only to retain his own lands (his title to which had, indeed, been disputed in favour of his nephew, Essel Falstaff, who, serving under his uncle, had been engaged in the action of the chalk pit, and died, leaving no issue), but to add to them the possessions of many gentlemen, his neighbours, who had perished in the glorious engagement above mentioned.

The Falstaff estates, on the settlement of the land, were found to be as spacious and wealthy as those of many powerful barons. Nevertheless, their holder was not suffered to take the rank of nobility, an honour he had been led to expect: nay, on his humble petition for the lesser dignity of knighthood—backed by a memorial of his services to the crown—he was informed that he should think himself fortunate to be allowed to retain possession of his estates, and that the honours of chivalry were not for a False Thief like him.

This *sobriquet* of *False Thief* stuck to him, and has been by many writers asserted to be the origin of the family name—corrupted into *Fals-taff*. Nothing is easier of refutation. In the first place, it is improbable that a gentleman should voluntarily adopt, as his family title, a term of ignominy and reproach. Moreover, the name is known to be of ancient Saxon origin, derived from *Fel-staf*—felling-staff, or cudgel; clearly tracing the antiquity of the house as far back as those barbarous times when the savage German warriors took their names from their favourite weapons. There is a curious old record (in the Strongate Collection), of the time of Edward the Elder, in which one Keingelt Felstaf appeals to the brethren of a Sodalitium, or fraternity of mutual protection, whereof he is a member, to subscribe two marks apiece towards the liquidation of a fine levied on him for the murder of three ceorles, which he is unable to pay, owing to the straitened circumstances of his family. He adds, that there is another fine against him for a like offence; but the victim in this case being only a Welchman, he believes he will be able to meet it without assistance.

Hundwulf Falstaff died in 1088, at the age of fifty-four, it is supposed of a broken heart, caused by the ingratitude of a monarch whom he had so efficiently and loyally served, aggravated by the unnatural conduct of his two daughters, whom, in pursuance of his cherished scheme of attaching himself to the Norman aristocracy, he had bestowed in marriage, with the dowry of a substantial estate apiece, on two poor knights of Guienne, — Philip le Borgne and Hugues le Bossu (surnamed Bandylegs). These ladies immediately after their marriage deserted their munificent parent for the gaieties of a court life ; refusing even to recognise him in the public thoroughfares, except on pressing occasion for pecuniary assistance. The Falstaff possessions were further crippled in this reign by repeated gifts to divers Norman noblemen, who being chivalrous gentlemen, with an instinctive abhorrence of wrong, got up frequent agitations against Hundwulf ; suggesting to their monarch the propriety of hanging up that chieftain for his glaring political immorality, and distributing his estates among themselves — men of spotless integrity. These agitations generally broke out at a time of national pressure, and Hundwulf found no means of allaying them but the one already alluded to. Thus, early after its acquisition, were the seeds of decay sown in the very system of the great Falstaff estate ; which, as the sequel will prove, may be likened to a strong man attacked with a mortal disease, who may live and struggle for years, but whose every effort to recover strength serves to hasten his dissolution.

The Falstaffs, in every reign, were staunch courtiers. Hundwulf's son and successor, Aymer de Falstaffe (the name had been Gallicised by his father), was a great favourite with William the Second, by whom he was knighted. In proof of the good fellowship that existed between the monarch and subject, the latter is not merely known to have lent his royal master repeated sums of money (which, owing to the troubles of the reign, were never accounted for), but is rumoured to have embraced the Jewish religion with that humorous monarch. This calumny remained as a stigma on the family for three generations, to the great annoyance of its representatives. Any suspicion, however, of leaning to the tenets of Judaism was triumphantly refuted in the reign of Henry the Second, by Roger de Falstaffe (fourth in descent from Hundwulf), who, lacking the means of keeping up his dignity at court, entrapped two travelling Jews into his castle, whom, with a view to making them divulge the secret of their hidden treasures, he placed upon hot plates over a slow fire, having previously extracted their teeth, according to the custom of the period. The cries of these wretches (who, with the obstinacy of their race, declared they were only poor Jewish youths, driven out of the Empire and in search of help from a wealthy kinsman in London) attracted the attention of a passing troop of King Henry's private guards. The leniency of that monarch towards the Jews has been commented on with due severity by the clerical writers of the period. It is certain that his persistent protection of those outcasts, in their lives and properties, was difficult of explanation to all well-disposed thinkers of that time, except on the ground of an utter absence of religious principle. Be that as it may, the king's guards besieged Falstaff Castle, and took the two Jews off the fire ere they were half done. Roger was tried for the offence, and sentenced to perpetual banishment, with confiscation of his estates.

Peter de Falstaffe, his son, followed Cœur de Lion to the Crusades ; and, in consideration of faithful services, was reinstated by that monarch in the possession of a considerable portion of his inheritance. Peter, who was an enthusiastic hero-worshipper, imitated his lion-hearted benefactor in everything — even to adopting the Royal mistake of wishing to be thought a poet. It was a received maxim among the critics of the period, that there was only one man living· capable of writing worse poetry than the king's — that man being Peter de Falstaffe. Falstaff Park, in his time, was known by the ignominious title of Fiddler's Green, in allusion to the droves of minstrels, troubadours, and illuminators who, with their wives and families, flocked to enjoy the munificent hospitality of Peter's mansion, where (strangely belying their ancient nomadic reputation) they took up their quarters as a permanency. Peter died in 1132, much in debt to the Gascon merchants of the Vintry, and deeply regretted — by the minstrels and illuminators.

The first act of Haulbert, his son, was to clear the premises of those gifted occupants ; in which work of ejection he was assisted by a faithful bulldog. He administered to his father's literary effects by tying them up in a bundle, and disposing of them for something under the cost price of the vellum to a Lombard broker in the city of London.

There is a blank in history as to the fate of Haulbert. He is known to have been a man of violent character, and to have died somewhere towards the end of Henry the Third's reign. In this reign, several noblemen and country gentlemen were executed for highway robbery.

Henry Falstaff (son of Haulbert, and seventh in descent from Hundwulf), in the time of Edward the First, restored the family name to its ancient spelling. Inspired by the successful efforts of this prince to fuse the various elements of the nation into one common English whole, he attempted to restore the old Saxon ways on his estate. He called himself Hengist; and, amongst other obsolete institutions, revived the Hirlas Horn, with the customs of Drink Hael and Waes Hael. These—by way of enforcing precept by example—he made frequent use of in his own person; till, like many other inventors and reformers, he fell a victim to his own devices. His death, however, was accelerated by a singular circumstance. He had a number of brass collars made, intending to fix them about the necks of his tenantry, or, as he preferred to consider them, his ceorles, after the manner of the ancient Saxon proprietors. Meeting with a prosperous farmer on his estate, one Snogg, the son of Huffkin, he requested the latter to kneel down that he might affix the badge of servitude, which, he assured him in the blandest and most engaging manner, was the old English way of doing things. Snogg replied, that he knew another old English way of doing things, namely, the way to give anybody a good thrashing who attempted any liberties with a free-born Briton. Snogg explained this method of proceeding in a practical manner, and left his landlord (already enfeebled by copious reference to the Hirlas Horn) for dead on the field. Snogg's life was declared forfeit; but as he was very popular among his labourers, and had some excellent pitchforks at his disposal, he succeeded in keeping the forces of the sheriff at bay for a considerable period, receiving the extreme unction at the age of ninety-seven, in the reign of King Edward the Second.

Uffa, son of Hengist Falstaff, was a wit, and court favourite in the reign of Edward the Second. None of his good things have been preserved; but as a proof that his facetious powers were of no mean order, it is on record that towards the close of Edward's reign he received a crown from the privy purse for making that unhappy monarch laugh; an achievement which, considering his Majesty's lively position at the time, could not have been easy. What the exact jest was is unknown; but it seems to have been levelled at Roger Mortimer, the leader of the queen's faction. For, on the seizure of the king's person, as Falstaff (dreading the resentment of the victorious party) was hastening to conceal himself on his estate, he was arrested by Mortimer himself, at the head of a troop. On being told the name of his prisoner, Mortimer said, " So! this is the knave who got a crown for a jest at my expense. He owes me a crown in common equity; and by the Lord he shall pay it. Let his head be lopped off straightway." Which sentence was put into immediate execution.

The above anecdote is in part mentioned by Hume.

Geoffrey Falstaff, son of the sprightly but ill-fated Uffa, lost a limb in the

Scottish wars, wherein he had greatly distinguished himself. Thus incapacitated from further service in the field, he resolved to devote himself to the improvement of his estate — which, to be sure, stood in need of something of the kind. The manner in which he set about the undertaking is characteristic. He ordered William of Wykeham, the celebrated architect (then engaged in rebuilding the king's palace at Windsor), to construct for him, on the site of the old tumble-down family mansion, — which, though dignified by the name of castle, was merely a dilapidated old Saxon grange, frequently altered and added to at the caprice of its successive owners, — a baronial residence, fit for a man of his rank and fame. William drew out his plans, and the works of demolition and reconstruction were set in hand. A splendid tower, which was to form the corner of an immense quadrangle, to be surmounted by a donjon keep in the centre, was all but finished, when it was discovered that money and building materials were no longer forthcoming. Geoffrey — always a bad accountant — was with difficulty made to understand that the mortgage or even sale of his entire possessions would not suffice to meet the cost of erecting two sides of the proposed quadrangle. As the good knight's building mania had already reduced his estate to a bare sufficiency for the maintenance of his household, the design was reluctantly abandoned. Fortunately, the main portion of the old structure had been left standing for purposes of temporary accommodation. The solitary tower with William of Wykeham's bill (in an unreceipted condition) were preserved by the family as colossal monuments of Geoffrey's magnificent intentions.

Geoffrey's son and successor was the father of our hero, that Gilbert Falstaff of whose character and financial condition a glimpse has been already obtained from his own writing. As he will appear personally in our narrative, we will dismiss him for the present with a brief allusion to his marriage. For the most part, the early Falstaffs seem to have married into the poorer branches of noble families, in order to support their aristocratic pretensions. This being impossible in Gilbert's case, owing to the scantiness of his patrimony, he wisely resolved on reversing the rule, and disposing of the honour of his alliance. He espoused Mistress Alice Bacon, the daughter of a wealthy merchant of the Wool Staple. The dower of this gentlewoman established the house of Falstaff — for some months at any rate — in a position of something like comfort and solvency. Sir Gilbert never ceased to remind his lady of the great sacrifice his love for her had induced him to make, in bestowing on her his name and protection. He was at the pains to do this, in order that she might feel assured he had made such sacrifice willingly, and to prevent her debt of gratitude to him from being burdensome.

There seem to have arisen no collateral branches of the Falstaff family.

The circumstances of the house, generally, make it improbable that there should have been any material provision for its younger sons. These seem usually to have left home, at an early age, to seek fortune; and as there is no record of any of them having found it, we must conclude that the evil genius of their race pursued them, and that they met with various dooms among the bands of free lances, condottieri, Brabançons, crusaders, rapparees, pirates, sheepstealers, rogues, thieves, and vagabonds, with which the history of those ages abounds.

III.

OF THE TRICK PLAYED BY LITTLE JACK FALSTAFF ON SIR THOMAS MOWBRAY
AND HIS FOLLOWING ; AND HOW JACK WAS CARRIED AWAY TO LONDON.

There is no merrier place in all Merry England — for it shall not lose the well-earned nickname, in spite of commercial enterprise and political economy — than the county of Kent ; that rosiest of the fair country's cheeks, which she so artfully presents on the side whence visitors first approach to salute her ; where the giant hops grow like Garagantua's vineyards, and where the larks fly about the tall corn nearly as big as partridges : the county of all counties, that is famous for fair maids, monstrous cherries, and all things that are ripe, ruddy, and wholesome !

Five hundred years ago, in the very heart of this laughing district, Falstaff Castle — or Folly, as it was irreverently styled by the neighbours — stood, at a distance of some twelve miles from the sea, and seven or eight from what was by courtesy called a road from Dover to Canterbury.

It was a quaint old building — situated in a wide, flat valley, between low, sloping hills. The site appeared too well chosen to have been the selection of any of the thriftless, blundering race who had held the soil for so many generations. Rumour, indeed, asserted that the estate had been wrested by an early Falstaff (taking advantage of an invasion of the heathen Danes to make war upon the professors of Christianity) from an order of Saxon monks. The rich surrounding plains — nicely watered by a brisk, gurgling stream, on the surface of whose waters the word "trout" was written in letters of burnished silver — and the thickly wooded uplands, certainly made it a very likely looking monastic site. Still, as the building itself presented no trace of ecclesiastical architecture, Rumour might be safely defied on this question.

The house was an old three-sided, one-storied Saxon grange, enclosing a quadrangle. Its original form, however, was not easy of detection at a glance. Here and there, where the thatched roof had fallen in, some ambitious proprietor had run up a turret, apparently with no other design than that of "playing at castles." In one place, a Gothic transept had been attempted, with a tolerably handsome mullioned window; but the hall, which the window had been intended to illuminate, not having been constructed, that ornament had been backed up with slanting thatch, and served only to enlighten the family cows, by whom its beauties were, doubtless, appreciated. Eccentric sheds, outhouses, and supplementary wings of all shapes and dimensions,—except the symmetrical or the grand,—clustered round the parent edifice like limpets on a stone. The whole was surrounded, at some distance, by a goodly moat (fed from the neighbouring trout stream), which had long been ceded as a perpetual seat of war between the ducks and tadpoles. The approach to the house was by a drawbridge, that had not been raised for many years, and was now incorporated with the common road, till such time as its rotten timbers should give way, and possibly precipitate a load of wheat or so into the ditch beneath. The bridge was backed by a small but well-built turreted gate of the early Norman school. In this there were the grooves for a portcullis. But if the iron grillage had ever been furnished, it had disappeared before the recollection of the oldest clodhopper. A low wooden gate had once supplied its place, but had lost its hinges, and lay half-buried in farm-yard refuse. The arched gateway, black with age and neglect, was surmounted by a dazzling, jaunty-looking freestone shield,—on which the arms of the family had been newly carved by no inartistic hand,—marvellously suggestive of a new patch on an old jerkin or a jewel in a swine's ear.

At some distance from the main building, and close inside the moat—for Geoffrey Falstaff's magnificent architectural dreams had conceived the covering of almost the entire enclosure—stood the really splendid tower of William of Wykeham, which had given the name of Folly to the family mansion. This was a most imposing and picturesque object. Though barely twenty years had elapsed since its construction, it presented all the aspects of a venerable ruin. Being built of soft Norman stone, which rapidly crumbles and darkens in our climate; being roofless and windowless in the upper stories; having been utterly neglected and being overrun by ivy and other creeping plants, nourished by a scarcely credible waste of farm ordures heaped on the soil beneath, the tower looked like the last proud relic of some mighty fortress long since swept away by the ravages of war—the original building appearing like a heap of ignoble fabrics constructed from its ruins.

On the compulsory abandonment of his building mania, Geoffrey Falstaff had been seized by a counterpoise one for economy. He had resolved on

converting the tower into a mill; and even went so far as to dam the moat
and construct a water-wheel. He was thinking about borrowing money to
purchase mill-stones, when he died. His son Gilbert, having no turn for
such ignoble pursuits, neglected to supply the deficiency. The dam was
allowed to stagnate and the wheel to rot—adding much to the picturesqueness
of the place.

Altogether, Falstaff Castle — viewed by the light of a dazzling May morning in the year 1364, on which we are supposed to make its first acquaintance
— presented as nice a higgledy-piggledy of improvidence, vanity, and eccen-
tricity as one could wish to see. And yet it was charming from its sheer
disorder! Every vagabond species of tree and shrub that would was suffered
to run riot up the sloping banks of the moat (strongly reminding the historic
student of the minstrels and illuminators in the time of Peter). Myriads of
birds kept up an incessant din. Communism reigned as an established principle among the domestic animals. The cows, from a defective wall in their
Gothic residence, had free access to the briar-grown orchard behind the
house. The philosophic pig was everywhere. Fowls, ducks, and pigeons
roamed wild without count or restriction among the shrubberies, building
where they pleased as *feræ naturæ*, and affording excellent sport and provender
to the house-dogs, with whom they were not on sufficiently intimate terms to
claim the immunity of neighbours.

There was one little oasis, of prim, quakerlike neatness, amid this unkempt
desert of thriftlessness. On the left wing of the building a little horn-latticed
door opened upon a garden leading down to the moat. Here the grass was shorn
like a friar's poll, and interlaced with shingle-walks as even and well-ordered
as the galloon on a lackey's coat. It was streaked with little beds of jet-black
earth that might have been dug with silver spoons and raked with my lady's
comb. On these the snowdrops and crocuses lay already dead, and the
primroses were drooping. But the daffodils still held their own bravely. The
Kentish roses were also budding about the walls and hedges in this enclosure — for it was a sheltered spot looking to the south, and the season
was early. On one side was a straight bed, showing as yet no vegetation,
but studded with little cleft pegs surmounted by wooden labels. This was
evidently the department of medical simples of the rarest virtues, and was
shut out from its more holiday neighbour by a hedge of apple-trees trained
espalier-wise. Two or three more fruit trees — cherry, apple, and plum —
rose above the flower beds, evidently of a choice description, and all
smothered in white or pink blossoms. There was also a goodly vine, trained
against the house, and forming a green porch over the latticed door.

There was no approach to this spot but from the house. The two sides leading down to the moat were jealously guarded by stout hedges of black-thorn and sweetbriar, overrun with luxuriant hop-bines, at that time a rarity, in what has since grown to be the hop-garden of the world.

This was the private garden of Lady Alice Falstaff, tended almost exclusively by her own hands. There was, haply, not such another at the time in all rich, improvident England. But Mistress Alice Bacon had been a travelled merchant's daughter, and had brought more than flower seeds with her from the land of the patient, thrifty Flemings.

A broad, uneven horse-track led from the front gate by a rough wooden bridge over the trout stream, and then wound its way to the right up what had once been Falstaff Chase, keeping in sight for full half a mile till it disappeared behind a hill.

Now, mark what happened at Falstaff Castle on the bright May morning I have spoken of.

There came, cantering and jingling over the hill and down the chase towards the castle, a gay troop of cavaliers, with pennon streaming and steel caps flashing in the sun.

Now, it was a time of peace. Had it not been, Falstaff Keep was in no condition to stand a siege. And yet, from the effect caused by the sight of these horsemen, an observer would have thought to hear drums beating and horns blowing — with drawbridge up and portcullis down in a crack of time. For no sooner had the sound of hoofs roused a neatherd from a comfortable nap by the banks of the trout stream (from crossing which it was his business to prevent the cattle in his charge — the pasturage on the other side being mortgaged to a neighbour), than he leaped to his feet, and, leaving his cows to enjoy themselves in the field opposite, scampered towards the house like one possessed, as fast as his hob-nailed cowskins would let him, and roaring at the top of his voice —

"Volk a horseback !"

There was only one point of strict discipline really enforced at Falstaff. This was, that on the approach of strangers, the lord of the castle, if at home, should be immediately apprised thereof. Many awkward accidents had occurred from the breach of this rule.

The neatherd rushed unceremoniously into the presence of Sir Gilbert Falstaff, and the lady Alice, his wife, cowskins, hob-nails and all. Fortunately, there were no carpets in those days.

The knight was pricking arms on vellum, at a little side table, with a flagon by his side. The lady Alice, helped by two neat little maids, was mending hose at a window.

"Volk a horseback coming down park," said the breathless messenger.

Sir Gilbert started up in alarm.

"How many ? What kind ? How far off ?"

"Ten or fifteen, mayhap. Steel-caps, speards, and a penance."

The knight wrung his hands, and rushed to the window to reconnoitre. It was pitiful to see his distress as he whimpered, —

"Alack ! alack ! 'Tis a knight and his following. Pestilence seize them ! What seek they here ? Certes some Lord of the Court, — and to see me in this plight—with darned hose ! Bar the shutters ! Say the knight and lady are at court—at their castle in the north—in Flanders. Plague on them ! Would I were dead !"

The hind moved to depart, scratching his head, with a confused notion as to his general orders.

"Stay, good fellow," the lady Alice said, rising from her seat. She was a comely English matron, well grown, with blue eyes and golden hair,—yet fair to look on ; though with a face harder in expression than it doubtless had once been, for she had been sorely tried in her married lifetime.

"Shame on you, Sir Gilbert Falstaff, to teach your hinds such base artifices ! How can you hope they will serve you truly ? Bid them welcome, Jankin, to such poor cheer as we can give them. Why, man ! there is not an inn within eight leagues."

"Jankin, go not. Art thou mad, woman ? Art thou mad ? Thou with nothing but a cloth kirtle, and I in this miserable —— But thou go to ! Thou art a true trader's daughter."

"Even so. One of those whose office it is to keep poor knights from starving." (It was a fault of this good dame's, that she would be bitter in her speech at times.) "I will not send these away an hungered. Come, maidens, away with the hose-baskets, and busily with me to the kitchen."

Lady Alice, followed by her two little maidens, left the room. The sound of the horses' feet approached rapidly. There was no time to be lost. Sir Gilbert clutched Jankin nervously by the arm, and said to him in hurried tones, —

"Take thou brown Crecy ; thou wilt find her in the orchard (if she be not loose in the wheat); saddle and gallop like wind to Sir Simon Ballard's. Bid him lend me his new green velvet surcoat, — that with the gold stars. Dost heed ? Say a nobleman of the court is with me, who desires one like it. Then to Dame Adlyn, the yeoman's wife. Say I have a wager with a certain earl, who lies here, that the weight of her gold chain is greater than his. Bid her lend it me for an hour. Spare not whip or spur, and I will owe thee a guerdon. Stay!—if these riders question thee, say the knight is gone out with his hawks. Speed !"

Jankin departed with a beaming face. He had no great faith in the promised guerdon, but he was fond of horse exercise.

The cavalcade was at the gate.

"A murrain on them!" Sir Gilbert muttered. "Would they were in the Red Sea! And yet I lack court news sorely. Pray Heaven that miser Ballard, and that farmer's jade, Adlyn, stand me in good stead."

Sir Gilbert having impressed upon the household the fiction he was desirous of keeping up, retired to bite his nails in a garret, till such time as Jankin should return with the borrowed plumes.

The visitors were met at the gate by one of Lady Alice's little maids. Falstaff was rather bare in the commodity of men-servants, and those it possessed were none of the most presentable. Master Lambert, the Reve or Steward, who was believed to be much richer than his master, had been called to Sandwich on business of his own, leaving his master's to take care of itself.

The leader of the cavalcade was a handsome young man of some one or two and twenty. He was

> ———— " a doughty swaine;
> White was his face as pandemaine,
>   His lippes red as rose.
> His rudde is like scarlet in grain,
> And I you tell in good certain,
>   He had a seemly nose.

> " His here his berde was like safroun,
>   That to his girdle raught adoun ;
>   His shoon of cordewane ;
>   Of Brugges were his hosen broun,
>   His robe was of ciclatoun,
>   That coste many a Jane."

Read further the description of Sir Thopas, and you will have a good idea of the sort of mediæval exquisite who announced himself to the little maiden as Sir Thomas Mowbray, who having, with certain other poor gentlemen of his company, mistaken his way, was desirous of paying his respects to the fair lady of the castle.

The little maid, with much blushing, but going through her task right cleverly, invited them to enter, and pointed out to them where their steeds might be bestowed. She then led the way to the hall, where spiced sack, and, what was then termed, a "shoeing-horn," but what, in this unpoetical age, we call broiled rashers of bacon, awaited them, spread temptingly on a snowy napkin.

Then the little maid told them, in a pretty set speech, that her mistress would be with them presently, if they would be so good as to entertain themselves the while; adding (and here the little maid blushed, as with positive shame,) that Sir Gilbert Falstaff was gone out with his falcons, but would doubtless be home in time to welcome his guests to their poor family dinner.

The visitors fell busily to work on the sack, and used the shoeing-horn unmercifully. It would seem that they required no other entertainment, having brought in some excellent jest with them, at which they had been laughing immoderately, when the little maid first met them at the gate, and which kept them laughing, at intervals, for a good half-hour after their being seated at table; at the end of which time Jankin was seen to gallop into the courtyard on Brown Crécy — now white Crécy with foam — with a bundle before him on the saddle. Jankin appeared in high spirits, and had indeed enjoyed his ride immensely.

The travellers only checked their laughter, when, a few minutes later, the hangings were raised, and Sir Gilbert Falstaff entered the hall, leading the lady Alice by the hand. The knight wore a green velvet surcoat, embroidered with golden stars, and twirled a massive gold chain, as became a gentleman of his rank and ancestry. His dame was clad in a plain cloth gown, without ornament, befitting her origin as a wool-merchant's daughter.

The visitors were welcomed by Sir Gilbert Falstaff with much ceremony.

"You take us by surprise, fair Sirs," he said, after the exchange of many formal salutations, "and must fain content you with our daily fare. Poor country folk, Sir Thomas! (How does your honoured father, Sir?) Had we known of your coming, then,—a welcome more befitting—— But I am glad to see you merry, gentlemen."

This was to Sir Thomas Mowbray's two esquires, who, not joining in the conversation, had bethought them of their late jest, and were convulsed once more.

Sir Gilbert liked not laughter in his presence. He always imagined himself to be its object.

"Nay, Sir Gilbert," said the young knight, "forgive their lack of manners. We have all had good cause for laughter, on our way hither, as you shall own when you have heard the jest."

Sir Gilbert felt relieved. They were not laughing at him. He twiddled Mistress Adlyn's gold chain with courtly ease, and simpered,—

"Doubtless some court pleasantry. Let me know it, I pray you. I am sadly behind date in such matters, gentlemen. But a fallen house, you know——"

"Nay!" Mowbray made answer; "the court would be a livelier place to live in, did it abound in such jests. But you shall hear. I should tell you first, we have come from Deal this morning, and were seeking a short cut to the Canterbury road, but missed our scent, like dull-nosed dogs as we are. When about six miles from here, we met a party of boys——"

"Boys !"

Sir Gilbert Falstaff and the lady Alice exchanged glances.

"Aye, real English, true Kentish boys,—a score of them perhaps,—of all sorts and sizes.   Ragged boys, warm-clad boys, shock-headed boys, and shorn boys,—after no good, I warrant me, for they were armed with bows and arrows, poles, cords, and knives."

Again Lady Alice glanced at her husband.   This time Sir Gilbert looked in another direction.

"However, their business was none of ours.   We asked them our way ; and one of them, who seemed to be their ringleader, a burly, flaxen-headed, blue-eyed urchin, of some fourteen,—who — the saints forgive me if I have spoken offence !—but now I look, he was the very image of your ladyship. *N'est-ce pas, Jean ?*"   Sir Thomas turned to a lazy-looking, handsome gentleman, of about thirty, who had dropped into a seat at his elbow.

"*Eh bien !   Quoi ?*"

"Excuse my friend.   He speaks very little English.   He is a French priest, though he does'nt look it."

The alleged priest was dressed in the wildest extravagance of the current fashion ; he had deep hanging sleeves, "purfled" with fur, and the toes of his Cordovan boots were a foot and a half long.

"*N'est-ce pas que ce garçon là ressemblait beaucoup à Madame ?*"

Monsieur Jean shook off his apathy, like a true Frenchman, at the mention of a lady's looks.   He bowed graciously, and showed a splendid set of teeth, as he replied,

"*Mais, parbleu !   est-ce que je n'aie pas déjà dit, qu'il était fort joli garçon ?*"

"I believe you are speaking of my own son, gentlemen," was the quiet reply of Lady Alice, who understood a little French.   "He left home at day-break ; on what errand, or in what company, I know not."

She looked a third time at her husband, who shuffled his long limbs under his chair uneasily.

"Then he is a son to be proud of !" said Mowbray heartily.   "But to end my story.   He advanced, cap in hand, to answer our inquiry ; and, with mock politeness, which made us all laugh, told us, that if we would turn down a certain lane in the forest, some two miles off, we would find ourselves 'in face of our ultimate destination.'   We were well amused at the lad's pedantic speech, but, never doubting his good faith, we turned down the lane as directed.   At the end of a few paces, we found ourselves in an open space in the wood, where there was — *a Gallows !* This was 'our ultimate destination.' We laughed good twenty minutes at the urchin's roguery—for which Maître Jean here gave him absolution on the spot—and have scarcely ceased laughing since. Our ultimate destination ! *Eh, Jean ? Nous allons tous finir par là ? "*

" *Possible !* " said Jean, shrugging his shoulders.

Lady Alice, in spite of the thoughtfulness that seemed to have possessed her, laughed till her bonny fat sides shook again.

Sir Gilbert looked wrathfully at her.

" The young villain ! Believe me, Sir Thomas, he shall be soundly whipped for this, if, indeed, it was our son, as I hope not. To pass so insolent a jest on a gentleman of your standing ! It is like you, wife, to, treat so grave a matter lightly."

" Nay, if the boy come to any harm through my betrayal," said Mowbray, kindly, " I shall consider myself cut out of all good fellowship for evermore. Besides, had he not led us astray, we had never caught sight of your splendid tower, as we did from an opening in the woods, and so should have lost your kind entertainment. This must have been a rare fortress in its day, Sir Gilbert."

" Held its own, Sir,—held its own,—and that indifferently. We are a fallen house. But be seated, Sirs, I pray you. Here comes our humble fare."

" On what errand did that boy leave home this morning ? " Lady Alice asked her husband, in a fierce whisper.

" Gentlemen, pray Heaven you are all too sharp-set to be dainty," said the knight, evading his wife's question. His face was deadly pale, and his hand trembled as he clutched the carving-knife, to do mischief on a smoking pig's head.

The dinner was substantial and abundant ; setting at glorious defiance that law of the period, for the restriction of luxury, which prescribed that "no one should be allowed, either for dinner or supper, above three dishes in each course, and not above two courses : " and which further decreed that " soused meat" should count as one of the aforesaid dishes. Nevertheless, conversation languished. The host, constantly making efforts to apologise to his guests for the humble fare set before them, seemed too ill at his ease to enjoy what was in reality a better dinner than he had sat down to for months. Lady Alice was attentive and hospitable ; but her last laugh had been forced from her, at the mention of her son's waggery, before dinner. Sir Thomas Mowbray was fain to talk in French with his friend, Maître Jean. His two esquires, and the men-at-arms below the salt, acted like sensible men : they eat and drank, and held their tongues.

Just after the hartshorn jellies, almond marchpanes, and cherry marmalades, had gone the way of their predecessors, the white broth capons, veal toasts, and chicken salads, and had been replaced by new cheese and old apples, Master Lambert, the Reve, was seen riding into the courtyard, — on a stout grey mare, — full of importance, and, as it shortly proved, of something else.

That faithful steward burst into the dining-hall, with the unmistakeable abruptness of an unpaid servant — saluting nobody.

"How now, Lambert ? " Sir Gilbert asked, with a sorry attempt at dignity. "What is the matter ? "

"Hanging matter, Sir Gilbert," answered the steward, in a thick voice. "Flogging matter at least, — caging matter for certain. But riding's dry work, and talking, drier. Save this fair company, — though I don't know 'em."

Master Lambert quietly drained Sir Gilbert's drinking cup, flopped himself down in an arm-seat beside the fire, blinked his eyes insolently at the company, and deliberately proceeded to take off his muddy boots.

"How now, knave ! art thou mad ? Dost thou know in whose presence thou art ? "

"Don't call me knave, Sir Gilbert Falstaff, knight," hiccupped the drunken steward ; "or I'll have the house over your head. You know I can do it. I ha'nt got coat armour, nor breeches armour ; but I can pay my way, and keep my sons from the gallows, — more than you can do at this time of day either one or the other."

Lady Alice turned deadly pale. Sir Gilbert's lank bones fairly rattled, as he fell back, half dead, in his chair. The guests looked at one another.

Lady Alice, with forced calmness, rose from her seat, and, approaching the drunkard, addressed him —

"Speak thy meaning, fellow — for thou hadst a meaning when thou camest into this room. What has given thee the right to insult thy master and myself, before our noble guests ?"

"Insult *you*, my lady ?" howled the steward, suddenly diverging into the maudlin state. "I couldn't do it. You're a sweet angel, you are, born and bred ; and I love the very ground you tread on ; always did. And when I see you thrown away on that snivelling gull——"

Whether the miserable sot meant gallantry or gratitude is uncertain. At any rate, utterly forgetting the questions asked him, as well as the presence he sat in, he made a staggering movement to take the Lady Alice's hand. Failing in the first attempt — the lady, rigid with astonishment, still remaining at his side — he rose, smilingly, to repeat it.

Sir Thomas Mowbray gave two strides from his seat, and felled the drunkard to the ground with a well-directed blow on the temples.

D

Master Lambert rolled, apparently lifeless, into the fire-place among the wood-ashes.

"You have killed him!" said Lady Alice, not without a grateful glance at her champion.

"I am afraid not," said Mowbray, cruelly enough, it must be admitted; "though, after all, we shall want him alive, to answer a question or two. How now! Sir Hogshead. Must we stave in that wooden head of thine to get anything out of thee?"

The young knight administered a ruthless kick to the prostrate steward, which sent that man of wealth rolling into the blazing embers.

The kick and the brisk fire roused Master Lambert Reve to something like consciousness and sobriety. He rose upon all fours (the threatening heel of Mowbray, armed with a terrible spur, and raised, from time to time, above his head, forbidding him to adopt a more dignified position), and whimpered out a lament that an honest serving-man should be thus treated after riding, at risk of neck and limb, to apprise his masters of a matter threatening their family honour.

"Come to the point," said Mowbray, raising his heel.

"Master Jack, with Tom Simcox, and Will the Tanner's son, and young Hob Smith, and others, stole a buck this morning. They have been taken by Sir Simon Ballard's keepers. Sir Simon swears he will have law of all, gentle and simple. They are in the cage at Maldyke," the steward rattled out, with marvellous clearness and volubility.

"So they were the lads we met. Fear nothing, Madam. My young wag shall come to no harm. Where is this Maldyke?"

"A league and a half from here, by the road you came."

"Enough. You may get up. Lads, to horse! *Jean, en veux-tu?*"

"*De quoi?*"

"*Des coups.*"

"*Toujours.*"

And Maître Jean put away a set of tablets on which he had been making some notes; and pulled on a pair of embroidered gloves, over which he was at great pains to draw on several jewelled rings. These warlike preparations completed, he declared himself — in the French language, and with a charming smile — ready for action.

The men-at-arms were soon equipped and mounted.

Sir Thomas Mowbray took a hasty farewell of his hostess, saying, as he did so —

"I perceive, Madam, your noble husband takes this matter greatly to heart. Either you lack his sensibility, or he your fortitude" (there was some irony in the speaker's tone as he said this). "Yet, fear nothing. I give you my knightly word to bring back your son safe and whole. We are strong enough to beat all the keepers in the county and bear the consequences. We owe you this trifling service in return for our entertainment. Farewell. Stay! There is yet a duty to perform."

Master Lambert, the Reve, lacking the stimulus of kicks, had relapsed into his arm-chair and a state of somnolency. Sir Thomas dragged the capitalist by his hood into the court-yard, dipped his head in a horse-trough, as a sanitary precaution, and shut him up in a log-house, placing a heavy invalid plough against the door for security.

And then Sir Thomas Mowbray with his friend Jean rode off at the head of their troop to rescue little Jack Falstaff.

Sir Gilbert had not spoken a word, nor moved an inch in his chair.

When they were alone, his wife approached him slowly, and said, in measured tones—

"Sir Gilbert Falstaff, from this day forth we are man and wife no longer."

"How! how!" said the knight, quivering with rage and shame. "That's well! that's well! All the world will desert me in my wretchedness— and you the first, I might be sure. It is in your blood. Would I were dead! To be seen in this plight by gentlemen of the court—insulted by my own groom—all in one day—and my son a felon——"

"For that he may thank his father," said the lady, coldly.

"It's a lie, woman!" the knight screamed. "I have done all I can to instil gentleman-like notions into him becoming his rank."

"You set him on to steal Sir Simon Ballard's deer—the man whose coat you are wearing. You have sacrificed my son and yours—body and soul, perhaps—to your liking for a certain dish of meat! You pitiful wretch! without the heart to rob a henroost for yourself!"

"'Tis a lie—a black, wicked, shocking lie!" the knight could only gasp; but it was plain to see with whom the lie was. "It is the low training you have given him, made him mistake my words—and the taste for bad company he had with your blood. I may have said, in the olden time it was thought good sport for young gentlemen of spirit to carry away a buck; as, indeed, it was, in the good old days when gentlemen were not meddled with in their sports by base hinds—for this Ballard is no better, for all he wears three-pile velvet, while his betters—— But 'tis no matter! All the world is against me. I am the most miserable wretch on earth!"

"I believe you are, indeed! My poor boy! My brave boy! whom I have tried to make good and honest, as God intended him to be!"

Lady Alice Falstaff sobbed as if her heart would break.

"Good! Good! Look to one's wife for comfort! Not a thought for my sufferings! But, if the young fool gets safely through this, I'll beat him within an inch of his life. And to try it in the day-time, too!"

"Enough! I will humble you no farther. You have heard my decision. Whether the kind, brave men who left us, to break the laws to spare our shame, — whether they bring me back my son or no, — whether he is to die a felon, or live an honest man, — from this time forth we two are strangers."

"You don't mean it," Sir Gilbert whined, in a half-imploring, half-threatening manner. "You would not have the base, black heart to leave me in my miseries — to be robbed and neglected by servants? You know I am ailing, and require little comforts. I can eat nobody's Warden pies but yours——"

"I have spoken my last word to you," said the lady, in an inexorable voice. And she left the room, to watch and pray for her son's safe return.

The poor mother spent a wretched hour, standing far out in the road, with strained eyeballs and compressed lips, watching the horizon. Her tribulation was shared by the entire household, by all of whom (with the exception of Master Lambert, the Reve, the favourite butt of young Jack's practical jokes) the young scapegrace in trouble was greatly beloved. Rough kitchen-maids and lumbering ploughmen were out on the road, watching as eagerly as their mistress — many of them with cheeks as wet as her own.

That hour seemed a lifetime to Lady Alice Falstaff.

Horses' hoofs were at length heard pattering over the hill.

"Here they be," roared Jankin, who had stationed himself as look-out in a high tree. "Hooray! they'm got'un."

The cavalcade burst down the chase. The mother's quick eye detected her son, in safety, at a glance.

In a few minutes the horses had thundered over the bridge, and little Jack Falstaff, leaping from Sir Thomas Mowbray's crupper, was in his mother's arms.

"My own boy! My brave, wicked boy!" the lady murmured, holding him tightly to her bosom. "God bless thee. God forgive thee! But what is this? Blood? Sir Thomas Mowbray, you promised me my son safe and whole. Jack! Jack! What is it? Have they killed thee?"

"No hurt, mother," said Jack. (I have called him little Jack; but he was a strapping urchin of fourteen, and, as Mowbray had said, the very image of his comely mother.) "Only scored across the costard. But he had it again. Eh, Sir Thomas? By the Lord! mother, this is a brave gentleman!"

"And thou art a brave rascal," said Mowbray, admiringly. "But get thee indoors. Lady Alice, there is no time to be lost. This Ballard is not a man to be trifled with. We found the doves trying to break their cage already, and had but to help them. There was a strong watch of keepers and constables set. Master Jack fought for his liberty like a hero of Troy, and has his wounds to show for it. But he is not safe here." Sir Thomas said this with a significance the lady too well understood. "He must to London with me. We have settled all. He is to be my page, and has promised to mend his manners."

"God bless you, sir," was all the mother could say through her sobs.

"Think of that, mother," said Jack, in the highest glee. "Page to a gentleman like Sir Thomas Mowbray! And going to London! Was ever such luck?"

"Luck, thou graceless varlet! when thou shouldest be on thy bare knees praying for forgiveness."

"Yes, that's all fair and good, mother," Jack answered, drily. "But, you see, the sheriff of Kent and his following might happen to come and interrupt my devotions. So I think horseback is safest."

"Away! Thou art incorrigible!"

"I hope not," said Mowbray. "But moments are diamonds. Find a horse for my page — I will see to the rest of his equipment. Why, how now, Jean! what the devil hast thou got there?"

"I don't know," said Maître Jean, in French, riding leisurely up after the rest. "I found the thing in the cage when we let the rest of the boys loose. It looked very small to be in prison. And its little pig's eyes twinkled so pitifully after its leader there, when you took him up behind you, that I was fain to carry the mite with me under my cloak. There, jump down, monkey."

And Maître Jean dropped among the straw of the courtyard a very small boy, clad in leather.

He was a remarkable boy — apparently about eight years of age, though from his countenance he might have been eighty. His eyes were very far apart, and surmounted by gravely frowning brows. He had a good deal of nose for his age, and mouth enough for any age. He walked with a sort of defiant straddle, and was altogether a stolid, grim, unrelenting sort of boy. But he was absurdly little.

"Let's have a look at it," said Mowbray, touching the stolid pigmy with his whip. "He's very funny to be sure. What's thy name? — Colbrand the Giant?"

The queer little boy returned no answer; but stood, with his legs further apart than ever, gravely confronting his interrogator, and waiting to be whipped again.

Young Jack Falstaff bustled up, leading out Brown Crecy,—the only good horse on the estate,—hastily saddled for the journey.

"Don't hurt little Peter, Sir Thomas," he said. "He would come with us this morning : when we talked of leaving him behind, on account of his size, he cried,—a thing he had never been known to do before, though he gets more thrashings than any boy in these parts. Indeed, it was he found the buck for us. It's no use trying to make him talk—he won't. Poor little man! he is very fond of me, and will be sorry to lose me."

A snort was heard from Peter, who was discovered, to the astonishment of all familiar bystanders, to be in tears, for the second time in his life.

"The son of a — ahem!—keeper of mine, Sir Thomas," put in Sir Gilbert Falstaff, who had sneaked out on the assurance of safety, and began to think, with the unexpected turn things had taken, that a little deer-stealing was no bad family investment. "I am ashamed that gentlemen of your rank should have been troubled by a single thought for such vermin. Out of the way, thou beggar's scum!"

Sir Gilbert aimed a fierce blow at Peter's head, which that philosopher avoided skilfully, and disappeared among the horses' legs.

"Have you aught to say to me, Sir Gilbert Falstaff, before I carry your son away with me? Time is short; and all the keepers and constables of the county may be upon us at any moment."

"Nothing, Sir Thomas—but—ahem!—a trifling matter. The horse that carries my son—being a steed of great value—albeit I shall never cease to feel bounden by your inconceivable kindness—yet, as the said horse—I am a poor knight, Sir Thomas, as you know—as it will be used henceforth in your service—seeing that Jack is to have the honour of being one of your household—I would merely say that——"

Mowbray cut him short by throwing two pieces of gold in the mud at his feet with a contemptuous oath.

"There's for your horse. Keep from the heels of mine. There is a certain kind of man he has a taste for kicking. Now, Jack! art ready? The sooner thou art out of this the better for thee. The air here is not good for thee, lad."

"All ready, Sir. Good bye, again, mother. God bless thee."

"God mend thee, my boy."

"Good bye, father!"

Sir Gilbert did not hear the parting salute of his son. He was busy picking up something in the mud—which he carefully pocketed, dirt and all.

Mowbray waved a gay farewell to Lady Alice. The poor lady had been playing listlessly with a withered rose-bud which she had stuck in her girdle, and forgotten in the day's troubles. She let it fall. Maître Jean leaped from his horse and picked up the treasure, pressed it to his lips, stuck it into a " love knot on the greter end of hys hoode," and vaulted again into his saddle with an air of triumph.

This was very kind of Maître Jean, for it made Lady Alice smile. And the poor mother stood in need of some such diversion, however passing.

" Now, lads," said Mowbray. " Whip and spur with a vengeance. No rest this side of Canterbury. And for London, ho !"

" For London, ho !" shouted Jack Falstaff, with a beaming face, looking more like a jovial young prince riding to tournament, than a rescued purloiner of animal food flying the constable.

And away they galloped.

" Jean," said Mowbray, as they rode up the chase, " do you intend to chronicle to-day's exploits among your *nobles aventures et faits d'armes pour encourager les preux en bien faisant?*"

" *Parbleu !* Why not ? I have put a good face on many a worse, before now."

That night, Lady Alice Falstaff begged a shelter with her good gossip Dame Adlyn, and never entered Falstaff Castle again.

That night, also, there was sore tribulation in the hovel of a ploughman on the Falstaff estate. Little Peter was missing.

IV.

OF JACK FALSTAFF'S COMING TO LONDON. — HOW HE SAW LIFE THERE, AND HOW HE BROKE SKOGAN'S HEAD AT THE COURT GATE.

Now you know how it was that the future Sir John Falstaff got his first start in life as page to that renowned knight Thomas Mowbray, more famous by his later title of Duke of Norfolk, who, though only a chivalrous well-bred young gentleman as we have seen him, afterwards became Mareschal of England, and what not, and learnt, in virtue of his high position, to betray sovereigns, and murder their uncles, and get himself banished, and altogether to play a great part in history. But with all that we have nothing to do. Edifying in the extreme is the moral of young John's advancement to this nobleman's favour, showing by what kind of achievement it behoves youths of spirit to draw upon them the early attention of those in power. Had young

John merely stopped at home, minding his book and heeding his mother, ten to one but he would have grown up with no higher ambition than to improve his father's estate and do justice to his tenantry, and might have lived till ninety and never been heard of beyond the sound of his parish bell, instead of —— But it is not the business of the chronicler to anticipate events.

Fain would I tell of the many novel and wonderful things which delighted Jack's eyes and ears on his memorable ride to London, pleasantly diverting his mind from dwelling upon disquieting themes, such as forest laws, broken-hearted mothers, and the like. That rough blacksmith fellow, for instance, — who, when they were about three miles on their way, came running out of his smithy, thrusting a mug of ale upon Sir Thomas, and thanking the knight and his troop for releasing his son Hob, one of Jack's cage-fellows, — begging them to drink to the confusion of all forest-lords, keepers, taxmen, and the like; how, when Sir Thomas declined the toast, and bade him teach his son better manners, he fell to cursing Sir Thomas roundly, saying he had thought him a true man, but found he was but a gentleman after all; and then fell to cursing Jack Falstaff for deserting the brave lads of Kent and leaguing with gentlemen and oppressors, till Jack was fain to draw Sir Thomas away, saying that Wat Smith was a good fellow and a rare cudgeller, only rather fierce when he got upon such topics as gentlefolks, keepers, and taxmen.

Much would it delight me, too, to tell you of the meeting at Canterbury — where the party rested for the night — between Maître Jean and an English gentleman, his friend, with a peaked beard and falling hood — also a clerk and scholar; how Sir Thomas Mowbray invited him to share their travellers' supper; of the compliments that passed between the two writers as to each other's wondrous gifts; how each would give place to the other at table, Maître Jean saying that the chronicler was less worthy than the poet, and the gentleman in the peaked beard prettily declaring that the mere stringer of idle fancies must yield to the grave compiler of history, and so forth, — until, after supper, Maître Jean having requested the gentleman in the beard to delight them with some of his new Canterbury verses, which the gentleman in the beard agreeing to with much alacrity, but not leaving off in time to give Maître Jean a chance of reading a trifle he had recently composed on the death of Estienne Marcel, with which he was anxious to favour the company, they fell to calling each other names; how the gentleman in the beard called Maître Jean "Scrivener's Clerk," to which Maître Jean retorted with "Town Bellman," and the like, until Sir Thomas Mowbray threatening to score them both across the costard and ordering in more sack, they became like brothers again, citing and lauding each other's works, and embracing at intervals, until they were taken up to bed.

Again, there was the odd adventure that befel them hard by Blackheath— of a strange, gaunt, ill-clad youth, with a small knapsack, who came limping up to them and seizing John Falstaff's bridle, declaring that our hero owed him a ride, seeing that he had once rescued Jack from drowning from a fishing-boat off Sandwich, by swimming to shore with Jack on his shoulders; which Jack recognising (though he had forgotten his preserver), Sir Thomas would have rewarded the lad with a gold piece; whereupon the latter said, No, he would take nothing that he had not earned; but having lamed his foot, and being unable to walk, he would claim a ride from John Falstaff as his due, and then cry quits: and, indeed, Jack was fain to ride into London with this strange fellow behind him, dropping him at the Southwark end of the bridge.

All these things, and many more such written in full, might fill many diverting pages; but, alack! if such time were given to each adventure in my hero's life where would this chronicle end? We have only yet got to the fourteenth year of one who led a long life, and, as some assert, a merry one. As to that we may be better able to judge by-and-by.

Well, here we have Jack Falstaff in London, in his fifteenth year, page to Thomas Mowbray, afterward Duke of Norfolk.* Let us see the sort of life he leads there. He lives in a fine house and is gorgeously dressed; the Mowbray badge on his arm he considers an honour and an ornament. He is very jealous of this, and will maintain its superiority over the badges worn by other pages, by blows if necessary, and if there happen to be bystanders. A private taunt in a back street he treats with contempt, unless repeated in public. He has nothing particular to do—his principal duties being to attend his master to the Court or tilt-yard; to kick his heels in anterooms at the former (where he rapidly graduates as a master of the arts of repartee and badinage, and acquires much edifying knowledge), and to pick up his master when knocked out of the saddle at the latter. Certain menial duties, such as brushing cloaks and polishing daggers, are his by virtue of office; but he early shows his powers of command by divining how these may be done by deputy. When there is a letter or message to be delivered he performs this conscientiously in person, such like commissions giving him an opportunity of studying the town and forming his opinions on men and manners. He is by no means a winged-footed Mercury; but can usually coin a good excuse for

* "There was Jack Falstaff, now Sir John, a boy, and page to Thomas Mowbray, Duke of Norfolk."—JUSTICE SHALLOW, *Henry IV*. Pt. II. act iii. sc. 2. The Justice naturally speaks of Mowbray by his later title, as we say, "Arthur Wellesley, Duke of Wellington."

delay, or, if detected, a jest to ward off punishment. He has plenty of
money ; for his master is liberal, and Jack is a great pet with the visitors to
the mansion — saying pretty things to the ladies and smart ones to the gentlemen, in return for which he is loaded with presents. Thus, much of his
income, even at this early period, is obtained by the exercise of his wits.
He mixes in the very best society. The princes of the blood are his
master's familiars ; they encourage him in his wit and impudence to crack
jokes upon their rivals or inferiors — occasionally getting one for themselves,
when Master Jack thinks fit to regulate the balance of society and teach
even princes their level. His observations of these great people, their habits
and capacities, imbue his young mind with the tenets of that philosophic
school of which the valets of heroes are said to be the head masters. He
has taken their measure in fact ; and, placing himself, mentally, back to back
with them, is — not disappointed to find them shortcoming, but complacently
satisfied with his own comparative dimensions. He thinks that perhaps
on a readjustment of the social scheme — but no matter ! He keeps his own
counsel and profits by his present opportunities. His acquaintance is much
sought after by numerous aspiring youths of the town — naturally, for he is the
companion of princes. Before these young men he is careful to keep up a very
high standard of the princely character, for those whom he acknowledges his
superiors must be proved great creatures indeed. He quotes a " merry jest
of John of Gaunt," or a " shrewd thing he heard Langley say upon such a
matter," — frequently the choicest and most elaborated sallies of his own
imagination. But he will allow no liberties with his royal patrons from
others. If any of his companions, inadvertently or presumptuously catching
his familiar tone, make inquiries as to the proceedings of " Clarence," or
" Young Thomas," he will rebuke them with " their Highnesses, the Duke of
Clarence and the Earl of Buckingham, if you please," and shroud himself
in dignified reserve for the rest of the evening, as one who has con-
descended too far.

It is natural that the society of a young man with such advantages should
be greatly courted : for, you see, every one of such a person's intimates is
enabled to retail his experiences to a still lower circle as having happened to
himself ; and so on, widening and weakening to the very borders of the
social pool.

One of Master Jack's familiars is a young gentleman from Gloucestershire,
Robert Shallow by name. As there must be language before there can be
grammar, and poetry before rules of composition, just so, long before our hero
had codified his laws of philosophy, he had learnt instinctively to obey a
maxim which he subsequently acted upon systematically, namely — always to

choose your associates from among your inferiors in wit who are your superiors in pocket. Master Shallow was descended from one of the oldest families in England, whose representatives were (and are still) to be found in every county. He had plenty of money—at least, his father had for him—and no wit. He was desirous of the honour and support of Jack Falstaff's acquaintance. Jack, striking a nice balance between humanity and justice, decided that Master Shallow should enjoy that privilege and pay for it: Master Shallow did both—enormously.

Master Shallow was a law student, and some five years our hero's senior; but, as usual, mind triumphed over matter (that is, to speak figuratively—materially there was not much more of Master Shallow than mentally). Jack patronised Shallow; Shallow aped, toadied, and swore by Jack. He was never tired of quoting our hero's sayings and boasting of his prowess. Nay, he even, in a measure, unwittingly contrived to make Jack pay his own expenses, for in such glowing terms did he describe his courtly patron in his letters home, that his worthy parents encouraged him in the outlay of money spent in the cultivation of so distinguished an acquaintance, and met his claims upon their purse liberally. It is possible that even the parents got some return for their expenditure, in the pleasure of humiliating their country neighbours with stories of their son's high favour with a young gentleman of the court. How little England has changed within five centuries to be sure!

In fact, Master Jack, with a handsome person, fine clothes, abundance of leisure and money, and, above all, a devoted toady, was in a most enviable position. And he lorded it finely over the youth of his own age, at taverns, ordinaries, and inns of court accordingly.

But, alas! what is greatness but a mark for envy? Many were the fingers itching to pick a hole in Jack's fine coat. At length an open seam presented itself. His courage was called in question. He was accused, in full cenacle, of having, in the most cowardly manner, deserted certain comrades—pages, students, and others —in a street row with 'prentices.

The accusation was perfectly just. Jack, on the occasion alluded to, wore a new doublet, and had no fancy to show himself at court in the morning with a broken head earned in a fool's quarrel. So he had walked quietly on, pretending to have heard nothing of the matter; urging, when accused, that having stayed out beyond his time, he had slipped away purposely when he saw his friends halting, as he supposed, to speak with some acquaintances.

The explanation was coldly received. Jack felt himself, figuratively, far on the road to that Coventry where years afterwards he distinguished himself in a material sense. He felt he must recover his position by a decisive *coup*. Mere single combat with one of his own age would be inadequate to the emergency. He walked homeward meditating.

He was attracted by a disturbance in a tavern. Except withheld by extreme prudential motives, he could never resist the temptation of a broil. He entered the tavern.

A burly black-bearded fellow of some five-and-twenty, far gone in his cups, was challenging a roomfull of people to make verses, quote Latin, fight, wrestle, or drink against him, declaring that he was the great poet cudgeller, or wrestling scholar, Henry Skogan. He brandished a scrap of greasy parchment, on which, he said, were written verses which Master Chaucer or Dan Virgil himself need not be ashamed of, as would be owned when he read them at the court gate in the morning to the Earl of Cambridge, in honour of whose twenty-seventh birthday they were composed. He volunteered to read them to the company, and dared any one to find them bad.

A stolid Thames waterman, with no soul for poetry, bade him hold his noise unless he wanted a cleft skull. They had had his trash a dozen times already.

" Aha ! what's this ?" said the gladiator poet. " One tired of life ? A worm 'neath Ajax's foot. Writhe hence or be crushed."

To make the scene brief, a cudgelling match ensued. The waterman was vanquished, and the poet resumed his swaggering antics with renewed extravagance.

Jack Falstaff walked home, musing as follows :—

" At the Court Gate to-morrow. The Court will all come out in procession to the tilt-yard. All the lads will be there. That fellow for all his swagger and bulk knows no more about cudgel-play than a pig. Three chances that poor waterman gave him, which, if he had been trained by Wat Smith, as I have, would have shortened the battle eight minutes. Pray Heaven he be not too drunk to keep his word in the morning !"

In the morning Jack presented himself at the Court Gate to wait for the coming out of his master, but earlier than his time of service required. There, as he expected, were a good sprinkling of his companions of the previous day assembled in the crowd to see the procession to the sports in honour of Prince Edmund's birthday. There too, to his delight, was the poet Skogan, parchment in hand, gesticulating and bullying as he had appeared on the previous evening—merely a little cleaner and apparently sober.

After listening to his rhapsodies for a few minutes, Jack approached his companions. They received him distantly. Even his staunch adherent and believer Shallow—who being an arrant coward dared not stand aloof from the majority—was constrained in his manner.

"I forgive you, gentlemen," said Jack; "you have had some reason to doubt my courage. I think I have an opportunity of proving it. This noisy fellow offends me; you shall see me thrash him."

"What—Skogan—the cudgeller—Jack?" gasped Shallow, in delighted astonishment.

"Pray you, some of you ask him to read his verses. I will find fault with them."

"Said I not—said I not?" said Shallow, in ecstasies.

One Master Thomas Doit, a law student, of Staffordshire, stepped forward, and in respectful tones begged the poet to favour him with a hearing of his verses.

The poet required no second bidding. Tucking his cudgel under his arm, he cleared his voice and began—

"Oh, royal Edmund, son of Edward Third, ——"

"You lie." said Jack, "he's the fourth son."

"Who spoke?"

"I did."

"Wilt be whipp'd, boy?"

"Ay—when thou goest a week without."

"He can do it! He can do it!" cried Shallow.

"Go on with the verses, Master Skogan," said the bystanders. "He is but young."

"True. Boy, another time——"

"'Though fourth in line ——"

"I told him so," said Jack. "He steals my very words."

"How now? cock-sparrow!"

"How now? hen-gull!"

"Send thy father here for a cudgelling."

"He sent me here to look for one," said Jack, "and I am not to go away without seeing one given."

"Take care, lad," said Skogan, raising his stick. Jack, seizing a cudgel from a bystander, knocked it out of his hand; and, following the movement up with a smart tingling blow across the bully's face, threw off his doublet nimbly and claimed a ring.

Skogan declined the combat on the score of his adversary's youth.

"Here's a fellow!" said Jack. "I heard him, drunk, last night challenge a score men—knowing well not one of them knew the use of a cudgel: now, sober, he fears to meet a boy who does."

"You must needs give him a lesson, Skogan," suggested a bystander, who was rather tired of waiting for the princes and wanted some amusement; "or farewell to your repute."

"Then just one bout to silence him," said Skogan, stripping.

The lists were soon formed and orthodox weapons provided. The combatants took their places. Master Skogan convulsed the bystanders by pretending to be terribly frightened. He shook all over in the most humorous manner; rejected half-a-dozen cudgels as not stout enough for so terrible an occasion; affected to look for a soft place to tumble upon; and hoped that some kind gentleman would have compassion on his wife and family in case of fatal accidents. The cudgel play commenced, and the spectators still laughed; but the mortifying conviction was soon forced upon Skogan that they were no longer laughing with, but at him. The poet had assumed a nonchalant patronising air, as who should say, "We will get this ridiculous business swiftly and mercifully over," which Jack imitated to the life, continuing, indeed, to burlesque every one of his adversary's movements throughout the encounter. Our hero parried every blow, easily. Skogan's jaunty smile deepened into rather an ill-favoured grin. He had made the serious mistake of underrating his opponent's powers. Jack, on the other hand, had well calculated the weight of the peril he was incurring, and now brought all his nerve, muscle, and intellect to bear in meeting it. He depended on a chance for a peculiar stroke—one of Wat Smith's teaching—of which he had seen Skogan to be ignorant. An opportunity for this offered itself. It was seized like lightning. A sharp ringing sound was heard. Skogan let fall his sword-arm, put his left hand up to his brow, and tried an unconcerned smile, as though the thing were a mere nothing, in the midst of which facial effort he fell senseless on his back with a fractured skull.

This was the manner in which Jack Falstaff broke Skogan's head at the Court Gate.

A loud shout burst from the spectators. Shallow wept tears of rapture—mingled with envy.

"Oh, if I could but do it! If I could but have such a thing to talk of! If I could but once say I had broken a head like that!" he exclaimed frantically.

"A word with you, sir," said a rough, shockheaded fellow, drawing him aside confidentially.

A flourish of trumpets announced the approach of the princes. Jack's companions flocked round him, overwhelming him with congratulations and apologies. Jack affected to treat the whole matter lightly; the knowledge that he had more than recovered his lost ground enabled him to still the

Drawn & Etched by George Cruikshank.

Published by Mess.rs Longman & Company.

Jack Falstaff, when Page to Thomas Mowbray, Duke of Norfolk, breaking Skogans head, at the Court gate., see Justice Shallow, Henry IV.th Part 2.d Scene 2.d

beatings of his heart. He had fought with wondrous coolness and apparent enjoyment, but had, in reality, suffered all the agonies which a keen intellect must always experience in an encounter with serious physical danger.

Skogan was carried away to be plastered. It is to be hoped his poem would keep till the next birthday.

By the time Sir Thomas Mowbray came out with the rest of the courtiers, he found his page fully equipped, and ready to accompany him to the tiltyard in Smithfield.

When they reached the ground, as Jack was struggling with a crowd of men at arms to get through the narrow gateway, he felt his sleeve pulled from behind, and an eager voice cried—

"Jack, Jack! don't go in yet. Look here; I've fought too!"

He looked round and saw Master Robert Shallow in a high state of excitement, dragging a man by the collar, whose head was bound with a cloth streaming with blood.

"Look, Jack! mind, say you saw it. Sampson Stockfish his name is—he's a fruiterer—I made him come here to show his broken head, or I threatened him with another."

"Another head?"

"I pray you let me go, sir," whined the wounded man; "you have hurt me sore enough for one day."

"There! you hear him confess," crowed the delighted Shallow.

"Out of the way, thou cobbler's end," said an authoritative voice. "What dost thou here among the Marshal's men?"

And Prince John of Gaunt, striding through the gateway, laid his sheathed sword across Master Shallow's head—reducing that warlike gentleman to the same condition as his blood-stained victim.

Master Shallow was led away howling, by the magnanimous Stockfish.

"Why what eelskin had'st thou got hold of there, Jack?" inquired the prince, looking after the discomfited champion.

"A Gloucestershire lamprey," answered Jack. "Your highness would have done well to kill him, for truly he puts your title in danger."

"How so?"

"Why your highness is no more Gaunt than he is. He fairly beats your name."

When Master Sampson Stockfish and his conqueror were alone, the former very considerately took the bandage from his own forehead—previously wiping off the superfluous sheep's blood—and bound it round his employer's head, as having more need of it. He then requested to be paid, as he wanted to get home.

"True; a silver mark it was, I think," said Shallow, who was not much hurt, handing the sum he named.

"A silver mark. Go hang! I'll have forty."

"Why it was thine own plan and bargain."

"All's one for that. I must have forty if I'm to keep counsel. If not, out comes the whole tale."

Master Shallow compromised the matter for twenty marks on the present occasion,—and, by occasional subsequent fees, was enabled to bind Stockfish over to permanent silence. He boasted incessantly of his victory, which he eventually led himself to believe he had gained. Moreover, he would have considered any price cheap for an adventure which led to his making the acquaintance of that renowned prince, John of Gaunt, with whom he was wont to declare he had enjoyed a most interesting conversation upon the political and theological questions of the day.

BOOK THE SECOND,

1381.

I.

HOW MR. JOHN FALSTAFF CAME INTO HIS PROPERTY, AND WAS KNIGHTED BY
KING RICHARD THE SECOND.

THERE is nothing in the latter and more publicly known portion of Sir John
Falstaff's career to make it surprising that he should have approached the
middle period of life without having acquired greater nominal celebrity
than that afforded by the registers of retail traders. Such greatness as he
afterwards attained to, having for its foundation a profound knowledge of
mankind, must needs absorb the study of a long life to develop its Aloetic
splendours.

Therefore, having clearly established my hero's antecedents, and seen him
launched on the sea of life, I might fairly take leave of him for many years
to come, as of an adventurous emigrant crossing the ocean, with the perils of
whose long voyage we have nothing to do, and who will only claim more
attention when he shall have cleared his forest and founded his colony on
the other side of the world.

But it must not be forgotten that we are treating of a knight and a
gentleman of the olden time. There are two events in the life of such a
person which, in justice to chivalry and noble birth, the historian may not
pass over: these are, 1. His accession to the inheritance of his ancestors.
2. The time and manner of his receiving the dignity of knighthood.

Sir Gilbert Falstaff, Knight, was gathered to his fathers early in the year
1381. The tidings of the melancholy event were conveyed to his son and
successor, then residing in the English town of Calais, by a faithful attendant
returning from England, whither he had been despatched on his young
master's business.

Master John Falstaff, at this period, occupied apartments in one of His
Majesty's fortresses in Calais, in favour of which he had vacated an official
suite in the Government-house of the same town. Here, for some months, he
had discharged the duties of an onerous but subordinate post, wholly unsuited
to his peculiar genius. Even at that early period the Government of England

was celebrated for a habit of injudicious selection in the matter of public appointments—putting usually the right man in the wrong place, and *vice versâ*. Falstaff—burning to distinguish himself in the service of his native land (and having his own private reasons for wishing to do so at a convenient distance)—exerted his court interest to obtain a colonial appointment. At the head of an invading army, or in command of a beleaguered city, there is no reason to doubt that he would have acquitted himself with satisfaction to all parties; but, Government having nothing more suitable to offer him than a deputy-collectorship of the wool duties (for which, it is true, he was certainly qualified on the grounds accepted by British Governments in all ages — his mother's father having been a wool-stapler), what could be expected but a directly contrary result? The exact deficit in the Falstaff accounts has not been preserved in the public records. But there is no reason to doubt that it was on a scale commensurate with the greatness of our hero's soul, inasmuch as, after a few months' probation, an intimation was forwarded to him that his resignation of office would be accepted. It is at least probable that the nation required his services in a wider and more honourable field. But of this we have no means of judging accurately, an adverse destiny placing it out of the ex-deputy-collector's power to avail himself of any such pending advantages. Adverse destiny, in his case, took the shape of an Anglo-French jailer.

Falstaff, in fact, like all men born to sway large destinies, had a lavish disregard of trifling expenditure. Like Julius Cæsar, he contracted debts; that is to say, as much like Julius Cæsar as possible — our hero lacking that arch-insolvent's facilities of obtaining credit. With two millions of somebody else's money (about the amount, I believe, on the Julian schedule), what would not Falstaff have done? It is difficult to answer. It may be safely stated, however, that it was from no fault of John Falstaff's that Julius Cæsar had the best of him in this respect.

At any rate, having started this historic parallel between these two great men, we may bring it to a triumphant close by stating that young Falstaff, like young Cæsar, was now a captive in the hands of pirates and waiting for his ransom.

It was in search of this talisman that the faithful attendant, alluded to in the opening of the present chapter, had been despatched, on a somewhat forlorn hope, to England. The faithful attendant returned without it, having no better substitute to offer than the tidings of Sir Gilbert's death. The prodigal but philosophic son declared, with a sigh, that, under the circumstances, he must try and make that do.

He sent for the pirate chieftains, — in modern English, for his detaining creditors, — a Flemish clothier and a Lombard money-lender. He informed them of the death of his obdurate parent, with whom he had been at variance for years, but of whose princely estate he was now the undisputed possessor. Now was the time for him to show his gratitude to the real friends who had stood by him in the hour of need; who had been long-suffering in his extravagance; lenient even in their tardy severity. What could he do for them?

" Pay us our money," suggested the matter-of-fact traders.

Falstaff treated the proposition with disdain. Of course he would pay them — a dozen times over if they liked. But he would be still in their debt. No; nothing would satisfy him but that his dear friends should accompany him to England, to assist him in taking possession of his inheritance. Falstaff Castle was close to the coast — they might see it almost on a fine day. He would want their assistance in refurnishing his ancestral halls. He must take them to court, and introduce them to his bosom friend the young king, with whom (now the unnaturally adverse court influence of his father was removed) he was all powerful. In a word, the heir of Falstaff would not be able to enjoy his fortune unless he secured that of two friends at the same time.

It is no discredit to the intellectual powers of these simple traders that they suffered themselves to be won over by the eloquence of their great-hearted captive. They agreed to release him from durance — previously securing themselves by the most terribly binding documents (such as our hero, at all periods of his life, was ready to sign with the greatest alacrity) — and to accompany him to England.

In those days the traveller crossed from Calais to Dover in an open galley; that is to say, when he crossed at all: for, in a large proportion of cases, the galley went down about half way and gave the traveller a premature opportunity of studying the engineering difficulties of the proposed submarine railway.

In a still greater frequency of cases the traveller waited several days at Calais for a fair wind. When it came, the gallant rowers hoisted what they called a sail, stuck an image of the Virgin in the prow of the boat, prayed to it — and became sick like men.

Jack and his faithful attendant, being Britons, and endowed with that peculiar native salt in their veins for which the analytical chemists have as yet found no name, were good sailors. The Fleming and the Lombard were bad ones, and howled dismally at the bottom of the boat. The crew were Frenchmen. No further explanation of their condition is necessary.

When the galley had made about three parts of her course, our hero's faithful attendant broke silence with —

"Don't you think now would be about the time, sir?"

"What for?"

"What for! why, to pitch them overboard, of course."

Falstaff wheeled suddenly round on his seat, and looked his faithful attendant full in the face. There was approval in the scrutiny, mingled with compassion.

"And do you suppose, young man," the master inquired, with a transparent assumption of severity, "that I am going to be guilty of such an act of treachery?"

"Then what the plague else did you bring 'em here for?" was the sulky reply. "They've got your bonds in their pockets. The sailors are all sick —none of 'em would be a bit the wiser."

"Away, tempter!" said Jack, with twinkling eyes. "How dare you lure an innocent youth to his destruction? *Avaunt* thee, fiend! *Vade retro Sathanas!*"

"Come! I'm not going to stand being called out of names."

"Then hearken to the voice of Wisdom. Suppose I were to commit the breach of confidence and gratitude you so insidiously propose, and, in your own words, pitch these worthy gentlemen overboard. What then?"

"Well, it would be a matter between ourselves and the lobsters."

"And pray, sir, in that case — WHO IS TO PAY OUR EXPENSES TO LONDON?"

The faithful attendant opened his eyes as wide as they would go, which was not very far, and a grin of intelligence dawned upon his usually stolid countenance. MUTUAL ESTEEM once more reigned between the master and servant.

A word as to this faithful attendant. Two years ago, having borrowed sufficient money for his continental outfit, and to liquidate such debts as might militate against his departure, our hero, with a serene mind and an easy conscience, had entered St. Paul's Church in search of a serving man. A certain aisle in the cathedral was at that period the central exchange or rendezvous for unhired domestics. A servant out of place would not attempt such profanation in the present day. In fact, a beneficent and considerate Dean and Chapter have wisely placed it beyond the means of such a person to do so.

Our hero passed a great many candidates for employment, some of whom he rejected as being all fool, others as too exclusively rogue. Neither of which elements, unmixed, would suit him. At length he came upon a stern looking young man, with straight thick eyebrows, a gash for a mouth, and a nose vermilion beyond his years. The red nose argued chronic and perennial thirst. This, in its turn, was suggestive of easily-purchased fidelity.

"My friend," said Jack to him of the proboscis; "I like your looks."

"You ought to," replied the salamandrine; "*I have been twelve years looking after you.*"

It was little Peter! subsequently nicknamed Bardolph, in honour of a fancied resemblance to a nobleman of the Court. What wonderful vicissitudes Peter may have undergone since the memorable evening when he straddled away from home in that very small leathern suit we may not pause to inquire. He was promptly retained by his old leader, whom he never quitted alive. Peter took kindly to the name of Bardolph; and, in the course of time, believed himself allied to the noble family from which it had been derived.

Falstaff and his travelling companions touched English soil between Dover and Deal. Who knows—for history delights in such coincidences—but it may have been on the very spot where some fourteen hundred years previously, that very identical Julius Cæsar, between whom and our hero so many points of resemblance have been established, landed on a similar errand —only with a few more people to back him?

The Fleming and the Lombard were put on shore alive, to their considerable astonishment. Bardolph was despatched to the nearest inn, on the coast, of which he knew every inch, in search of horses.

Our hero reviewed his position.

"I don't quite know what to do with them, now I have got them," he meditated. "I am afraid they won't find the Falstaff Estates quite up to my representations. I must make it out that I have been robbed by servants during my exile. At any rate, one thing is decided. THEY DON'T GO WITHOUT PAYING FOR IT."

Bardolph returned running, with yellow cheeks, purple lips, and a blue nose,—altogether a remarkable facial chromatic phenomenon.

His tidings were startling.

The lads of Kent had risen in open rebellion, and were devastating the land with fire and sword. They had burnt and sacked every gentleman's seat in the county, having hanged such of the proprietors as they could lay hands on, and were now marching on to London. Horses, shelter, or provisions were out of the question.

Falstaff was delighted. Had he been Destiny itself, he could scarcely have pre-ordained things more in accordance with his present wishes. He mastered his real emotion, and counterfeited another. He tore his hair, and threw himself writhing and moaning on the beach.

His visitors were naturally curious to know what had happened.

The matter was this, he told them—when he could collect his scattered thoughts : — he was a ruined man. The peasantry were in arms — had declared themselves against the landowners. His ancestral castle had doubtless, ere this, perished in the flames. Nothing remained for him but a nameless grave, which he would thank his companions to dig for him on the beach.

The commercial mind is sceptical in all ages. The Fleming and the Lombard — not by any means sure that they had acted wisely in the first instance in trusting themselves to the mercies of their plausible debtor — became doubly suspicious. They held a brief consultation apart, the result of which was a somewhat lugubrious proposal that they should proceed experimentally to Dover.

Towards Dover they walked ; Falstaff mechanically yielding to his conductors, as one whom despair had robbed of volition.

Remarkable as the statement may read, it soon proved that Bardolph had spoken the truth. Smoking homesteads, trampled crops, with here and there a smouldering rick or coppice, too well corroborated his story. Scared and crouching figures, emerging from concealment, warned the travellers not to approach the town as they valued their lives. Numbers of the rebels, maddened with success, were still in possession of the neighbourhood, vowing destruction to every man with a delicate skin and a whole coat over it.

What was to be done ?

Falstaff, magnanimously forgetting his own troubles in his anxiety for his guests, suggested that the latter should return to whence they came, leaving him to his fate. In another hour it might be too late. Their boat would be seized.

Not if the commercial gentlemen knew it. If every rebel in ten thousand rebels had been in ten parts, and every part a rebel, they would have faced the entire insurgent camp rather than those terrible waves a second time in the same day. Besides, the thing was out of the question. The gallant crew — including the body servants of the two merchants — learning that plunder was the order of the day, had hastened in divers directions across country to enrol themselves under the national banner like the truest imaginable Britons. The unlucky foreigners begged of our hero not to desert them, promising that, if he would see them safely through the present difficulty, he should have no cause to complain of their — ahem ! — leniency.

John winked—aside ; and repressed an inclination to execute, there, on the beach, what might have anticipated the invention of hornpipes by some centuries.

He wrung the hands of his two friends, and vowed that, at all hazards, he would stand by them. Still he was at a loss to decide for the present emergency. ——

The merchants suggested that they should proceed to the Falstaff Estate. It was possible that the incendiary spark had not yet reached so far. The fact was, these two gentlemen were rather anxious for a glimpse of the princely domain, of which they had heard such glowing accounts, under any circumstances. Even its blazing ruins would be a consolation, as proving that they had not been utterly taken in.

Falstaff appeared to brighten at the proposal. Yes, he declared, there was hope in it. The people had been wronged and oppressed, and there was some excuse for their violence in certain quarters. But when he reflected what indulgent, beneficent masters — if, indeed, parents were not the fitter word — his ancestors had always been to their tenants : — no ! for the sake of human nature, he could not believe in such black ingratitude as to suppose Falstaff had come to any harm. It would still be in his power to give his friends a cordial welcome. He led the way almost cheerfully, deploring only that the journey must be performed on foot.

At the first opportunity he whispered Bardolph —

" Slip on before us, borrow a horse, steal an ass, or run like mad. The lads may have spared the old den for my sake. If you find it standing, set a light to every room. I'll detain these gulls so as to give you time. Burn every stick and rag except Wykeham's tower. Fire won't touch that."

Exit Bardolph in advance at a brisk trot.

His master explained.

" I have sent him on to herald us, and to meet us with horses ; if, as I still hope, honesty and good faith be not extinct upon earth."

Our hero was taken ill frequently on the road ; the result of his agitation and irrepressible misgivings. It was found necessary to solace him with repose by the wayside, and refreshments from the private stores of his companions.

" Oh, my friends !" said Jack, in a voice wherein gratitude struggled bravely against exhaustion ; " How shall I ever repay you for this kindness ? And if it should be too late — too late !"

" Come ! come ! Don't give way. We cannot have far to go now. We shall soon know the worst."

" True ! let me strive to be a man, and remember that I am answerable for the safety of others."

They reached Maldyke, six miles from Falstaff.

Here the sight of a goodly castellated mansion, gutted and smoking in the centre of a forest of charcoal, reduced our hero to a state of prostration. He threw himself on his face, imploring, as a last act of friendship, that his companions should despatch him with their knives.

The gateway of this mansion was situated on the public road. From the raised portcullis of this gateway swung a human body, dead, and half-naked.

Yesterday, this estate had belonged to Sir Simon Ballard. To-day, Sir Simon was its sole remaining occupant. But the rebels had hanged him by the neck, and he was dead.

Falstaff groaned piteously.

" Rouse, man, rouse!" said the Fleming. " Surely this is not your castle?"

" It's—it's—" sobbed Jack, spasmodically ; "IT'S ONE OF THEM ! ! !"

Then, falling upon his knees before the corpse of his old enemy, he clasped his hands, and exclaimed, piteously,

" My poor uncle ! my poor uncle George ! And is this the reward for your devotion to my interests ?"

The two merchants led him away compassionately.

For several roods they passed through the crops and woodlands of the ill-fated Ballard. The rebels had spared nothing.

" You see, gentlemen," said Falstaff, appealing to the devastation on either hand, " to what they have reduced me."

There could be no harm in Jack's assuming right of property in the defunct Ballard's possessions. In the first place, those possessions were no longer particularly worth having. In the second, it were unreasonable to suppose that their late proprietor could possibly have any further use for them.

The Fleming and the Lombard felt extremely sorry for their unfortunate guide and debtor. Nay ; they even hoped that, in the upshot of things, he might prove still to be in the possession of something valuable, as an excuse for their assisting him with further advances.

As they neared the Falstaff Valley, Jack's uneasiness increased visibly.

" It is my home, gentlemen," he explained, " where I first saw light.* It may be that they have spared me that. I scarcely dare hope it. But we shall know anon."

They reached the summit of the hill overlooking the valley,—down which, fourteen years ago, Sir Thomas Mowbray, now Earl of Nottingham, had come, laughing and cantering with his friend Maître Jean, the Chronicler, now curé of Lestines, and a most respectable clergyman.

Falstaff gave a rapid glance in the direction of his paternal mansion, then drew a long breath.

" Enough ! I know the worst," he said ; and seemed all the easier for the knowledge.

---

* See Book I. Chapter I. in explanation of this glaring breach of veracity.

Not a trace of Falstaff Castle was standing except William of Wykeham's Tower. The rest was mere smouldering dunghill.

Bardolph had been spared the crime of arson. The rebels had been before him. He had found the castle in the state I have described it, and —— Master Lambert, the Reve, hanging by the heels from a beech tree, with his skull cleft. The travellers discovered the faithful messenger contemplating this edifying spectacle with mingled philosophy and satisfaction.

At the sight of the steward's corpse Falstaff uttered a piercing cry, and fled.

"Follow him!" cried Bardolph, eagerly (he had caught and appreciated a flying wink from his broken-hearted patron), "or he will do himself a mischief."

The ruined landowner, after some search, was discovered in the orchard with his girdle slung to the arm of a pear tree. Into a noose, at the nether extremity of this, he was about to slip his neck, when his privacy was invaded. The rescuing party uttered a cry of thanksgiving for their timely arrival. They needed not to have hurried themselves. Our hero's inherent good breeding would have induced him to wait for them under any circumstances.

The merchants tried verbal consolation.

Futile in the extreme! The intending suicide assured them that they had but frustrated his purpose for a time. He could have borne the loss of home and fortune—his friends might judge, from the sole remaining tower, of what a dwelling the rebels had deprived him (though, of course, they could have no conception of the extent of the family jewels, plate, &c.); but what he could not bear was the sight of his faithful steward. hung by the heels like an unclean beast, doubtless as a punishment for his fidelity!

"Bardolph!" sobbed the ruined man. "How we loved him!"

"Don't speak of it, sir!"

Bardolph himself was so overcome that he did not venture to show his face, which he concealed within his palms. The latter, it should be stated, were more than capacious enough for the purpose.

"He loved you, Bardolph!"

"Like a mother, sir. But don't!"

The Flemish merchant then tried vinous consolation from his private flask. Falstaff rejected it. Bardolph didn't.

Falstaff—calmed in a measure, but determined—begged of his friends to make the best of their way to London, and leave him to die. He had now nothing left in the world but his sword. That, he was now too broken-hearted to turn to advantage. Would they be kind enough to go, leaving

F 3

him their forgiveness for the trouble he had so unwittingly caused them. That was all! Stay — another boon — a dying man's request. Would they promise to be kind to his faithful Bardolph, the last of a thousand devoted retainers?

"Don't, sir!" that valuable relic gasped, kicking out his right leg spasmodically.

Now, the Lombard creditor, in spite of his being a trader in money, was a good-natured fellow. He hit upon a third and more efficacious means of consolation — to wit, the pecuniary.

"Come, Master Falstaff," he said kindly, in the cosmopolite French of the period. "Things are not at the worst. You are young and strong, and, with a good name to back you, may recover lost ground. Who ever knew an outbreak of peasants last over a few days? If a few hundred marks will set you on your legs for a time, they are yours; and no questions about the past till you are ready to answer them. Remember you have promised to bring us to London and show us the Court. We are in your hands."

Jack leaped to his feet and dried his eyes. He was rebuked. This was no time for selfish considerations. His eyes were opened.

"When I reflect," he said, "that, without me, your lives are not safe; that those fierce Kentish rebels will spare nobody, unless guaranteed by the safe conduct of a true man of Kent; for, after all, they must respect my presence —come, gentlemen, I will see you safe to London, and the young king shall hear of your devotion."

What a good sort of fellow this poor ruined, broken-hearted Jack Falstaff was after all!

They led him away from the scene of devastation. At a few paces from the ruins, he declared he must return for a minute or two. His friendly gaolers, for so they had constituted themselves, looked at each other. Was their prisoner to be trusted alone?

"Gentlemen," said Jack, with much earnestness, and real tears starting from his eyes, "I give you my honour, as a man and a soldier, that I will return immediately."

They let him go, and waited for him.

Jack scrambled hastily over a heap of seething fragments, what had once formed the right wing of his father's dwelling, and found himself in a patch of ground sloping down towards the stagnant moat.

It was a wilderness of charred weeds. Nothing remained to tell that the spot had once been a dainty garden.

Yes. One thing.

A hardy Kentish rose-bush still asserted its life above a mass of filth, bricks, and potsherds. It bore one flower.

Jack tore this fiercely from its stem, and concealed it in his bosom, as if he had been stealing a diamond. He hastened to rejoin his companions with the most unconcerned look he could assume.

"What's afoot now?" growled Bardolph, *sotto voce*. The worthy hench-man was merely anxious to catch the new order of the day, if any.

"Hold your tongue!" said his master angrily, and looking very much ashamed of himself, "Don't speak to me!"

Lady Alice Falstaff had been dead four years. The long loved son who should have closed her bonny blue eyes, was away at the time;—never mind where, or what doing. The last flower of her pretty garden withered and dried up beneath Jack's doublet. He never noticed its final disappearance. you see his time was so much occupied.

This was the way in which Master John Falstaff came into his property, the residue of which he disposed of some few weeks later for the price of three new suits and a couple of horses, but which he never ceased to speak of as a princely inheritance, of which the troubles in 1381 had deprived him. Of course he found great advantage in this; for such is the inestimable value of rank and possessions, that the mere recollection of them—nay, the bare assertion of imaginary claims to them—will often procure for a gentleman credit and esteem.

The manner of Sir John Falstaff's attaining to the honour of knighthood, is a sequel to the same adventure.

He conducted his foreign guests faithfully towards London, as he had promised. On their way, they were beset by several companies of rebels, amongst whose numbers Jack recognised old acquaintances, to whom he made himself known, and who were glad to let him and his company pass free, for the sake of old times. On all such occasions our hero was careful to have it impressed upon the merchants that they owed their safety entirely to his countenance; and the gratitude of those poor travellers knew no bounds. Still, great precautions were necessary. In the first place, Jack counselled them strongly to destroy all written papers they might have about them; assuring them, that of all public evils, the men of Kent looked upon the art of writing as the greatest, considering it a Norman invention, to which they owed the bulk of their misfortunes. Admitting the policy of this precaution, the merchants destroyed Jack's bonds before his eyes. Next to manuscripts, he assured them the most dangerous thing they could possibly carry about with them was money. He courageously took upon himself the onus of bearing their purses for them, of the contents of which he distributed a considerable portion as *largesse* to the insurgents. The purses were faithfully restored to their owners.

At Blackheath our travellers came up with the body of the insurgent camp, commanded by Jack's old master of fence, Wat Smith, who had assumed the name of Tyler. Here it was Jack's good fortune to rescue the Princess of Wales, the young king's mother, from the fury of the malcontents, whom their honest but mistaken leader was unable to control. Jack asserted himself as a man of Kent, and claimed immunity for the princess as a Kentish woman — for had she not been known in the heyday of her beauty as the Fair Maid of Kent? Was she not the widow of the Black Prince, who had humbled the pride of the haughty Frenchmen, to whom it was notorious that all such evils as taxes, game laws, bad harvests, and expensive beer, were attributable? The princess, he assured them, had just been on a pilgrimage to Canterbury, to pray at the shrine of St. Thomas à Beckett for an extension of the peerage, by which every man of the age of twenty-one would be entitled to landed property and a seat at His Majesty's council. In conclusion, he would simply state, that, in order to prove her sisterly affection, the princess was anxious to kiss them all round — a proposition whereat the populace was highly amused, and to which the princess readily assented, only too glad to be let off so easily.

Thus did Jack Falstaff rescue the Princess of Wales from imminent danger, at no greater cost to her highness than a little sacrifice of personal dignity, and much subsequent expenditure of soap and water — all of which I have told briefly, seeing that the main incidents of the scene (doubtless taken down from the words of Falstaff himself) have been already chronicled by our old friend Maître Jean Froissart, curate of Lestines — and from his cheerful pages copied into the books of Hume and others.

For this good service to the royal family was John Falstaff knighted, on the same day which saw the like honour conferred upon one William Walworth, a fishmonger, for knocking out the misguided brains of poor Wat Smith — a much honester man than himself. Jack witnessed the perpetration of this murderous act of snobbishness, and took a deeply rooted dislike to Sir William Walworth ever afterwards.

Wat Tyler did not die unavenged. Sir John Falstaff dealt with Sir William Walworth for fish. When Walworth sent in his bill, he began to understand the meaning of Nemesis.

Bardolph greatly distinguished himself in the sacking of London by the Kentish rebels, several of whom he had the honour of bringing to justice on the pacification of society.

BOOK THE THIRD.

1410.

I.

FOR THE MOST PART A TREATISE ON HEROES AND KNIGHTS-ERRANT.

WHY should we call Time old, when we constantly find him playing tricks like a schoolboy? Here we have him at the beginning of the fifteenth century, amusing himself by rolling Sir John Falstaff down a hill, which men have agreed to call Life, like a snowball—Sir John getting rounder, and bigger, and whiter, at every push.

And now we approach that period in our hero's life, when his acts are public history. Our task grows lighter, our responsibility heavier. Hitherto we have had to treat merely of Achilles in girl's petticoats, Cæsar at school, Cromwell at the mash-tub, Bonaparte besieging snow castles. Now we are in sight of our hero's Troy, Rubicon, Marston Moor, Toulon — whatever the reader pleases.

Sir John Falstaff will next appear in these pages as the ripe full-blown Falstaff of Shakspeare, the fat knight *par excellence,* the hero of Gadshill and of Shrewsbury; on the eve of the former of which great engagements we are supposed to resume the thread of our narrative.

And here it may be as well that the historian and his reader should at once understand each other as to the purport of this work.

It is impossible that a man should take the pains of research and compilation necessary for a voluminous biography without the preliminary inspiration of deep sympathy with, and exalted admiration for the character of his subject. This is, at any rate, indispensable to the satisfactory execution of his task. None but a man with a turn for such achievements as usually result in solitary confinement could have written the "Life of Robinson Crusoe." The "Newgate Calendar" would not be the work it is, had not the last and present centuries been prolific in writers who, under a trifling depression of circumstances, might have changed places with their heroes.

I do not mean to say, that had I lived in the fifteenth century I should have been a Sir John Falstaff. Morally, in his position, I should have cut as sorry a figure as, physically, in his garments. Boswells need not be Johnsons. Sympathy and admiration, I repeat, are the necessary qualifications. I sympathise with, and admire the HEROIC CHARACTER as developed in all ages ; and I look upon Sir John Falstaff as the greatest hero of his own epoch.

Earthly greatness, like everything else to which the same adjective applies, is comparative — to be measured only by besetting difficulties.

The Italian captive, who blots down his autobiography on fragments of old linen, with his forefinger nail nibbed into a pen, and dipped in an exasperatingly gritty fluid of soot and water, is not to be tested by the same severe rules of criticism as the literary patrician, writing in his well filled library, to the mellifluous gurgle of his eastern pipe, and with every advantage that Bath post, gold pens, Webster's dictionaries, and the most carefully annotated editions of Lindley Murray can offer. As just would it be to compare the struggling unguided crudities of a mere Shakspeare or Æschylus, with the more polished productions of a modern dramatist, in the enjoyment of private means, and a *troisième* on the Boulevard des Italiens, having a running contract with the nearest theatrical printer for the earliest first-proof sheets of his publications. Mr. Hobbs, the American locksmith, with his multifarious means and appliances of picklocks, " tumblers," and what not, is entitled to our respect as a skilful mechanician ; but placed in comparison with Jack Sheppard and his rusty nail, what becomes of Hobbs and his reputation ?

It has been beautifully observed of Sir John Falstaff (by no less an authority than himself), that having more flesh than most men, he should be excused for displaying a greater amount of that frailty to which flesh is heir. On the other hand, having fewer advantages than most heroes, he may easily be proved to have displayed a more than proportionate share of heroism.

I consider it too late in the day to attempt a new definition of the word hero. The world has been agreed for ages upon the only acceptation of which it is susceptible,—namely, a man who takes a more than common advantage of his fellow-creatures in furtherance of his own interests, or those of his nation, county, township, street, row of houses, family, or self. Exclusive devotion to the latter interest marks the real hero. But this is a demi-god pitch of excellence rarely attained. Even Sir John Falstaff fell short of it.

Achilles was invulnerable (with a contemptible exception of which the oversight is a disgrace to the shoe-making science of the period), and had a supernatural mother to look after him. I think little of his heroism. Cæsar, as we have seen, had the vast advantage of almost unlimited credit. Cromwell had the majority of a nation at his back ;—so had Napoleon.

Sir John Falstaff won a hero's laurels, and attained a hero's ends) which may be briefly summed up as the privilege of doing pretty much as you like at the expense of other people), by the almost unaided exercise of his head and arm. Is he to be blamed for only having gained purses, where Cæsar or Alexander pocketed kingdoms? As ridiculous would it be to find fault with him for making no greater speed than four miles an hour from the disputed field of Gadshill, because swift travelling carriages had not been invented. Imagine Napoleon with fifty-eight years and thirty stone of flesh at his back, and none but pedestrian means of exit from Moscow before him! Who would ever have heard of Waterloo or St. Helena?

It may be objected, that of the recognised heroes I have cited for comparison, two at least (the last mentioned of the number) were originally actuated by the desire to free an oppressed people. Here, even, the parallel does not fail. Sir John Falstaff, too, had his subjects and followers, whose condition required ameliorating. It is true that these were limited in number, and that their most stringent oppressions were the severe debtor and creditor laws of the period, aggravated by a season of scarcity in the matter of wages. But, as I have said before, every thing in this world is comparative.

A great deal of misconception as to my hero's real character, may be traced to a deplorable ignorance of the time in which he lived. Many celebrated writers on the Falstaffian era (that is to say, people who know nothing at all about it) have declared the age of chivalry, in that great man's time, to have been extinct. This has led modern thinkers—who, according to the improved lights of their age, look upon speculations on the Stock Exchange, joint-stock banks, Samaritan institutions, cheap clothing warehouses, the adulteration of coffee, pickles, &c. &c., as the only legitimate means of plundering your neighbours—to apply harsh names to the more primitive mode of transferring capital adopted by our hero. The fact is, *Sir John Falstaff was a knight-errant,*—the only one of his time, perhaps—the last ray of the setting sun of chivalry, if you will; but its most gorgeous! To paraphrase the words of an eminent historian, "he was the greatest, as well as the last, of those mighty vagabonds who formerly overhauled the purses of the community, and rendered the people incapable of paying the necessary expenses of their legal prosecution." He was, in short, the Earl of Warwick of knight-errantry.

Let us prove our theory by an extension of the parallel lines.

The knight-errant of antiquity rode out, armed at all points, to win renown. Even in the most Arcadian times, the acquisition of that commodity appears to have been contingent on the display of a certain amount of spoil, in the shape of weapons, prisoners, ransoms, and so forth. The public enemies against whom the knight-errant's attention was chiefly directed, were—

1. *Giants.*

Which, I take to mean, people who had grown so big as to require more land and larger houses to live on and in than their neighbours.

 2. *Magicians; i. e.* people rather cleverer than their non-conjuring fellow-citizens.

It will be admitted that Sir John Falstaff did a great man's best to reduce the influence of these two varieties in his own favour.

The knights-errant had their esquires and men-at-arms, who were allowed the privilege of fighting under their leader's banner. It was not customary for the chroniclers of the period to mention the names of these subordinate personages. The dawn of a more equitable state of things, in this respect, may be traced to the time of Falstaff. The names of his immediate followers have been honourably preserved.

The list is as follows :—

 1. P. Bardolph, *Esquire.*

[The ancient title of Esquire has been recently much abused ; being assumed by mere writers, painters, and even members of the legal professions. Though it originally meant nothing more than " ostler," in those barbarous times, when manual labour was not a positive disgrace, yet, in the heyday of chivalry, it was promoted to an equivalent of " bearer of arms." Esquire-ship was the brevet rank of knighthood. The esquire, in order to become a knight, having served his lord faithfully for a certain number of years, was expected to sit up all night watching the arms by which he had earned distinction. These, in the case of Bardolph, adopting the heraldic acceptation of the word "arms,"—may be described as a bottle gules, on an oak table proper, with a corkscrew trenchant, supported by thirst rampant. These Bardolph is known to have sat up watching, not merely all one night, but for several hundred nights in succession. And yet this gallant soldier never attained to the distinction of knighthood. It is true that gentle blood was an indispensable qualification for the honour. Bardolph's blood was *not* gentle, but of the most obstinately opposite description. Coax it as he would, it persisted in flying to his nose.]

 2. Pistol, *Ancient.*

[Ancient—pardon the apparent contradiction of terms,—is a comparatively modern expression, certainly not dating further back than the time of Falstaff. The term has been corrupted into " Ensign." In those days, the most " ancient " and proved soldier in the ranks was supposed to earn the right of bearing the standard of the troop. I say "supposed," because I would not have it imagined that, even then, folks were so uncivilised as invariably to promote common people for mere desert. Then, as now, a loud tongue, a timely service, or a family connection, were excellent substitutes for personal merit. The individual under notice was a striking example of this truth. The distinguishing mark of the ancient in Pistol's time, was a white feather.]

  3. Peto.

  4. Gadshill.

[Two subordinate officers belonging to a class described by the convertible terms of " knaves," " villains," or " varlets."]

  5. Nym, *Corporal.*

[The Corporal in our time is distinguished by two stripes. In those days a deserving officer was more liberally treated ; Corporal Nym having marks to show for a thousand. Neither Nym nor Pistol make their appearance till rather late in the Falstaff annals ; each doubtless having his period of time to serve in another sphere of action.]

  6. Robin, *Page.*

[Also a late acquisition to the Falstaff forces, to be noticed more particularly in his fitting place.]

The knight-errant had the privilege of putting up, with his retinue, at the most hospitable mansion he found in his way.

He never paid rent.

Formerly this billet system was applied to the mansions of powerful barons. A succession of anti-chivalric monarchs had weakened the hospitable resources of these establishments. Taverns were their modern substitutes. Our hero, even as the commercial traveller in the present day (latest type of the knight-errant) is fain to put up with Railway carriages, where he once enjoyed his own gig,—accommodated himself to the change. But, whatever alteration had taken place around him, he himself was still true to the traditions of his order. Yes ! John Falstaff could lay his hand on his heart and say,—that he never entered the meanest hostelry without treating the host and hostess exactly as, two hundred years earlier, he would have treated a baron and his lady. The favoured mansion at present enjoying his high consideration in this respect, was the renowned Boar's Head Tavern in Eastcheap — of which more anon.

The knight-errant of old occasionally acted as the tributary vassal to a powerful prince. Herein is the vast superiority of Falstaff manifest. *He* made the most powerful prince of his time act as tributary vassal to him.

Yes; it is not the smallest laurel in the Falstaffian crown, that our hero alone, of all men that ever lived, could boast of having conquered the Conqueror of Agincourt. That he did so is unquestionable. The prince himself, like a true Englishman, who never knows when he is beaten, was not aware of the fact himself. Those who may be inclined to doubt it, are requested to study the lives of the two men, and to decide calmly whether, in the long run, Sir John Falstaff had or had not decidedly the best of His Royal Highness, the Prince of Wales, afterwards Henry the Fifth.

This young prince was a very great prince indeed; and has been justly held up as an example to the youth of succeeding generations. His claims to admiration are indeed somewhat remarkable, being founded apparently less upon the fact of his having proved a respectable character in later life, which might be questioned by detractors, than upon that of his having been an intolerable reprobate at the outset of his career — as to which there can be no doubt whatever. I cannot too highly commend the conduct of school-masters and writers in encouraging young people to the adoption of this effective principle of, what may be termed, Rembrandt Respectability, — a little streak of pure light looking so excessively brilliant when touched on to a background of utter darkness. Oh! my young friends, declaimers of Pinnock and readers of Goldsmith! adopt the Henry the Fifth philosophy as you hope to rise and be honoured. Would you aspire to a reputation for excessive humanity? In that case, kick your grandmother daily for ten years; then suddenly leave off and present the old lady with a new bonnet in a neat speech on gentleness. Is sobriety your ambition? Get intoxicated two or three times a day up to the age of, let us say thirty. By that time you will have sufficiently disgusted your neighbours with your life and conduct to make your sudden appearance in the character of a healthful, temperate, and well-ordered citizen (which, of course, it will be the easiest thing in the world for you to assume at a moment's notice, throwing off your old habits like a harlequin's cloak), matter of startling commentary. Would you shine by the light of your honesty? Then begin with robbing orchards, and proceed in due order to shop-tills, culminating with bank-safes and plate-baskets. Having thus attracted the public attention, you need only send your five pounds to the Chancellor of the Exchequer for unpaid Income Tax, and take your place amongst the honest folk, who will be delighted to receive you.

It is true, that for the modern commoner the same advantages do not exist for the safe pursuit of this line of conduct as were enjoyed by the crown prince of the fifteenth century.   But, for the last time, let it be stated that greatness is to be measured by its besetting obstacles.   Above all, there can be no harm in trying.

The Prince of Wales acted on this principle of contrast through life. Being a slim, well-built young gentleman, he liked to be seen walking with a stout overgrown elderly gentleman like our hero.   Knowing he would be a king some day, when he would find it as advantageous to be thought an honest man as it would be easy to hang anybody who might say he wasn't, he considered that his future would shine all the brighter from present companionship with rogues — such as a prejudiced society agreed to consider Falstaff and his followers.   So Prince Henry studied the first crude principles of taxation by plundering his father's subjects on the public roads in company with Sir John Falstaff.   And Sir John Falstaff, like a sagacious treasurer, had usually the first pickings of the revenues thus acquired.

Prince Henry, in his princely heart, had a great contempt for Sir John Falstaff, whom he looked upon as a mere tool to be thrown aside when no longer needed.   It is to be feared that he had not properly calculated the sharpness of the implement, nor its probable effect upon his own fingers.   It would have been gall and wormwood to his Royal Highness to know that, in the estimation of our philosopher. he ranked no higher than a second edition — more neatly got up, and with gilt edges — of Master Robert Shallow, formerly of Gray's Inn, and now of His Majesty's Commission, in the county of Gloucester.

Sir John was willing to be led wherever His Royal Highness pleased, and to dance to any tunes of the Prince's dictation.   Only it invariably happened that His Royal Highness had to pay the piper !

And now we have carefully reviewed our hero's position ; we have ascertained the site of his head-quarters, the number of his forces, the strength and disposition of his allies.   Pegasus, bestridden by the historic muse, snorts impatiently for his first feed of warlike beans.   Let us cling to the tail of the noble animal, and suffer him to drag us (with no more than necessary interruptions) to the field of Gadshill.   At any rate, let us close the chapter ; for we shall not come across such a splendid classical peroration again in a hurry.

II.

THE reader is invited to assist at a council of war.

The scene is a private room in the palace of Westminster. The members present are, 1. His Royal Highness the Prince of Wales. 2. Sir John Falstaff, Knight. The latter gentleman in the chair (which he finds rather a tight fit).

Sir John Falstaff opened the proceedings by asking His Royal Highness what time of the day it was.

THE PRINCE OF WALES.—"Thou art so fat-witted with drinking of old " sack, and unbuttoning· thee after supper, and sleeping upon benches after " noon, that thou hast forgotten to demand that truly which thou wouldest " truly know. What a devil hast thou to do with the time of day? unless " hours were cups of sack and minutes capons ?"

For the remainder of His Royal Highness's speech (the language of which is not strictly parliamentary) see Mr. William Shakspeare's verbatim report ; where, indeed, all particulars of the meeting are minutely·chronicled. It is the present writer's business merely to offer a brief summary.

After some general discussion (in the course of which Sir John moved for the Abolition of the Punishment of Death for larcenious offences, in the ensuing reign, but was induced to withdraw his motion by a promise of office under the crown, as public executioner), the meeting proceeded to the order of the day.

HIS ROYAL HIGHNESS.—"Where shall we take a purse to-night, Jack ?"

SIR JOHN FALSTAFF.—"Where thou wilt, lad ; I'll make one: an I do " not, call me villain and baffle me."

Carried nem. con.

At this juncture, a new member entered the council chamber in the person of Master Edward Poins. This was a young gentleman of good family, but bad morals ; that is to say, for the present. He was one of those loyal natures who, in all ages, are to be found attaching themselves instinctively to some great man, taking their tone and colour in all things from the illustrious model. Mr. Poins cut his hair and his conscience in exact imitation of the Prince of Wales. The existing court fashions, as established by the Prince, were long hanging sleeves, pointed shoes, late hours, intoxication, and

Drawn & Etched by George Cruikshank.

Pub.d by Mess.rs Longman & Comp.y

The Prince & Poins. driving Falstaff, Gadshill, Peto & Bardolph, from their Plunder. at Gadshill – 1.st Part of Henry IV – Act 2.nd – scene 2.nd

roystering. Mr. Poins followed them all with scrupulous fidelity; but was quite ready to change them for sad-coloured doublets, square toes, early rising, temperance, and respectability, at a moment's notice.

The following debate ensued upon the order of the day:—

MR. POINS.—"But my lads, my lads, to-morrow morning by four o'clock, "early at Gadshill! There are pilgrims going to Canterbury with rich offerings, "and traders riding to London with fat purses." (Hear, from the chair). "I "have visors for you all, you have horses for yourselves: Gadshill lies to-night "in Rochester: I have bespoke supper to-morrow night in Eastcheap; we may "do it as secure as sleep. If you will go, I will stuff your purses full of "crowns: if you will not, tarry at home, and be hanged."

SIR JOHN FALSTAFF.—"Hear me, Yedward; if I tarry at home, and go "not, I'll hang you for going."

MR. POINS.—"You will, chaps?"

SIR JOHN FALSTAFF.—"Hal, wilt thou make one?"

THE PRINCE OF WALES.—"Who, I rob? I a thief? not I, by my faith."

SIR JOHN FALSTAFF.—"There's neither honesty, manhood, nor good fel- "lowship in thee, nor thou camest not of the blood royal, if thou darest not "stand for ten shillings."

THE PRINCE OF WALES.—"Well, then, once in my days I'll be a "madcap."

SIR JOHN FALSTAFF.—"Why, that's well said."

THE PRINCE OF WALES.—"Well, come what will, I'll tarry at home."

SIR JOHN FALSTAFF.—"I'll be a traitor then, when thou art king."

THE PRINCE OF WALES.—"I care not."

MR. POINS.—"Sir John, I pr'ythee, leave the prince and me alone; I will "lay him down such reasons for this adventure, that he shall go."

SIR JOHN FALSTAFF.—"Well, mayst thou have the spirit of persuasion, "and he the ears of profiting, that what thou speakest may move, and what he. "hears may be believed, that the true prince may (for recreation sake) prove a "false thief; for the poor abuses of the time want countenance. Farewell; "you shall find me in Eastcheap."

THE PRINCE OF WALES.—"Farewell, thou latter spring! Farewell All- "hallown summer!"

The meeting then, as far as concerns Sir John Falstaff, broke up. The Prince of Wales and his friend Poins, may be left to their own devices.

Thus do we see how a great man works silently to his own ends by en- couraging his inferiors to think for him. Here was the campaign of Gadshill ready planned and arranged down to the very moment of attack, and the equipment of the forces, without a personal effort on the part of our hero.

Forestalling the policy of a more modern general, Louis the Fourteenth—who never showed himself on a field of battle till he was assured that his subordinate officers had made victory certain, and who then, in the most considerate manner, always came up in time to take the credit of it out of their hands—the task of Falstaff was simply to gather the ripened fruit, which, *but for the blackest and most unparalleled act of treachery that ever disgraced the annals of warfare* —— But let us not anticipate.

Had I the pen of Homer (who, by the way, supposing that fabulous person to have existed, could not possibly have known the use of such an article) I might write out a list of the warlike preparations made by Sir John Falstaff and his followers, in the course of the day, that might equal, in vivid dramatic interest, the famous catalogue of ships. Mine would it be to enumerate the scores of Kentish oysters, the hundreds of Gloucestershire lampreys, the skins of Canterbury brawn, the breasts of capons, the green-goose pies, the veal toasts, the powdered mutton, the marchpanes, the hartshorn jellies, the stewed prunes, the pippins and the cheese, stowed away in the vast resources of our hero's commissariat department, as provisions for the approaching campaign. Then would ye have, in succession, the vast and irresistible phalanx of sturdy oaths and light-winged cajoleries arrayed against the hostess of the tavern (a married woman, it must be admitted, but whose husband was already ailing) to induce her to yield further credit for the victualling and liquoring of the troops, resulting in the entire rout of her scruples, and the unconditional surrender of her cellar keys. Nor would be forgotten the hundreds, nay thousands, of matchless LIES, by which Patroclus Bardolph obtained a new saddle for his master from a dealer in Watling Street, and released the knight's steed from the spells of enchantment, which a cruel magician (in what we should now call the livery stable interest) had cast about the animal for some weeks.

All these details, and many more—down to a list of the snores of the thunder-vying Falstaff as he took his after-dinner nap to fortify himself for the coming fatigues, and of the glasses of strong waters tossed off by the lightning-shaming Bardolph while his master wasn't looking—would I enumerate had I the pen of Homer.

But as it has been already satisfactorily proved that neither I nor any other writer, ancient or modern (especially Homer), could ever have enjoyed the possession of that article, I will not attempt anything so ambitious.

III.

THE BATTLE OF GADSHILL.

Now did the chaste Diana despatch Mercury with a message to her brother Phœbus, requesting the latter to pull up his horses for an hour or two, so that Sir John Falstaff might not be incommoded by the light of his solar gig-lamps; promising the messenger that, if he would make haste back, she would show him a little sport in his own line. It is not positively on record that, on the morning of the battle of Gadshill, the sun rose two hours later than his regular appointment with society. But, on the other hand, historic fairness compels me to state that there is no proof whatever to the contrary.

Then did Diana throw her hooped petticoat of clouds over her head, so as to conceal the silver light of her countenance — merely reserving a peep-hole large enough to enable her to wink at the doings of her chosen minions.

She could not resist the temptation of showing her full face just once, to bestow an Endymion kiss upon a solitary pedestrian who emerged from the wood of Gadshill into the chalk-white Rochester Road. The Moon embraced him coquettishly — and hid herself immediately. He was a fine looking man, and portly — albeit advanced in years. There was certainly every excuse for the Moon. However, as she has quite enough scandals to answer for, let us hope that nobody saw her.

The stout person was of martial aspect, and clad in the terrible panoply of war. I will not say he was armed *cap-à-pie*. A full suit of armour to his measure would have had a terrible effect, not merely upon the wearer, but on the iron market of the period. But he bore weapons, offensive and defensive, sufficient to indicate the most desperate intentions. To add to the terror his presence was calculated to inspire, the warrior was under the influence of a passion which, though ridiculous in its influence on ordinary mortals, becomes sublime and awful when in possession of an heroic nature. I allude to ANGER. Sir John Falstaff was in a towering rage. It is no stretch of poetical license to say that the earth shook beneath his angry tread (there had been a little rain in the night, and the soil was tremulous). Streams of perspiration poured from his massive brow. His breathing was short and thick. Several times he essayed to speak, but rage impeded his utterance. At length he cried, in a voice of thunder —

" Poins !"

It must be understood that the thunder of Sir John's voice was rather of a muffled and distant character. Thunder, to be heard distinctly, requires a favourable wind — an advantage not enjoyed by Sir John Falstaff at this period of his existence.

Mr. Poins, against whom the culverin of Sir John's wrath, primed and loaded to the muzzle, was especially directed, had withdrawn himself prudently from the range of that fearful ordnance, and returned no answer.

It was about four o'clock in the morning. The enemy, that is to say, the travellers, were momentarily expected to make their appearance. At this critical juncture, Mr. Poins had removed the knight's horse, and tied the animal its owner knew not where. What is the knight at any time without his charger — especially when he labours under physical disadvantages which make "eight yards of uneven ground" a journey as terrible as "threescore and ten miles afoot?" This was the case with Sir John Falstaff. Here he was, burning with martial ardour; Victory, as it were, about to rush down hill into his arms; and the treachery of an inferior had placed him utterly *hors de combat!* There is only one point of view from which the conduct of Poins appears at all excusable: it was an act of real humanity to the horse.

"Poins! and be hanged; Poins!" the knight repeated.

"Peace, you fat-kidneyed rascal!" said the Prince of Wales, from a neighbouring hedge. "What a brawling dost thou keep!"

"Where's Poins, Hal?"

"He is walked up to the top of the hill: I'll go seek him."

And the Prince walked up the hill in an airy and unconcerned manner, *pretending to seek Poins.* Herein is exemplified the habitual duplicity and dissimulation of this young prince's character. He knew as well that Poins was close behind him, grinning in a hollow tree, as that in their own hearts (much hollower than the tree, by the way, only not nearly so big) they were gloating over a scheme of malice and treachery, of which their unsuspecting senior was to be the victim. "A plague on't," as that moralist himself observed, a few seconds afterwards, "when thieves cannot be true to one another!"

Sir John himself was the soul of honour among —— men of his own order.

"If I travel but four foot by the square further afoot," said the knight, sitting on a fallen tree and chafing like a caged lion — still more like a stranded whale, "I shall break my wind. Well, I doubt not but to die a "fair death for all this, if I 'scape hanging for killing that rogue. I have "forsworn his company, hourly, any time these two-and-twenty years;* and

---

* Either this is an illustration of the hereditary Falstaff looseness as to dates and figures, or a proof of our hero's marvellous insight into human character. Accepting the latter

"yet I am bewitched with the rogue's company. If the rascal have not "given me medicines to make me love him, I'll be hanged! it could not "be else. I have drunk medicines. Poins! Hal! a plague upon you both! "Bardolph! Peto! I'll starve ere I'll rob a foot further."

Sir John felt sick of rogues. In his wrath he even meditated the terrible vengeance of turning honest, and thus depriving his false-hearted comrades of the advantages of his counsels and alliance. But it had needed a more implacable nature than our hero's to carry animosity to such a deadly pitch. Moreover, Sir John, for one, would not set the base example in the camp of sacrificing duty to private feeling. Besides, there was another weighty consideration — he was in want of money.

These and other reflections calmed our hero; so much so, that by the time Gadshill, their scout (evidently from his surname a native of Kent, son, perhaps grandson, of one of Jack's deerstalking comrades in the days of yore; who knows?), arrived with tidings that there was money of the King's coming down the hill and going to the King's Exchequer, Sir John was himself again; forgetting fatigue, danger, and resentment, everything but that there was money of the King's going to the King's Exchequer.

"You lie, you rogue!" he said, "'tis going to the King's Tavern."

"There's enough to make us all," said Gadshill.

"Be hanged," put in Jack, in the highest spirits imaginable.

"Sirs," said the Prince, "you four shall front them in a narrow lane. *Ned Poins and I will walk lower. If they 'scape from your encounter, then they light on us.*"

And will any one make me believe that this man won the battle of Agincourt? — unless, indeed, by some parallel stratagem. There, as at Gadshill, I doubt not but he had his Falstaffs, Bardolphs *, and Petos to bear the first brunt of the battle, while he and his congenial fellows *walked lower* — reserving themselves to enjoy the fruits of victory. Never tell me what historians have said! I am an historian myself; and I know that there are some people of that profession who will write anything — provided they are properly paid for it.

"How many be there of them?" General Falstaff inquired, previous to arranging his plan of battle.

"Some eight or ten."

---

hypothesis, Sir John must have discovered Mr. Poins to have been a dangerous acquaintance in embryo, before that young gentleman had emerged from his cradle.

* This unpremeditated association of the names of Bardolph and Agincourt causes the historian to drop a tear on his proof sheet, in anticipation of a painful event that inexorable duty will compel him to chronicle by and by.

A prospective difficulty, such as could not have been foreseen by any but a comprehensive mind capable of embracing all emergencies, presented itself to our hero, who exclaimed—

"ZOUNDS! WILL THEY NOT ROB US?"

"What, a coward, Sir John Paunch!" asked the Prince, mockingly.

"Indeed, I am not John of Gaunt, your grandfather" (a favourite play on words with our hero); "but yet no coward, Hal."

"Well, we leave that to the proof."

"Sirrah Jack!" said Poins, as he sneaked away to 'walk lower' with the Prince of Wales; "thy horse stands behind the hedge: when thou need'st him there thou shalt find him. Farewell, and stand fast."

"Now cannot I strike him if I should be hanged!" exclaimed the magnanimous John.

Footsteps sounded, lanterns glimmered on the summit of the hill.

"Now my masters," said Jack, grasping his broadsword. "Happy man be his dole, say I; every man to his business."

They withdrew into "the narrow lane." This was a short cut, down which the travellers would probably walk, leaving their horses to be led round by the high road. Such proved to be the case. The travellers, four in number, were plebeians of the vulgarest description; shopmen, farmers, carriers, and the like,—people with large hands and coarse minds, such as in all cases have been reserved by destiny as the legitimate prey of the superior classes: the only observable variation of their treatment being in the manner of levying taxation.

Four terrible figures rushed out of the darkness, and four terrible voices cried :—

"Stand!"

The unfortunate travellers would have been most happy to do so, only they were too frightened. They fell on their knees instead, and roared.

As you may suppose, this was not the way to get rid of the assailants. The four terrible figures attacked the four terrified ones. The leader of the former, a man of colossal stature and intrepid behaviour, let fall in his fury some remarkable words—

"Strike! down with them, cut the villains' throats! * * * Bacon-faced knaves! *they hate us youth*."

Sir John Falstaff was the speaker. Who shall presume to count a great man's life by years? Sir John, in the heat of action, was a mere boy again. Nay, in proof that his weight of flesh even sat no heavier on him than his weight of years, he exclaimed almost in the same breath :

"Hang ye, gorbellied knaves, are ye undone? No, *ye fat chuffs!* I would your store were here. On, bacons, on! What, ye knaves; young men *must live.*"

Why prolong the scene? Surely the mere statement that a man like Sir John Falstaff *fell upon four travellers*, is fully equivalent to saying that the latter were completely crushed.

The enemy retreated, leaving their stores in possession of the victors. The glorious field of Gadshill was unstained by a drop of blood. Nor was there a single prisoner taken. In fact the victory was undisputed, which appears to me the most desirable kind of victory. A man who will not let you get the better of him without a great deal of trouble, is obviously almost as good a man as yourself. And pray what is the object of a battle, except the establishment of decisive superiority?

Flushed with victory, and laden with spoils, Falstaff and his companions sat down on the grass to divide the latter. No signs were visible of the Prince or of Poins. Public opinion went strongly against those defaulters, who were treated as mere amateurs, with no real soul or aptitude for business. Of course, it was decided unanimously that neither of them should derive any benefit from the proceeds of an action wherein they had taken no part.

" There is no more valour in that Poins than in a wild duck," said our hero with trenchant scorn.

Had the selection of good Master Cruikshank's subjects rested with me, I would have pointed out, as the theme for one picture, Jack Falstaff, sitting on the ground, with a bag of silver between his thighs, stirring it round unctuously with his hand from right to left, sniffing its odour, as it were, and smacking his lips over it as over the ingredients of a choice pudding, whereof he knew the flavour and nutritive qualities by anticipation. To this, though, honest Master George might well object that Falstaff remained not long enough in that attitude to sit for a picture. Time rarely favours the world with a sublime moment, scarcely ever with many of them in succession.

" Your money! " cried a strange voice.

" Villains! " cried another.

And two men in buckram suits, with masked faces, rushed out of the wood and attacked the freebooters.

I will state the issue of this second and most unforeseen engagement, briefly, and then comment upon it. Falstaff and the rest, after a blow or two, *ran away, leaving their booty behind them.*

Now perhaps you have fallen into the vulgar error of imagining Sir John Falstaff a coward? Allow me to help you out of it.

The reflections and decisions of genius are instantaneous and almost simultaneous. The instinctive conclusions of Sir John Falstaff, on being thus unexpectedly attacked, may be summed up and classified as follows :—

1. That men, who can afford buckram suits (defensive armour of the period, of considerable costliness), are not common men.

2. That men out of the common seldom venture upon a dangerous undertaking without plenty of satellites in reserve.

3. That no sensible man will attack superior numbers unless supported by the reasonable certainty of some advantages.

4. That a man who watches a thief rob an honest man, and then takes upon himself to rob the thief, is decidedly a sensible man.

5. That a purse of silver is more easily replaced than a forfeited existence.

6. That the men in buckram hit rather hard ; and that the sensation of being thrashed was decidedly unpleasant.

7. That he, (Sir John), had better be off.

Acting upon these rapid convictions, Sir John Falstaff performed one of the most renowned manœuvres in his warlike career—the retreat from Gadshill.

Ordinary prose is inadequate to the emergency of describing this great event. A moment's grace, reader, while the historian calls on the poetic Muse—just to see if she be at home. Yes. It is all right.

> Flashing sparks from clashing blows
> Dimm'd the glare of Bardolph's nose ;
> Gadshill, Peto, screaming ran,
> (Warriors prompt to lead the van !)
> Falstaff last withstands the pressure,
> Strikes three blows to guard the treasure ;
> But the warrior braving death
> Can but fight while he has breath :
> Falstaff's stock is quickly done ;
> Foes are on him two to one.
> What's of martyrdom the fun,
> Or of gold the value ? None—
> When compared to flesh and bone
> To the weight of half a ton !
> White as moon three-quarters done,
> Hot and moist as autumn sun ;
> Round and swift as shot from gun,
> Down the valley see him run——
> Thus was Gadshill lost and won !

IV.

THE DAY AFTER THE BATTLE.

THE Boar's Head Tavern, in Eastcheap — the head-quarters of our hero, and where he drew his last breath — like the Old Swan, near the Ebgate Stairs, where he uttered his first cry — like the church of St. Michael, Paternoster, where his mortal remains found honourable asylum — was utterly destroyed in the memorable fire of London. Authorities differ as to the exact site of this famous hostelry. Some maintain that it stood at a certain distance, in a given direction, from some part of the present Cannon Street — the immediate vicinity of the Old London Stone being, not improbably, the implied locality. Others are of a contrary opinion, and insist stoutly that it stood elsewhere. Many archæological writers, whose verdict would have placed the matter beyond question, are silent on the subject. It is to be hoped that the antiquarian reader is satisfied.

Towards this establishment, on the night after the battle of Gadshill under the friendly cover of darkness, rode Sir John Falstaff — and the remains of his discomfited army. Do not be alarmed. No one had been killed. The only loss of numbers had been caused by the desertion of the Prince and Poins. But the march to London had been terrible. The troops were utterly without provisions. The exchequer was empty. Foraging excursions had been attempted, but in all cases had failed. To the horrors of war had succeeded those of famine — still worse of thirst. To give you an idea of the desperate condition to which they were reduced, it is actually on record that Esquire Bardolph was seen to *drink water* from a horse-trough near Deptford. Singular phenomena are said to have attended on this prodigy. It is asserted that, on the gallant officer bringing his face to a level with the noxious element, a hissing sound was heard, and a rapid cloud of steam ascended from the surface. The water, on the warlike gentleman's withdrawal, was discovered to be lukewarm, as if a heated iron had been thrust into it. Sir John Falstaff is the authority for these remarkable occurrences — which probably were but the creations of a distempered fancy, the result of his own exhausted bodily condition. At any rate, it is certain that the Falstaff troops reached the metropolis sadder and lighter men.

Still I would not have my readers imagine that I have fallen into the common view with regard to the issue of the battle of Gadshill; namely, that Sir John Falstaff was utterly routed, discomfited, and bamboozled in that engagement; that he was made by it a butt. a laughing-stock, and a victim ; that he lost fame, wealth, and standing by it ; that he repented, and was ashamed of it for the rest of his days.

For much of this erroneous impression, we are, no doubt, indebted to certain players, who, taking advantage of the dramatic form of Shakspeare's Chronicles, have attempted the personation of Sir John Falstaff on the public stage. I have frequently been moved almost to tears by the temerity of these people in daring to disport themselves in the lion skin of Falstaff. I have never been deceived by any one of them for a moment. Even before they have commenced braying, I have invariably recognised them by the patter of their hoofs, even though some of them have been the greatest ——— creatures of their species. These ——— creatures stuff themselves out with certain pounds of wadding, glue on a pair of white whiskers, ruddle their countenances, and say to themselves, "Now I'm Falstaff;" just as on the previous night they may have rolled an extra flannel waistcoat or so into a lump between their shoulders, and conceived themselves Richard ; just as on the following night, in virtue of a goat-like beard, a long gown, and a stoop in the shoulders, they will constitute themselves Shylock ! What is the Falstaff of which these libellers give you an idea ? A bloated, ridiculous poltroon. Now, in the first place, cowards do not get fat. They are a nervous race — unquiet and dyspeptic. The stage Falstaff runs away from Gadshill like a boy from a turnip-ghost; not like a sensible man with a respect for his skin, having reason to believe the latter in some peril. He lies about his adventures as if he expected Prince Hal to believe him — or cared two pins whether he did or not. On being detected in his fictions, I have invariably observed the stage Falstaff conduct himself in the following manner. He covers his face with his shield, hides in a corner like a school-girl, and kicks out one leg behind him in a fashion peculiar to baffled old gentlemen on the stage. At Shrewsbury he behaves so like an arrant nin-compoop, as to make it preposterous that he should ever have shown his face on a field of battle, let alone have been entrusted with the command of a troop. Altogether he appears before us a ridiculous, giggling, spluttering, snorting, inconsistent pantaloon, — a personage widely differing from the majestic figure faithfully copied, line for line, by my excellent friend George Cruikshank from the immortal full-length drawn by William Shakspeare, — and a man whose life I would no more condescend to write than that of the next potato-man who may become bankrupt through lack of brains to roast his merchandise properly for the market.

Those who wish to have my opinion of Gadshill in the abstract and in its upshot, as proving Sir John Falstaff the real master of the situation after all, are requested to accompany me critically through a chapter in the great

Universal History of Shakspeare, section Falstaff. Refer to the Chronicle of King Henry the Fourth, part the first, act the second.

The scene is the Old Boar's Head (interior). The time midnight, succeeding the Gadshill engagement. The persons first present are the Prince of Wales and Mr. Poins, his obsequious companion in infamy. (It is quite right to abuse the Prince at this period of his life, when it was his own wish to be thought a scoundrel. When he becomes a great man, I hope I shall know how to conduct myself towards him with becoming respect.) They have been in London some hours. There are no travelling difficulties for princes.

His Royal Highness has been amusing himself for a quarter of an hour or so by a series of practical jokes on a harmless waiter, which the Prince himself appears to have thought excessively clever, but which Shakspeare and the present writer have agreed to consider excessively stupid. Even the obliging Poins has not been able to see the jest. He is trying his hardest to discover it; and is determined to be convulsed with laughter, or perish in the attempt, when the landlord makes his appearance in the room, announcing the arrival of Sir John Falstaff and his followers.

A word as to this landlord,—though, indeed, he is scarcely worth it. This is the first and last we hear of him. In the course of a few weeks we find his wife a perfectly reconciled widow, and sole mistress of the establishment. There are two hypotheses as to the sudden disappearance of her husband from the scene. The first—which I have already formally adopted—is, that, at the period alluded to, he was ailing,—probably from the fatal facility of the bar-parlour;—that he died soon afterwards; that he was a fool, and not worth regretting or remembering. The second is, that his fair helpmate (of whom we shall have much to say hereafter) being a credulous woman, with a defective sense of legal obligation, had been entrapped into a fragile marriage,—whereof the only consolation existed in its fragility. It is not óf the slightest consequence: the vintner has made his sole appearance, and has been sent about his business to introduce Sir John Falstaff. Neither you nor I need care two-pence what became of him. At any rate, I don't;—you, reader, being a free-born Englishman, are at liberty to do as you please.

And now I will save myself the trouble of writing the next three or four pages, by allowing Shakspeare to speak for me without interruption. I shall be happy to hear anybody find fault with the substitution, and will even go so far as to consider it a compliment.

MR. POINS. — Welcome, Jack. Where hast thou been?

SIR JOHN FALSTAFF. — A plague of all cowards, I say, and a vengeance too! marry, and amen!—Give me a cup of sack, boy.—Ere I lead this life long, I'll sew nether-stocks, and

mend them, and foot them too. A plague of all cowards!—Give me a cup of sack, rogue.—
Is there no virtue extant ?   [*He drinks.*

THE PRINCE OF WALES.—Didst thou never see Titan kiss a dish of butter? pitiful-
hearted Titan, that melted at the sweet tale of the sun! if thou didst, then behold that
compound.

SIR JOHN FALSTAFF.—You rogue, here's lime in this sack too : There is nothing but
roguery to be found in villainous man : Yet a coward is worse than a cup of sack with lime
in it; a villainous coward.—Go thy ways, old Jack; die when thou wilt, if manhood, good
manhood, be not forgot upon the face of the earth, then am I a shotten herring.   There
live not three good men unhanged in England; and one of them is fat, and grows old :
God help the while! a bad world, I say.   I would I were a weaver; I could sing psalms
or any thing : A plague of all cowards, I say still.

THE PRINCE OF WALES. —How now, wool-sack ! what mutter you ?

SIR JOHN FALSTAFF.—A king's son! If I do not beat thee out of thy kingdom with a
dagger of lath, and drive all thy subjects afore thee like a flock of wild geese, I'll never wear
hair on my face more.   You prince of Wales !

PRINCE OF WALES. —Why, you abominable* round man ! what's the matter ?

SIR JOHN FALSTAFF. —Are you not a coward ? answer me to that ; and Poins there?

MR. POINS. — 'Zounds ! ye fat paunch, an ye call me coward, I'll stab thee.

SIR JOHN FALSTAFF. —I call thee coward ! I'll see thee damned ere I call thee coward :
but I would give a thousand pound I could run as fast as thou canst. You are straight enough
in the shoulders, you care not who sees your back.   Call you that backing of your friends ?
A plague upon such backing! give me them that will face me. — Give me a cup of sack : —
I am a rogue, if I drunk to-day.

THE PRINCE OF WALES. —O villain ! thy lips are scarce wiped since thou drunk'st last.

SIR JOHN FALSTAFF. —All's one for that. [*He drinks.*]   A plague of all cowards, still
say I.

THE PRINCE OF WALES. —What's the matter ?

SIR JOHN FALSTAFF. —What's the matter? there be four of us here have ta'en a thousand pound this day morning.

THE PRINCE OF WALES. —Where is it, Jack ? where is it ?

SIR JOHN FALSTAFF. —Where is it ? taken from us it is : a hundred upon poor four
of us.

THE PRINCE OF WALES. —What, a hundred, man?

SIR JOHN FALSTAFF. —I am a rogue, if I were not at half-sword with a dozen of them
two hours together. I have 'scap'd by miracle. I am eight times thrust through the doublet ;
four through the hose ; my buckler cut through and through ; my sword hacked like a hand-
saw, *ecce signum*. I never dealt better since I was a man ; all would not do. A plague of
all cowards ! — Let them speak : if they speak more or less than truth, they are villains, and
the sons of darkness.

THE PRINCE OF WALES. — Speak, sirs ; how was it ?

MR. BARDOLPH. — We four set upon some dozen,——

SIR JOHN FALSTAFF. — Sixteen, at least, my lord.

MR. BARDOLPH. — And bound them.

MR. PETO. — No, no, they were not bound.

SIR JOHN FALSTAFF. — You rogue, they were bound, every man of them ; or I am a Jew
else, an Ebrew Jew.

MR. BARDOLPH. — As we were sharing, some six or seven fresh men set upon us, ——

---

* I have ventured to modify a few of the old dramatist's expressions. My sole motive
for doing so has been a natural objection to being pointed out in the streets as the one living
writer who never did anything towards the improvement of Shakspeare's text.—BIOGRAPHER.

Drawn & Etched by George Cruikshank

Pub.ᵈ by Longman & Company, Paternoster Row —

Falstaff, giving his account of the affair at Gadshill —

" I made me no more ado, but took all their seven points in my target, thus . — Henry 4.ᵗ part thisᵗ. Act 2ᵈ scene 4.ᵗʰ

SIR JOHN FALSTAFF. — And unbound the rest, and then come in the other.

THE PRINCE OF WALES. — What, fought ye with them all?

SIR JOHN FALSTAFF. — All? I know not what ye call. all ; but if I fought not with fifty of them, I am a bunch of radish : if there were not two or three and fifty upon poor old Jack then am I no two-legged creature.

MR. POINS. — Pray God you have not murdered some of them.

SIR JOHN FALSTAFF. — Nay, that's past praying for : I have peppered two of them : two, I am sure, I have paid ; two rogues in buckram suits. I tell thee what, Hal, — if I tell thee a lie, spit in my face, call me horse. Thou knowest my old ward ; — here I lay, and thus I bore my point. Four rogues in buckram let drive at me, ——

THE PRINCE OF WALES. — What, four ? thou saidst but two, even now ?

SIR JOHN FALSTAFF. — Four, Hal ; I told thee four.

MR. POINS. — Ay, ay, he said four.

SIR JOHN FALSTAFF. — These four came all a-front, and mainly thrust at me. I made me no more ado, but took all their seven points in my target, thus.

THE PRINCE OF WALES. — Seven ? why, there were but four, even now.

SIR JOHN FALSTAFF. — In buckram.

MR. POINS. — Ay, four, in buckram suits.

SIR JOHN FALSTAFF. — Seven by these hilts, or I am a villain else.

THE PRINCE OF WALES. — Pr'ythee, let him alone ; we shall have more anon.

SIR JOHN FALSTAFF. — Dost thou hear me, Hal?

THE PRINCE OF WALES. — Ay, and mark thee too, Jack.

SIR JOHN FALSTAFF. — Do so, for it is worth the listening to. These nine in buckram, that I told thee of, ——

THE PRINCE OF WALES. — So, two more already.

SIR JOHN FALSTAFF. — Their points being broken, ——

MR. POINS. — Down fell their hose.

SIR JOHN FALSTAFF. — Began to give me ground ; but I followed me close, came in foot and hand ; and with a thought, seven of the eleven I paid.

THE PRINCE OF WALES — O monstrous ! eleven buckram men grown out of two !

SIR JOHN FALSTAFF. — But, as the devil would have it, three mis-begotten knaves, in Kendal green, came at my back, and let drive at me ; — for it was so dark, Hal, that thou couldst not see thy hand.

THE PRINCE OF WALES. — These lies are like the father that begets them ; gross as a mountain, open, palpable. Why, thou clay-brained guts, thou knotty-pated fool, thou villainous, obscene, greasy tallow-keech, ——

SIR JOHN FALSTAFF. — What ! art thou mad ? art thou mad ? is not the truth, the truth ?

THE PRINCE OF WALES. — Why, how couldst thou know these men in Kendal green, when it was so dark thou couldst not see thy hand ? come tell us your reason : what sayest thou to this ?

MR. POINS. — Come, your reason, Jack, your reason.

SIR JOHN FALSTAFF. — What, upon compulsion ? No ; were I at the strappado, or all the racks in the world, I would not tell you on compulsion. Give you a reason on compul-sion ! if reasons were as plenty as blackberries, I would give no man a reason upon com-pulsion, I.

THE PRINCE OF WALES. — I'll be no longer guilty of this sin ; this sanguine coward, this bed-presser, this horse-back-breaker, this huge hill of flesh ; ——

SIR JOHN FALSTAFF. — Away, you starveling, you elf-skin, you dried neat's tongue, you stock-fish, — O, for breath to utter what is like thee ! — you tailor's yard, you sheath, you bow-case, you vile standing tuck ; ——

THE PRINCE OF WALES. — Well, breathe awhile, and then to it again : and when thou hast tired thyself in base comparisons, hear me speak but this.

MR. POINS. — Mark, Jack.

THE PRINCE OF WALES. — We two saw you four set on four ; you bound them, and were masters of their wealth. —— Mark now, how plain a tale shall put you down. — Then did we two set on you four, and, with a word, out-faced you from your prize, and have it ; yea, and can show it you here in the house : — and Falstaff, you carried your guts away as nimbly, with as quick dexterity, and roared for mercy, and still ran and roared, as ever I heard bull-calf. What a slave art thou, to hack thy sword as thou hast done ; and then say, it was in fight! What trick, what device, what starting-hole, canst thou now find out, to hide thee from this open and apparent shame ?

MR. POINS. — Come, let's hear, Jack ; What trick hast thou now ?

SIR JOHN FALSTAFF. — By the Lord, I knew ye, as well as he that made ye. Why, hear ye, my masters : Was it for me to kill the heir apparent ? Should I turn upon the true prince ? Why, thou knowest, I am as valiant as Hercules : but beware instinct ; the lion will not touch the true prince. Instinct is a great matter ; I was a coward on instinct. I shall think the better of myself and thee, during my life. I for a valiant lion, and thou for a true prince. But, by the Lord, lads, I am glad you have the money. —— Hostess, clap to the doors ; watch to-night, pray to-morrow. — Gallants, lads, boys, hearts of gold, all the titles of good fellowship come to you ! What ! shall we be merry ? shall we have a play extempore ?

THE PRINCE OF WALES. — Content ; — and the argument shall be thy running away.

SIR JOHN FALSTAFF. — Ah ! no more of that, Hal, an thou lovest me.

Now, reader, do you know the opinion I have formed, after a careful study of the above historic dialogue ? Perhaps you will not guess, as it is widely remote from the common one. It is, that Sir John Falstaff DID KNOW IT WAS THE PRINCE. I don't mean to say in the heat of battle, when the outside of the knight's head monopolised all his attention ; but I believe, on after reflection, by calmly putting that and that together, he would have more than a shrewd guess at the character of his assailants. Why, then, all the lies and subterfuges ? Why the hacking of the Falstaffian sword with the Falstaffian dagger ? Why the tickling of the noses with spear grass to draw blood ? and the subsequent "beslubbering" of their garments therewith, under pretence of its being the blood of true men (a stratagem somewhat unworthily betrayed by Lieutenant Bardolph) ? Wherefore all these devices, with the certainty of detection ?

The answer is very simple.

It was Sir John Falstaff's object to make the Prince of Wales *believe himself a much cleverer fellow than he really was;* and I maintain that he succeeded most triumphantly in the present instance.

Well, the money was safe. The Prince was satisfied — Falstaff perfectly contented. Credit was unlimited — sack abundant. Nothing remained but to make a night of it. A night was accordingly manufactured ; the principal ingredient in its composition being the first specimen of a now popular class of entertainment on record, — namely, an amateur play, in which Sir John Falstaff, with much dignity, sustained the character of King Henry the Fourth, the Prince of Wales being represented (on that occasion, and by

Drawn & Etched by George Cruikshank

Published by Mess.rs Longman and Comp.y

Falstaff, enacting the part of the King ———— Henry 4.th part 1.st scene 4.th

particular desire), by His Royal Highness in person. The two leading comedians subsequently exchanged parts. The performance was received with thunders of applause by a select, if unfashionable, audience. For the libretto of this highly successful production, the reader is referred to the collected works of the able dramatist who has already met with such frequent and encouraging notice in these pages.

V.

HISTORIC DISSERTATION UPON THE GREAT CIVIL WAR WAGED BETWEEN THE REVOLTED HOUSES OF PERCY AND MORTIMER, ABETTED BY THE WELSH CHIEFTAIN, OWEN GLENDOWER, AND THE SCOTS, UNDER ARCHIBALD EARL OF DOUGLAS, ON THE ONE SIDE; AND KING HENRY THE FOURTH AND SIR JOHN FALSTAFF, WITH THEIR ALLIES AND FOLLOWERS, ON THE OTHER: WITH THE ARMING OF SIR JOHN FALSTAFF'S TROOPS, AND THE MARCH TO COVENTRY.

IN order to appreciate fully the position of Sir John Falstaff amid the stirring national events succeeding upon the action of Gadshill, it behoves us to quit, for a while, the private park of Biography, and turn into the high road of History; that is to say, to leave Sir John to his fate for a page or so, and give some passing attention to the doings of practitioners in his own line, but in a more extensive way of business.

In the commencement of the fifteenth century, the Scotch, obeying the hereditary instincts of their race, made repeated incursions into England— not, it should be stated, with that invariable success which has attended their more modern attempts in a similar direction. After various reverses, the flower of Scottish chivalry, commanded by Hepburn of Hales, were effectually routed by an English force, under the Earl of March, at Nesbit Moor, in the spring of 1402.

Archibald, Earl of Douglas, " sore displeased in his mind for this overthrow, procured a commission to invade England." So writes Hollinshed. It appears singular to us, that a Scottish gentleman should, at any time, have thought it necessary to apply to his government for permission to fulfil a portion of his natural destiny; but, of course, every age has its own manners. The Douglas, with an army of ten thousand men, advanced as far as Newcastle, but finding no army to oppose him, he retreated, loaded with plunder, and satisfied with the devastation he had committed, and the terror he had produced. The King, at this time, was vainly chasing Glendower up and down his mountains; but the Earl of Northumberland, and his son, Hotspur, gathered a powerful army, and intercepted Douglas on his return to Scotland. This army awaited the Scots near Milfield, in the north of Northumberland, and Douglas, upon arriving in sight of his enemy, took up a strong post upon Homildon Hill. The English weapon, the long bow, decided the contest, for the Scots fell almost without fight. Douglas and the survivors of his army were made prisoners.

Events immediately ensuing upon this engagement led to a rupture between King Henry the Fourth and the family of the Percies. The origin of the quarrel is thus described by Hollinshed: —

"Henry, Earl of Northumberland, with his brother Thomas, Earl of Worcester, and his son, the Lord Henry Percy, surnamed Hotspur, which were to King Henry, in the beginning of his reign, both faithful friends and earnest aiders, began now to envy his wealth and felicity; and especially were they grieved, because the king demanded of the earl and his son such Scottish prisoners as were taken at Homildon and Nesbit, for, of all the captives taken in the conflicts fought in those two places, there was delivered to the king's possession only Mordake, Earl of Fife, the Duke of Albany's son, though the king did at divers and sundry times require deliverance of the residue, and that with great threatenings: wherewith the Percies, being sore offended, for that they claimed them as their own proper prisoners and peculiar prizes, * * * * came to the king unto Windsor (upon a purpose to prove him), and then required of him, that, either by ransom or otherwise, he would cause to be delivered out of prison Edmund Mortimer, Earl of March, their cousin-german, whom (as they reported) Owen Glendower kept in filthy prison, shackled with irons, only for that he took his part, and was to him faithful and true.

* * * "The king, when he had studied on the matter, made answer, that the Earl of March was not taken prisoner for his cause, nor in his service, but willingly suffered himself to be taken, because he would not withstand the attempts of Owen Glendower, and his complices; therefore he would neither ransom him nor release him.

"The Percies, with this answer and fraudulent excuse, were not a little fumed, insomuch that Henry Hotspur said openly: 'Behold, the heir of the realm is robbed of his right, and yet the robber with his own will not redeem him.' So in this fury the Percies departed, minding nothing more than to depose King Henry from the high type of his royalty, and to place in his seat their cousin Edmund, Earl of March, whom they did not only deliver out of captivity, but also (to the high displeasure of King Henry) entered in league with the foresaid Owen Glendower."

The rapidity with which I have dashed off the foregoing paragraphs convinces me that I must have a vocation for what is called the higher walk of history. It is true that this, my first attempt of the kind, has been favoured by great facilities such as I might not always be so fortunate as to meet with; seeing that the whole of the above—quotations from Hollinshed included—has been copied out of a printed book now lying open before me (the name of which I see no necessity for divulging), with but few interpolations and excisions. Perhaps if I were to push on a little further in the same path, I might be able to surmount greater difficulties than have yet presented themselves. I say nothing. But time and the publishers say something to me,—namely, that I have no business to trouble myself with writing the History of England in these pages, at all events except so far as it concerns Sir John Falstaff. Therefore, I must reserve myself for a future occasion.

However, as Sir John Falstaff took a most active part in the civil dissensions excited by the feud above alluded to, the Knight's biographer must be permitted to dwell awhile upon the merits of that quarrel, ere resuming the thread of his personal narrative.

The "merits" of the case, in one sense of the term,—namely, according to the logic of the young naval officer who was ordered to report upon the "manners" of a barbarous people, may be briefly summed up, in the words of that marine authority, as "none whatever." It was simply a carboniferous contest between the forces of King Pot on the one side, and those of the revolted chieftain Kettle (aided and abetted by divers of his brother Smuts) on the other. Do not suppose me capable of wilfully depreciating great names and achievements below their legitimate value. Only, let us have justice. My especial business is with the reputation of Sir John Falstaff. If, in spite of my convincing arguments and unanswerable facts, certain wrong-headed moralists will adhere to the opinion that my hero was a mere thief, and as such to be reprehended, I, in defence of my own position, must insist—upon the showing of my adversaries—that King Henry the Fourth, Hotspur, Glendower, and Company, only differed from Sir John Falstaff as pilchards do from herrings, "the pilchard being the greater."* Hold me my

---

* *Vide* the Clown in *Twelfth Night*, an Illyrian wit of the Middle Ages, who was indebted for most of his *bons mots* to an acquaintance with Sir Toby Belch, an English *emigré* of the period, and, obviously, a personal friend of Sir John Falstaff. A companion work to the present (in two volumes octavo, on thick paper, with plates), to be entitled *Sir Toby Belch; his Life and Difficulties, with his Inducements to Foreign Travel*, has not yet been commanded by the publishers. The author bides his time.

knight virtuous ; accept me the moonlit field of Gadshill as glorious ; and I will honour Bolingbroke, glorify Shrewsbury, and weep over Percy with the most orthodox among you. But I will have no two laws,—one for the rich, the other for the poor. If Sir John is to hang, he shall make a fat pair of gallows. All the Harries of the period—old Harries and young Harries— shall hang with him !

Have the kindness, with all your dignity of History and what not, to show me the difference between the Gadshill expedition and the war of the Percy rebellion. What is it but one of magnitude? The King and the Percies had been in league to take advantage of certain Scotchmen—a people who, at that barbarous period, (however incredible it may appear now-a-days,) were not very well able to protect themselves—just as had been the King's son and the Falstaff fraternity, *quoad* the helpless Kentish travellers. The Percies took all they could lay their hands on, and wanted to keep it. The King was jealous, and would'nt let them. History delights in these *bizarre* coincidences. At the same time, it is remarkable that the chief bone of con- tention should have been the right of proprietorship in a few Scotchmen, — a commodity which must have been much more scarce, and proportionately precious, in England at that period than in our own favoured time, when the supply of the article may certainly be pronounced equal to the demand.

The story abounds in instructive morals. In the first place, the Earl of Douglas ought not to have attempted to return to his own country. It was an unnatural proceeding in a Scotchman ; and the Nemesis of his people overtook him accordingly. It is but just to state that on his being made prisoner he remained in England as long as was practicable, even on the condition of fighting under the banner of his late conqueror ; and only recrossed the Tweed upon compulsion. But the atonement came too late.

Enough of these wholesale dealers in the general Falstaff line for the present. Suffice it that the Percies were in the field at the head of a powerful army ; and were known to all loyal subjects (*i.e.* cautious people waiting to see the issue of hostilities) as "the rebels ;" an offensive epithet, but they were used to it. They had been rebels more than a dozen years before, when they had stolen a crown for Henry Bolingbroke, who was then a rebel with them. Henry was a king now, and had turned round on them ; just as his son was foredoomed to turn round upon Falstaff, Bardolph, &c., a few years later. It was in the blood, you will say ? Possibly. Still it is a plague when princes and warriors cannot be true to one another.

The leaders on the Royalist side were the King himself, the Prince of Wales, some more princes, dukes, and earls, whose names are of no importance, and
    SIR JOHN FALSTAFF !

It will readily be believed that under these terrible circumstances the rebels had their work cut out for them.

Sir John Falstaff stood in need of warlike excitement. In his own words, "he had fallen off vilely since the last action." Many things had occurred to sadden him. In the first place, the Prince of Wales, with characteristic meanness, had refunded the spoils of Gadshill to its original owners ; and Sir John "liked not that paying back," properly considering it "double labour." He had grown hypochondriac, and took strange fancies. Amongst others, he preposterously imagined that he was becoming thin. Mistress Quickly, hostess of the Boar's Head Tavern, knew better than this, having recently taken the knight's measure for a dozen holland shirts, at eight shillings an ell, provided at her own expense, and supplied to Sir John on the faith of his knightly promise to pay. These shirts were a sore subject with Mistress Quickly. Let us respect the memory of her feelings, even at this distance of centuries. None but a sailmaker, who has equipped, on credit, an Indiaman, which has gone down with all the wealth of its owner on board, could fully appreciate them. Altogether, Sir John was out of sorts : he lacked society. The Prince of Wales—an amusing young man enough in his better moments—was busily preparing his programme for the future astonishment of the world. Mr. Poins was, of course, in close attendance upon his highness, and rarely showed. Gadshill and Peto were uninteresting plebeians, only to be used when wanted. Bardolph was very well in his way ; but his way was not an enlivening one, at the best of times ; he so rarely opened his mouth, except to put something into it. With regard to Mrs. Quickly, she was becoming intolerable : she wanted her bill.

Also, with regard to Mrs. Quickly, at this juncture of our narrative (when I say "our," reader, I mean yours and mine—I have no intention of adopting the mysterious "we" of conventional literature) it behoves the writer to digress and apologise. The latter let us consider done. The former process I will get over as rapidly as possible.

I professed, a few pages back, to have done with Mistress Quickly's husband for good and all. Justice to my view of the lady's character— which is one of high admiration—compels me to allude to that shadowy person once more. I have stated that I believe him to have been ailing, giving the most probable cause of his indisposition. At this period, I believe his malady was approaching the final crisis, and that he lay on his deathbed —babbling, not like Sir John Falstaff, some years later (in the same chamber —who knows ?) of green fields, but of black cats and other flitting shapes— phenomena, I am informed, frequently witnessed by sufferers in the last stages of a complaint caught in the dangerous atmosphere of a spirit cellar too easy of access. I am sure there was some such domestic calamity harassing poor Mrs. Quickly at this time. There were heavy apothecaries' bills to be met; and, perhaps, tradesmen's accounts, (for which she had given her husband the money months ago, believing it duly paid,) pressing upon her. Otherwise she would never have troubled Sir John Falstaff as she did—for pitiful dross. Poor lady! it was not in her nature to give pain, and she knew how distasteful such questions were to the sensitive organisation of her illustrious guest. But that she had pressed him somewhat warmly is evident. For had not Sir John been compelled, in self-defence, to ward off her importunities by something in the shape of un-knightly fiction, as to certain valuables abstracted from his pocket in her house? There was no way else. The woman would not be appeased save by money or plausible excuses. If Sir John had possessed plenty of the former, and not had the slightest occasion for its immediate use, he would doubtless have paid her, in coin, and honourably commenced a fresh account. Having none, he could only offer her the substitute alluded to. The loss of " three or four bonds of forty pound a piece, and a seal ring of my grandfather's," is surely a fair reason for a gentleman of moderate means being temporarily straitened. After all, there was some truth in the matter. Sir John Falstaff's pocket *had* been picked (by those miscreants, the Prince and Poins—*vide* Shakspeare), and in Mrs. Quickly's house. The details of the robbery are of secondary importance. Nòthing can be justly called a lie save that which is utterly divested of truth!

Worthy Dame Quickly! I regret to find that it is the custom to consider her a very ridiculous and improper personage. I think she was a very good woman in her own foolish way. If Hero Worship be a true creed, she deserves honour amongst the foremost ranks of the faithful. She believed, rightly or wrongly, in one whom she considered a great man; and clung to him till the last, suffering for her faith in purse and credit, like a simple-minded, illogical, immoral, ungrammatical martyr, as she was. I believe myself that she was right. Her powers of perception were limited, but correct, as far as they could range. She had just wit enough to see the good that was in Sir John Falstaff—no more; and obeyed him like a slave or a soldier, pandering with unquestioning loyalty to his very vices, on the principle that the king can do no wrong.

To dispose of Mrs. Quickly's husband at once and for ever. I have already said that nothing certain can be ascertained about him; but a well-supported theory on the subject may be some consolation to those restless Shakspearian commentators who spend their lives in hunting after the unpublished facetiæ attributable to Juliet's nurse's husband—who write folios upon the probable birthplace of the undertaker's journeyman in *Richard the Third,* who doesn't want the Duke of Glocester to interfere with his professional duties,—and the like. It is, then, my confident opinion, that Mrs. Quickly became a widow at about the time of the battle of Shrewsbury — that is to say, if a lady can be said to become a widow who has never been legally married. That Mrs. Quickly had believed herself married let us hope. She was the most likely person in the world to be imposed upon, in this, as in other matters. But, assuming a legal contract to have taken place, how could she have preserved her maiden name? That Quickly was her maiden name is certain. For, in the *Merry Wives of Windsor,* Shakspeare introduces us to a second Mistress Quickly, housekeeper to the celebrated Dr. Caius, who wrote the well-known treatise on English dogs*, a spinster, and most obviously the sister of our hostess — the family likeness being, indeed, so strong between them, as to have led to a confusion of their identities by the ignorant and unobserving. It is no doubt in search of sisterly consolation from this second Mrs. Quickly, in a time of great tribulation, that the heart-broken hostess of the Boar's Head, in the third scene of the second act of the history of King Henry the Fifth, implores to be "carried to Staines," near Windsor.

Ha! an unexpected solution to the moral difficulty! one that may remove the last taint of suspicion from the lady's reputation. May not our Mrs. Quickly have been celebrated as the hostess of the Boar's Head in her spinsterhood? May she not have taken to herself a husband, changing her name, to the church and the law, but not to her customers, according to the practice of queens, opera singers, poetesses, and other celebrated women? The conclusion is at least charitable; and those who like, are at liberty to adopt it. For my own part, I cling to the belief that her husband, "the vintner" of the first part of *Henry the Fourth,* was a sponge and an impostor, one who probably made a trade of marrying unprotected landladies for their taps and cash-boxes, who most likely had half-a-dozen wives living, whom he had fleeced and ill-treated, of which fact Mistress Quickly, his latest victim, had full knowledge; but was, nevertheless, kind to her betrayer, in an upbraiding, petting, devoted, inconsistent, womanly fashion, to the very last. I may be doing gross injustice to the memory of a most harmless and respectable citizen; but I am supporting my theory of Mrs. Quickly's character admirably. Argument, like progress, according to a modern imperial authority, cannot march without its martyrs and its

---

* First printed in the reign of Elizabeth — with interpolations : hence the erroneous belief that Dr. Caius was a physician of that later period.

victims. If the vintner, in his lifetime, were really a good man, he would have forgiven me. So that upon the whole, we may consider the matter settled.

Sir John Falstaff, at the suggestion of Prince Henry, was entrusted with a charge of foot. It was all very fine to laugh at Sir John in time of security. When danger made its appearance, they were only too glad to rush to him for assistance. Prince Henry had staked his future reputation on the issue of the coming struggle, and chose his officers accordingly. Historians fix the date of the battle of Shrewsbury on the 21st of July, 1403. I am inclined to regard this as a proof that historians know nothing about it. At that period, the Prince Henry (who, it must be admitted, distinguished himself honourably in the action), could not have been more than fifteen years of age. Was this the sort of person, likely, not only to inspire the renowned and terrible Hotspur with jealousy of his fame and valour, but, moreover, to have previously obtained advantages, however temporary, over a man like Falstaff? I think not. Besides, the historians betray their habitual looseness in making Hotspur himself thirty-five years of age at the same period. This is simply preposterous. Would a weather-beaten warrior, *whose spur had ne'er been cold* since his thirteenth year, at a time of life approaching that, when, in the words of a chivalric bard, "grizzling hair the brain doth clear," express thus passionately his eagerness for a personal encounter with an unfledged stripling : —

> " Come, let me take my horse,
> Who is to bear me, like a thunderbolt,
> Against the bosom of the Prince of Wales ;
> Harry to Harry shall, hot horse to horse,
> Meet and ne'er part till one drop down a corse . . ."

Who says the above speech is not historical? I tell you, I find it in Shakspeare, who is for me the most authentic of historians. He may be wrong, occasionally, in a date or a name, and may, perhaps, at times allow his imagination to run away with him. What then? if in nine cases out of ten, as I believe to be the case, his imagination, in two or three bounds, carries him nearer to the truth than the plodding foot-passengers of history can ever reach in their life's time, encumbered as they are with their thick-soled shoes, clumsy staves, and ponderous knapsacks? In matters of remote history, we must take many things for granted, and can only sift the true from the false by our own instinctive sense of probability. When I compare a history of Shakspeare's with a more prosaic record of the same events, the odds of verisimilitude are infinitely in favour of the former ; and — as the less must be contained in the greater — when I find a man invariably right upon matters of real importance, why should I suppose him wrong upon trifles? Never tell me that a great mind will not stoop to the consideration of petty details, however essential. That is a weak invention of the incapable, who dread an invasion of the giants in their own little territory. The great mind knows that the world is made up of atoms, and can see a fly as well as a dragon. Virgil, in the present day, would have been a better authority upon steam ploughs and liquid manure than Mr. Mechi, of Tiptree Farm; Herodotus could have written a better sixpenny catechism of geography than Pinnock; I warrant Raphael Sanzio knew how to sharpen a crayon in less time, bringing it to a better point, and with less damage to his penknife, than any School of Design boy of the present century.

And so, upon the whole, I have decided to pin my historical faith—for great and for small, for positive and for doubtful—upon the representations of Shakspeare, as many wise men have not been ashamed to confess, in solemn assemblies, they have done before me.

This decision leads me to fix the date of the battle of Shrewsbury at the 21st of July (I yield the day of the month to Hollinshed and Co.), in the year 1408. At this time the Prince of Wales—history is generally pretty correct as to the birth of princes—was in his twenty-first year, and being a handsome youth, well trained to warlike exercises, with of course a princely command of ornamental outfit, would justify Sir Richard Vernon's glowing description:—

> "I saw young Harry, with his beaver on,
> His cuisses on his thighs, gallantly arm'd,
> Rise from the ground like feather'd Mercury,
> And vaulted with such ease into his seat,
> As if an angel dropp'd down from the clouds,
> To turn and wind a fiery Pegasus,
> And witch the world with noble horsemanship."

Sir John Falstaff at the same date would be (alas!) in his sixty-second year. Hotspur, according to the new reading I am sanguine of establishing, could not have been born earlier than the year 1382.

It must have been on or about the 10th of the same month (*i. e.* July, 1408) that Sir John Falstaff, having got the nucleus of his troops in marching order, prepared to lead them against the enemy, proceeding from London in a north-westerly direction.

The departure of the Falstaff troops from the metropolis, though an event, judged by its results, worthy of celebration by the historic pencil, was not, *per se*, one of sufficient importance to call forth any such public demonstrations as the closing of shops, the erection of triumphal arches, or of

balconies for spectators, the turning out of municipal authorities, the reading
of addresses, &c. &c.   The Lord Mayor of London on that day attended to
his business, cuffing his 'prentices and mixing his wines, stretching and
powdering his broadcloth, washing his stale ribs of beef with fresh blood,
or prematurely ripening his hides with marl and ash bark,—according to
the civic chair in that year happened to be filled by vintner, clothier, butcher,
or tanner,—just as though nothing were going forward.   There was
not even so much as a procession of virgins to scatter flowers before the
warriors' footsteps; not even a band of music to play before them; not
so much as a wooden barrier to keep off the crowd that did not come to look
at them !

There were two good reasons for this apparently contemptuous indifference
on the part of the public.   In the first place, it was not then customary
to celebrate great victories until after they had been obtained.   In the
second place, the Falstaff troops were not, at their setting forth, conspicuous
either by numbers or equipment.   They amounted altogether to certainly not
more than fifteen warriors, for the most part indifferently armed and clad.
Of these, two were our friends Bardolph and Peto, the latter holding the rank
of Lieutenant, to Captain —or, as he would now be called, Lieutenant-Colonel
Sir John Falstaff.   The exact grade of Bardolph in the expedition is not
easy of definition: it is to be presumed he officiated as a sort of aide-de-camp,
varying his titular distinction according to his audience.*   The remainder of
the troop were, it is true, men of some considerable renown, but owing their
celebrity to achievements which made their gallant leader by no means over
anxious to be seen in their company ; so that the march from London was
commenced in an unobtrusive, not to say straggling manner, Sir John Falstaff
himself not taking horse till his forces had been some half-hour before him
on the road to glory.

And was this intrepid chieftain actually about to risk the chances of battle
against the armies of Percy, Douglas, and Glendower, with such fearful
disadvantages of number and discipline as these ?   No, reader.   Let us guard
against exaggeration.   There are limits to everything —even the heroism of
Sir John Falstaff.   We must not lose sight of the fact that our hero would
have a king, with several princes and noblemen, with their followers, to

---

* A distinguished member of the Shaksperian Society has, I am informed, a quarto in
preparation devoted to the solution of the following vital question .—" Was Gadshill killed at
the battle of Shrewsbury? and if not, how is it we hear no more of him after the date of
that action ? "   I can answer the question in two lines.   Gadshill was hanged at Dulwich,
ten days before the setting out of the expedition, for robbing an aged farmer of two geese,
and a pair of leathern inexpressibles.

Drawn & Etched by George Cruikshank.

Falstaff's Ragged Regiment —

Pub.d by Major Longman & Company

support him in his expedition;—moreover, he was to recruit forces as he went along.

The mode of raising soldiers in those days was very simple, and much more efficacious than at present. There was, then, no occasion for foreign legions, militia nurseries; and such tedious devices. The king, who could only do one wrong—namely, that of allowing himself to be kicked off the throne by the other king—when he was in want of soldiers, resorted to the simple expedient of taking them. That is to say, he appointed his officers—who, instead of having to ruin themselves in scarlet cloth, bullion lace, sabres, feathers, and horseflesh, as in the present day—were merely expected to find their own soldiers, a commodity as cheap as dirt, and treated accordingly. This the king's commission enabled them to do with great facility. Armed with the royal authority, the officer entered a parish or township, and said he wanted a certain number of men. The local authorities were compelled to furnish the number required, subject to the officer's approval ; and the men selected were compelled to go, whether they liked it or not. This admirable system of recruiting, subjected to slight modifications, is still in vogue on the continent. Its discontinuance in our own country fully accounts for the fact —so often pointed out to us by our neighbours, who of course are more qualified to judge of us than we are ourselves—that we have long ceased to be a great military nation ; a fact which, though humiliating, is incontrovertible—witness the notorious incapacity of our Guards in the late Crimean war!

Sir John Falstaff was empowered to press into the service of King Henry the Fourth a hundred and fifty men. Amongst them there may have been several who looked upon that monarch as an usurper, and might object to fighting against the partisans of Mortimer, Earl of March, who, if English law meant anything, was certainly their lawful monarch. This was no business of Sir John Falstaff's.

And how did Sir John speed with his recruiting ? Admirably, as he did in most of his undertakings. His number was soon complete. Of the quality of his troops and his manner of raising them let him speak for himself. No description of mine could approach his own inimitable picture. (Let it be premised, in justification of this great captain's occasional regard of his own interest in the matter, that the commanders of regiments in those days had no such privileges as tailoring contracts, &c., and were fain to avail themselves of such advantages as offered.)

" If I be not ashamed of my soldiers I am a soused gurnet. I have misused " the king's press most damnably. I have got, in exchange for a hundred " and fifty soldiers, three hundred and odd pounds. I press me none but good

K

" householders, yeomen's sons : inquire me out contracted bachelors, such as
" had been asked twice on the banns ; such a commodity of warm slaves as
" had as lief hear the devil as a drum ; such as fear the report of a caliver
" worse than a struck fowl or a hurt wild duck. I pressed me none but such
" toasts and butter, with hearts in their bellies no bigger than pins' heads,
" and they have bought out their services ; and now my whole charge
" consists of ancients, corporals, lieutenants, gentlemen of companies, slaves
" as ragged as Lazarus in the painted cloth, where the glutton's dogs licked
" his sores : and such indeed as were never soldiers ; but discarded unjust
" serving-men, younger sons to younger brothers, revolted tapsters and
" ostlers trade-fallen ; the cankers of a calm world and a long peace ; ten
" times more dishonourably ragged than an old-faced ancient : and such have I
" to fill up the rooms of them that have bought out their services, that you
" would think that I had a hundred and fifty tattered prodigals lately come
" from swine-keeping, from eating chaff and husks. A mad fellow met me
" on the way, and told me I had unloaded all the gibbets, and pressed the
" dead bodies. No eye hath seen such scarecrows. I'll not march through
" Coventry with them, that's flat :—Nay, and the villains march wide betwixt
" the legs, as if they had gyves on ; for, indeed, I had the most of them out
" of prison. There's but a shirt and a half in all my company ; and the half
" shirt is two napkins tacked together, and thrown over the shoulders like a
" herald's coat without sleeves ; and the shirt, to say the truth, stolen from
" my host at St. Alban's, or the red-nosed innkeeper of Daintry ; but that's
" all one ; they'll find linen enough on every hedge."

The above profound reflections (which every officer of irregular infantry
would do well to lay to his heart) were made by Sir John Falstaff, on the
occasion of a review of his troops near Coventry — at which the Prince of
Wales and the Earl of Westmoreland assisted. I am inclined to fix the date
of this important military display on the third day previous to the battle of
Shrewsbury. The Royalist forces were proceeding towards that city by
forced marches. Sir John Falstaff, as is well known, came upon the field in
ample time to give battle to the rebels ; and it is improbable that any system
of forcing could have got him over sixty miles of ground in less than
three days.

Whether or not the knight found the hedgerows of Warwick, Stafford, and
Salop of such fruitfulness — in the matter of linen — as he had anticipated,
the historian has no means of ascertaining. The shirt in those days, it should
be stated, was a comparatively recent invention — nor had the art of the
laundress been brought to its present perfection.

V.

HOW SIR JOHN FALSTAFF WON THE BATTLE OF SHREWSBURY.

EVEN had the Royalist side been deprived of the immense weight of Sir John Falstaff's counsels and support, the issue of the struggle could not have been doubtful. Fortune seemed to have declared against the rebels from the outset. The Earl of Northumberland was taken ill at Berwick, and unable to join his gallant son in the field. The Welsh under Glendower did not come up in time for the battle. All the efforts of their gallant and patriotic chieftain to bring his troops past the neighbouring cheese districts of the border county of Chester had proved ineffectual.

Nevertheless the rebels determined on giving battle, which was perhaps a superfluous piece of generosity on their part, as the king, the princes, and Sir John Falstaff had come determined to take it. Hotspur—the warmth of whose heels would not seem to have produced in him any remarkable coolness of head—sent, on the eve of the engagement, an epistle to the king, which is strikingly illustrative of the knightly courtesy of the period. In this document he accuses Henry of murder, perjury, illegal taxation, obtaining money under false pretences, kidnapping, and bribery at elections.* The crimes of garrotting and stealing drinking vessels from the railings of private dwellings were not then known, or it is more than probable that these too would have entered into the wholesale list of accusations. Such a document, it will be admitted, was not calculated to dispose the king to leniency or placability. He was a monarch of the bilious temperament, and not at any time remarkable for excessive amiability or good humour. A popular historian has informed us that "he was subject to fits, which bereaved him for a time of reason."† The effect of such a communication on a monarch so constituted may be imagined.

Whether it was that the insurgent chieftains had formed a mistaken estimate of the king's nature, and imagined that he required a great deal of provoking before he could be induced to give them the thrashing they seemed so ardently to desire, it would be difficult to say. At any rate, on the morning

---

* Hall, folio 21—22, &c.

† *Pinnock on Goldsmith*—a work that has not come within the sphere of my observation for many years. The passage quoted, however, and many others from the same, were indelibly impressed on my memory at the time of perusal by a system of mnemonics now unhappily falling into disuse.—BIOGRAPHER.

of the battle, Sir Thomas Percy, the Earl of Worcester, thought it advisable to look in on the royal camp, as he happened to be passing, with a flag of truce, and favour his Majesty with a *vivâ voce resumé* of some of the heads of his nephew's spirited epistle of the preceding night, which might have slipped the royal memory. To Percy's address—which has been put into excellent blank verse by Shakspeare—the king replied with a proposal that the rebels should lay down their arms and go home quietly, which he knew would not be accepted. Percy departed, and the royal council of war at which he had been heard—and at the deliberations of which the Princes Henry and John, with Sir Walter Blunt and Sir John Falstaff, had. assisted—broke up to prepare for action.

The rival armies were drawn up on a large plain near the town of Shrewsbury overlooked by Haughmond Hill. The character of the ground is indicated in the opening lines of the fifth act of the chronicle of " Henry the Fourth " (Part I.) :—

> " How bloodily the sun begins to peer
> Above yon bosky hill ! The day looks pale
> At his distemperature."

Herein we have one of ten thousand proofs of Shakspeare's fidelity to historic and natural truth on all occasions. Mr. Blakeway says that great author has described the scene as accurately as if he had surveyed it. " It still merits the appellation of a bosky hill." " Bosky" must be taken in its ancient and poetical sense, signifying " wood-covered," and not in its more modern and familiar acceptation, which the presence of Sir John Falstaff, Bardolph, and other warriors of their way of living, might have rendered applicable to the aspect of the country.

The opposing forces were about equal in number, each army consisting in round numbers of twelve thousand men. In point of discipline and training the advantages were also fairly balanced. The light infantry, under Sir John Falstaff, consisted, as we have seen, of raw recruits, indifferently clad and nourished. But, as an offset to this must be taken into consideration the condition of the Scots under Douglas—large numbers of whom, being from the northern highlands, were, according to English notions, of necessity more imperfectly clothed than even the Falstaff troops themselves. For courage on either side there could not have been much to choose ; Englishmen and Scotchmen could hit as hard, and were quite as fond of doing it, then as in the present day.

Hume, writing of this decisive engagement, says :—

" We shall scarcely find any battle in those ages where the shock was more

" terrible and more constant. Henry exposed his person in the thickest of
" the fight : his gallant son, whose military achievements were afterwards so
" renowned, and who here performed his novitiate in arms, signalised himself
" on his father's footsteps ; and even a wound, which he received in the face
" with an arrow, could not oblige him to quit the field. Percy supported that
" fame which he had acquired in many a bloody combat ; and Douglas, his
" ancient enemy, and now his friend, still appeared his rival amongst the
" horror and confusion of the day. This nobleman performed feats of valour
" which are almost incredible : he seemed determined that the King of England
" should that day fall by his arm : he sought him all over the field of battle ;
" and as Henry, either to elude the attacks of the enemy on his person, or to
" encourage his own men by the belief of his presence everywhere, had
" accoutred several captains in the royal garb, the sword of Douglas rendered
" this honour fatal to many : but while the armies were contending in this
" furious manner, the death of Percy, by an unknown hand, decided the victory,
" and the royalists prevailed. There are said to have fallen on that day, on
" both sides, near two thousand three hundred gentlemen ; but the persons
" of greatest distinction were on the king's : the Earl of Stafford, Sir Hugh
" Shirley, Sir Nicholas Ganoil, Sir Hugh Mortimer, Sir John Massey, Sir
" John Calonly. About six thousand private men perished, of whom two-
" thirds were of Percy's army. The Earls of Worcester and Douglas were
" taken prisoners : the former was beheaded at Shrewsbury ; the latter was
" treated with the courtesy due to his rank and merit."

The above account is substantially correct. To the list of killed and
wounded it is necessary to add the names of Sir Walter Blunt amongst the
two thousand three hundred gentlemen, and amongst the six thousand
private men, one hundred and forty-seven hapless warriors whose particular
fate will be presently mentioned. Sir Walter Blunt was one of the several
captains whom the king had " accoutred in the royal garb," with the
view " either to elude the attacks of the enemy on his person, or to
encourage his own men by the belief in his presence everywhere." The
reader may accept which theory he pleases. I myself incline to the former,
having the greatest confidence in Henry Bolingbroke's wisdom as a general
and sense of his own value as an individual.

Of the violence of the shock between the conflicting armies, one circumstance alone is sufficient corroboration. Sir John Falstaff, emulating his
royal chieftain, also " exposed his person in the thickest of the fight"—nay,
may very reasonably be asserted to have been " the thickest of the fight
himself." We will not pause to dwell upon the magnitude of risk incurred by
Sir John—much greater in proportion to his bulk than that of the slender

and dyspeptic monarch—in exposing so vast a target to the arrows of the enemy. Our knight's heroic achievements are too numerous to need any stress to be laid on one solitary instance. Suffice it, that Sir John, at an early stage of the battle, conducted his troops to a position of the greatest danger, where they perished almost to a man. In his own light-hearted words, uttered amidst the most terrible carnage and peril, "he led his ragamuffins where they were peppered!"

"There's not three of my hundred and fifty left alive!" said Sir John, wiping his brow, that was clotted with dust and blood, "and they are for the town's end, to beg during life."

And with this historic fact staring them in the face, there are not wanting people to pronounce Sir John Falstaff a coward! Well, well! Sir John himself has told us what the world is given to!

The heroism of the Douglas and his gallant Scots has not been exaggerated by their compatriot historian, in whom exaggeration on the subject might well be pardoned. Those intrepid warriors—their movements, for the most part, unencumbered with nether garments—performed prodigies of valour and ubiquity. It was said of the field of Shrewsbury in the fifteenth, as of the four quarters of the globe in the nineteenth century, "You found Scotchmen everywhere!"

Amongst the Royalist gentlemen with whom the gallant Scotch leader had the honour of crossing swords in the course of the day, but to whom the reciprocal honour was not "fatal," as Hume has told us it had been to so many, we must class Sir John Falstaff. The fact that the hero of these pages was sought out for single combat by the "hot, termagant Scot," is a proof of the high estimation in which our knight's valour was held even by his enemies. The Douglas could not have mistaken him for the King, of whom he was in such active pursuit. Sir John's costume and personal appearance must have placed that out of the question. At any rate, they met and fought. After a brief encounter—in which the training of poor Wat Smith, the Maldyke cudgeller, was doubtless not forgotten—the fortune of war decided against our hero. He fell wounded,—not dangerously, or even severely, but wounded. The Douglas seeing his formidable enemy *hors de combat*, and—let us assume—espying one of the King's counterfeits in the distance, retreated without following up his advantage. I might revive national jealousies, which had better be left at rest for ever, were I to hint that the unquestionably brave Caledonian had *possibly had enough of it*, and had found his stalwart English adversary rather more than he had bargained for. I will content myself with the statement that the Earl of Douglas quitted the scene of action abruptly, leaving Sir John Falstaff alive,—not seriously injured, but for the moment incapable of doing mischief.

And now I approach what I confess to be a most delicate question, and one whereof the solution causes me much perplexity. The question is—

"WHO KILLED HOTSPUR?"

Hume, as we have seen, asserts that the young Northumbrian fell by an unknown hand; Shakspeare, as the world knows, represents him to have been slain by the Prince of Wales, after a brief hand-to-hand combat.

Which is the truth? Is either the truth?

As I have professed to abide by the representations of Shakspeare on all occasions, in preference to those of other historians, consistency bids me to adopt his views on this momentous problem. But I hesitate. After all, even Shakspeare was but a man. May not the wish to glorify a popular favourite have lulled his conscience to sleep just for once, and induced him to crown one hero with another's laurels? He *has* been known to falsify history for the gratification of popular feeling—in one instance most glaringly. Has he not loaded the shoulders of Richard the Third with more hump and iniquity than that monarch is historically licensed to carry? And why? Because he happened to be writing in the time of Henry the Seventh's granddaughter, and the name of the last Plantagenet was still execrated in the land; just as was that of the now respected Cromwell in the fine old English reign of the great and good King Charles the Second.

Let us, however, calmly consider Shakspeare's view of the case in point, and sum up the probabilities before coming to any definite decision.

According to Shakspeare, at the moment when the Earl of Douglas *was running away from Sir John Falstaff*—I repeat that I impute no unworthy motives to that possibly intrepid act on the part of the noble Earl—while the Earl of Douglas was running away, and Sir John Falstaff lay panting and bleeding (the Prince of Wales saw him bleed) on the field of battle, the two young Henrys, Percy and Plantagenet, had met, at a short distance from the scene of the last recorded struggle, and were exchanging formal civilities previous to the laudable operation of cutting each other's throat, after the chivalrous manner of our prize-ring gladiators, derived traditionally from the practice of the Dacian Pet and the Herculaneum Slasher, as chronicled in the writings of Tintinabulus.* The Game Chicken, from the wilds of Northumberland, complimented the Larky Boy—champion of the Westminster Light Weights—with some irony rather implying a regret that the latter bantam should be in a recently hatched and inadequately-fledged condition, and scarcely entitled to the honours of immolation at the hands, or rather the red-hot spurred heels of himself, the Northumberland Chicken, which he

* Vita in Roma . . . De Pugnatoribus. Cap. I.

K 4

declared the Larky One was nevertheless foredoomed to undergo; to which
Larky replied by advising his adversary not to crow prematurely, nor too
loudly, nor yet to waste arithmetical calculation upon chickens whose
incubation was at least problematical. He admitted that he was not an old
bird, but at the same time implied that he was not to be caught by the
peculiar species of conversational bait of which his opponent was so over
liberal. Briefly, they flapped their wings, and, without further cackling,
flew to the attack.

"The pen of Homer" has been worn by myself and others into a rather
stumpy condition for the recital of warlike encounters. Let me borrow the
pen of Jones, the latest London successor of the graphic Tintinabulus, to
describe the event in question, which Shakspeare represents as having "come
off" at Shrewsbury.

ROUND THE FIRST.

The two plucky ones were in admirable condition. At first it might have
been feared that the Westminster Boy, who had bolted from his training
a short time previously, would not be able to come to the scratch; while it
was presumed that the Northern Customer, having been for some weeks out of
collar, and at grass, might have accumulated a troublesome superabundance
of pork; whereas it proved ——

But no! The penholder of Jones is too much for the grasp of my
attenuated fingers. I cannot manage it. I may not attempt to particularise
the various fibbings, sloggings, grassings, and chancery suits to which the
conflicting champions subjected one another. I will confine myself to a
statement in plain language,—that the gallant Percy, having more than once
drawn claret from the heroic Plantagenet, and the latter mountain of courage
having given birth to a ridiculous mouse under the left ogle of his opponent,
both champions having repeatedly kissed the old woman*, and risen from
that filial process in a piping condition, the future winner of the Agincourt
belt had it all his own way, until the terror of the Scottish borders was
eventually gone into and finished.

After all, there is nothing like plain, straightforward, intelligible, unadorned
English!

Then, says Shakspeare, the Prince of Wales, having wiped his ensanguined
sword, and, let us assume, briefly congratulated himself on being well out of
a serious difficulty, delivered a funereal oration over the body of his late
adversary, which proved his Royal Highness to be gifted with the most

* Mother Earth. Vide "Tintinabulus." London edition, 1857.

Drawn & Etched by George Cruikshank.

Pub.d by Major, dragman. Str. Ludgate Lan

Sir John Falstaff's grand manœuvre, at the Battle of Shrewsbury !

·eminent qualifications for a popular lecturer. This burst of eloquence being terminated to his own satisfaction, he looked round with the pardonable vanity of a public speaker, to see if anybody had been listening to him. He was disappointed to ·discover no one but Sir John Falstaff, apparently dead, on the ground.

However, being in the oratorical vein, his Royal Highness was not to ·bè deterred from speaking, by so contemptible a reason as the absence of a living auditory. He accordingly let off the following· speech, addressed to what he considered a dead gentleman. A foolish proceeding, if you will, but princes are privileged :—

> " What! old acquaintance! could not all this flesh
> Keep in a little life? Poor Jack, farewell !
> I could have better spar'd a better man.
> O! I should have a heavy miss of thee,
> If I were much in love with vanity.
> Death hath not struck so fat a deer to-day,
> Though many dearer, in this bloody fray.—
> Embowell'd will I see thee by and by;
> Till then, in blood by noble Percy lie."

Having delivered himself of this laboured composition, the Prince of Wales went away to tell his father what a clever thing he had done.

And then Sir John Falstaff—GOT UP ! He had had ample breathing time, and felt, upon the whole, much better. He had sufficiently recovered his faculties to overhear and understand the concluding phrases of the Prince's soliloquy.

"Embowelled !" said Jack, rising slowly (the expression is Shakspeare's); " if thou embowel me to-day, I'll give you leave to powder me, and eat me " to-morrow. 'Sblood, 'twas time to counterfeit, or that hot, termagant Scot " had paid me scot and lot too. Counterfeit! I lie; I am no counterfeit. " To die is to be a counterfeit, for he is but the counterfeit of a man who hath " not the life of a man ; but to counterfeit dying, when a man thereby liveth, " is to be no counterfeit, but the true and perfect image of life indeed. The " better part of valour is — discretion ; in the which better part I have saved " my life."

The unapproachable wisdom of these words, which have claimed the discussion of the subtlest modern commentators, it is too late in the day to dwell upon.

And then Sir John Falstaff looked round and saw the dead body of poor Harry Percy. He was frightened, and confessed himself so. But let it be borne in mind *he only confessed it to himself.* The bravest are subject to fear. The faculty of apprehension implies comprehension. Lord Nelson had a dread of the sea to his dying day, because he knew it would be sure to make him sick for the first few days of a voyage. "You were frightened," said a bantering subaltern, after the Battle of Inkermann, to a veteran whose cheeks had turned as white as his hair on entering the action. "Quite true," said the brave old man, who had been nearly cut to pieces; "if *you* had been half so frightened as I was, you would have run away."

Let Sir John Falstaff speak for himself on the occasion:—

"Zounds! I am afraid of this gunpowder Percy, though he be dead. How if he should counterfeit too, and rise?"

Quite possible! Sir John knew very little of the defunct Percy's character. How was he to divine that Hotspur had but been distinguished by the worser part of valour—brute courage? For aught he knew, the young Northumbrian might have been as sensible a man as himself. But let us not interrupt the knight's soliloquy.

"I am afraid he would prove the better counterfeit. Therefore I'll make him sure; *yea, and swear I killed him.* Why may not he rise as well as I? Nothing confutes me but eyes, and nobody sees me."

(This episode of the civil war may be supposed to have taken place in a sheltered ravine of the plain of Shrewsbury, then intersected by the numerous branches of a stream, the source of which—on the hill of Haughmond—is now dried up.)

"Therefore, sirrah, with a new wound in your thigh, come you along with me."

Saying these words, Sir John Falstaff inflicted a gash upon the still warm body of Percy, which he proceeded to hoist on his shoulders. Not an easy task, considering our knight's bulk; but he was born to face and conquer difficulties!

The native impetuosity of the Prince of Wales's character cannot be better illustrated than by his impatience to procure a witness of some kind or another to his recent achievement. In the absence of a better, he pounced upon his little brother John, Prince of Lancaster, and possibly the most uninteresting character in English history. He dragged that mild prince to the scene of action, which they reached just in time to meet Sir John Falstaff bearing off the mortal remains of the illustrious Percy.

Bewilderment and utter confusion of the distinguished visitors—especially Prince Henry.

"Now then, Hal," said Prince John (I translate the stilted versification of Shakspeare into familiar prose); "I thought you told me this stout party had gone to that thingamy from which no what-do-you-call-it returns?"

"Ahem! so I did," replied the elder, stammering and blushing a little.

"I saw the individual in question in a positively door-nail condition, not ten minutes ago; and I can scarcely believe my senses ——"

"Mr. Paunch—*are* you dead?"

No reply.

"Because, if you are, be so kind as to say so—like a man. Seeing is by no means believing in this exceptional case. I should be an ass, indeed, if I were to say I am all ears; but I listen attentively for your own testimony as to whether you are what you appear to be, or not."

"No, that's certain," replied Sir John, throwing down his body (I now quote the chronicler textually). "I am not a double man. There is Percy: if your father will do me any honour, so; if not, let him kill the next Percy himself. I look to be either earl or duke, I can assure you."

The Prince of Wales scratched his ear, and looked very uncomfortable. The Prince of Lancaster eyed his brother with an unmistakeable expression of opinion that the latter was the greatest humbug in the family—which was saying a good deal.

"Why,—" Prince Henry stammered awkwardly, addressing himself to Sir John Falstaff,—"Percy I killed myself, and saw thee dead."

Prince John of Lancaster whistled a popular melody in a low key.

Sir John Falstaff lifted up his hands, and exclaimed—

"Didst thou? Lord, Lord, how this world is given to lying! I grant you I was down, and out of breath; and so was he: but we rose both at an instant, and fought a long hour by Shrewsbury clock. If I may be believed, so; if not, let them that should reward valour take the sin upon their own heads. I'll take it upon my death, I gave him this wound in the thigh: if the man were alive and would deny it, I would make him eat a piece of my sword."

Prince John of Lancaster continued to whistle, and implied that the story was, to say the least,—singular. It was evident he was inclined to attach more credit to the representations of Sir John Falstaff than to those of his elder brother. You see, they had been at school together. No man is a hero in the eyes of the valet who takes off his boots when he is not in a condition to remove them himself; or in those of the little brother whom he has fleeced, fagged, and bullied at a public college.

Appearances were certainly against the Prince of Wales, and he was, at any rate, philosopher enough to make the best of the difficulty. For once, the conqueror of Agincourt—Englishman and warrior as he was—knew and confessed himself beaten. He felt that in this particular contest Sir John Falstaff had got decidedly the best of him, and morally yielded his sword with princely grace.

He contented himself with remarking to the Prince of Lancaster,
" This is the strangest fellow, brother John."
And then, addressing Falstaff,

> " Come, bring your luggage nobly on your back.
> For my part, if a lie may do thee grace,
> I'll gild it with the happiest terms I have."

At this juncture a retreat was sounded, proving that the fortune of war
had decided in favour of the Royalist faction. The two princes hastened to
their father's tent, Sir John Falstaff following, with the body of Hotspur on
his back, soliloquising as follows :

" I'll follow, as they say, for reward. He that rewards me, Heaven reward
him ! If I do grow great, I'll grow less ; for I'll purge, and leave sack, and
live cleanly as a nobleman should do."

The above is the Shakspearian account, and — as I have already stated —
in consistency I am bound to adopt it. But what I want to know is this, —
why, if the Prince of Wales really killed Hotspur, the paid chroniclers of the
period have not reported it ? I admit I can come to no definite conclusion
upon the subject, and will confine myself to the expression of an opinion that
the death of Hotspur is still an open question, — with the supplementary
reminder that Sir John Falstaff, being only a private gentleman of limited
means, could not hope for the historic recognition of an honour disputed with
him by the heir-apparent of England. And — to come to the point at once
— I really believe that Sir John Falstaff *did* kill Hotspur, and that his royal
patron bore him a grudge on that account to his dying day. It is the
only logical explanation of Henry the Fifth's notorious ingratitude to his
former boon companion, whom it would have been so easy and natural for
him to load with honours.

The Earl of Douglas, as we have seen, was punished by being sent back to
Scotland. Sir John Falstaff, contrary to his reasonable expectations, was not
made either Duke or Earl, in recompense of an achievement for which,
whether really performed by him or no, he at least obtained credit in the
opinion of many impartial persons. Herein we find not merely an illustration
of the proverbial ingratitude of monarchs, but also one, by implication, of the
personal jealousy of Prince Henry towards Sir John Falstaff, whom, as the
sequel will show, the Prince of Wales treated with the most pointed malignity
from the date of the Shrewsbury action to that of the knight's death.

I will merely remark that Henry Plantagenet — fifth English king of that
name — *was not a man to do anything without a motive.*

What Sir John Falstaff really gained by his glorious victory of Shrewsbury
shall be seen in future chapters. It will be found that he was not a loser

by the transaction. I will conclude the present chapter by a quotation from our knight's expressed opinions before entering the field of battle :—

"Honour pricks me on. Yea, but how if honour pricks me off when I
"come on? How then? Can honour set to a leg? No. Or an arm? No.
"Or take away the grief of a wound? No. Honour hath no skill in surgery
"then? No. What is honour? A word. What is that word honour?
"Air; a trim reckoning! Who hath it? He that died o' Wednesday?
"Doth he feel it? No. Doth he hear it? No. Is it insensible, then?
"Yea, to the dead. But will it not live with the living? No. Why?
"Detraction will not suffer it ;—therefore, I'll none of it. Honour is a
"mere scutcheon, and so ends my catechism."

I think the above observations prove that Sir John Falstaff knew rather more about honour than most people of his time, and therefore deserves a prominent position amongst the honourable men of the age he lived in.

BOOK THE FOURTH.

1410—1413.

I.

OF THE SIGNAL VICTORY GAINED BY SIR JOHN FALSTAFF OVER THE LORD
CHIEF JUSTICE OF ENGLAND.

THERE is reason to believe that Sir John Falstaff remained for some months
in the north-west of England, doubtless employed in pursuit of the scattered
remnants of the rebel forces. Some considerable time must have elapsed
from the date of the battle of Shrewsbury to that of his next appearance in
London of which we have any positive record. Sir John was most favour-
ably received on his return to the metropolis, where he was more than
compensated for the ingratitude of the court by the hospitable treatment of
the citizens, at whose expense he and his retainers feasted in great profusion
for many weeks, solely on the strength of the glowing accounts received
(never mind from what source) of our knight's achievements in Shropshire.

But a warrior like Sir John may not long rest on his laurels. A new
enemy had to be faced, arising in an unexpected quarter.

One of the most eminent men of the reign of Henry the Fourth (after Sir
John Falstaff) was William Gascoigne, Knight and Chief Justice of England.
The biography of this wise and excellent judge will be found in Master
Fuller's work upon English Worthies ; a book which would be irreproachable
but for the culpable and glaring omission of a personage so eminently
entitled to prominence in such a collection as the hero of these pages. The
anecdote of Sir William's courageous committal of the Prince of Wales for
contempt of court—in the celebrated criminal action of the King *versus*
Bardolph—is too well known to need recapitulation here. It is true that,
bearing as it does on two of the most conspicuous characters in this narrative,
some slight discussion might be opportunely employed on the occurrence ; for
instance, as to the nature of the offence which originally got our rubicund friend
" into trouble," and what was the real extent of the magnanimity displayed
by the Prince, on the one hand, and the Lord Chief Justice, on the other. It

would be valuable to the cause of historic truth to make quite certain whether the whole affair was, or was not, what, in the parlance of modern criminal jurisprudence, is called a "put up concern" between the two distinguished actors, having for its object a harvest of mutual popularity. The fact that Bardolph *was at liberty* in an incredibly short space of time after the event, lends a slight colour of such suspicion as I have hinted at to the transaction; but the rights of the matter are involved in such hopeless obscurity as to render all investigation on the subject worse than idle.

Though in the enjoyment of much and well-merited court favour, and public approbation, and being a man of modest integrity, it is still not unnatural or inexcusable that Sir William Gascoigne should feel some little jealousy of the more brilliant attainments and more enviable renown of a warrior, statesman, wit, and scholar like Sir John Falstaff.

The weakness of envy is perhaps the most difficult of all Adam's legacy for the best of us to rid ourselves of. History, ancient and modern, abounds in illustrations of the tenacity of this vice, even in the noblest natures. Dionysius the elder, and the great Cardinal Richelieu, though the one an absolute monarch of the fairest island in Greek colonised Europe, and the other the virtual master of the most warlike and polished realm of the seventeenth century, were both jealous of the pettiest scribblers of their respective days. The author of "The Vicar of Wakefield," and "The Citizen of the World," could not see a mountebank throw a summerset but he must risk the scattering of his valuable brains in an attempt to do the same thing better. To seek an illustration nearer our own time, have we not the celebrated little boy of the United States of America, who, though he had carried away the prizes for writing and arithmetic, committed suicide because an inferior mathematician of his own class defeated him in the correct spelling of "phthisic!"?

Is it then a great wonder that the Lord Chief Justice of England (an office which, after all, was then of little more importance than that of a police magistrate of the present day) should have felt envious of a man so vastly his superior in every way (except in the trifling matters of solvency and conventional honesty), as Sir John Falstaff, and should have sought to annoy his brilliant rival by every means in his power; of which, considering the official position of the one man, and the habits of the other, there could have been no scarcity?

Amongst other illustrations of what must be called *petty persecution*—(for, in a work of this serious description, things should receive their right names without respect to persons)—on the part of Sir William Gascoigne towards Sir John Falstaff, it may be mentioned that the former chose to consider the Gadshill expedition as a grave offence, punishable by the defective criminal code of the period. He summoned Sir John to appear before him to answer the charge. Sir John treated the invitation with the contempt it deserved, and went off to kill Percy—stay, that is a slip of the pen—I should say, to distinguish himself in the glorious field of Shrewsbury.

It will hardly be supposed that the tidings of Sir John Falstaff's safe return from action under a perfect forest of fresh-grown laurels were particularly agreeable to Sir William Gascoigne. Gall and wormwood, on the contrary, may be assumed to have been the flavour imparted by them to the chief judicial mind. At any rate, it is indisputable that his lordship had not many days heard of our hero's safe arrival and honoured treatment in London when he took a walk, attended only by a single follower, for the express purpose of taking Sir John Falstaff into custody. There is but one consideration which makes such a proceeding *wholly inexcusable*—namely, that the Justice should have nursed his vindictiveness for a period of so many months. This, it must be admitted, argues a relentless and unforgiving nature.

The Chief Justice was an artful man, as will be believed from his having risen to high rank in the legal profession. He thought it prudent to veil his malignant design even from his attendant.

"What's he that goes there?" He enquired, breaking off a general conversation to point towards a stout gentleman whom he saw walking leisurely down the street followed by a diminutive page.

"Falstaff, an't please your Lordship."

His Lordship affected absence of mind.

"He that was in question for the robbery?"

The robbery! You observe, reader? There was but one robbery present to his Lordship's mind, and that one committed possibly more than a twelvemonth back.

"He, my Lord: but he hath since done good service at Shrewsbury; and, as I hear, is now going with some charge to the Lord John of Lancaster."

"What, to York?"

The countenance of his worship fell considerably. These tidings were baffling to his hopes of vengeance. Sir John Falstaff was once more in the king's commission, and consequently not liable to arrest. Still Sir William was loth to let his prey slip wholly away from him.

"Call him back," he said to his servant.

There was some difficulty in getting the knight to arrest his course.

In the first place, he was afflicted with a sudden deafness. This temporary obstacle overcome, he showed an obtuseness of understanding as to what was said to him that was really surprising in a man of his intellectual antecedents. At length the Justice attacked him personally, with—

" Sir John Falstaff, a word with you."

The Chief Justice had his wish—rather more than his wish, in fact. Sir John Falstaff's manner of gratifying it shall be given in the exact words of the chronicler * :—

SIR JOHN FALSTAFF.—My good lord ! God give your lordship good time of day. I am glad to see your lordship abroad ; I heard say your lordship was sick : I hope your lordship goes abroad by advice. Your lordship, though not clean past your youth, hath yet some smack of age in you, some relish of the saltness of time ; and I most humbly beseech your lordship, to have a reverend care of your health.

CHIEF JUSTICE.—Sir John, I sent for you before your expedition to Shrewsbury.

SIR JOHN FALSTAFF.—An't please your lordship, I hear his majesty is returned with some discomfort from Wales.

CHIEF JUSTICE.—I talk not of his majesty:—You would not come when I sent for you.

SIR JOHN FALSTAFF.—And I hear, moreover, his highness is fallen into this same villainous apoplexy.

CHIEF JUSTICE.—Well, heaven mend him ! I pray you, let me speak with you.

SIR JOHN FALSTAFF.—This apoplexy is, as I take it, a kind of lethargy, an't please your lordship ; a kind of sleeping in the blood, a rascally tingling.

CHIEF JUSTICE.—What tell you me of it ? be it as it is.

SIR JOHN FALSTAFF.—It hath its original from much grief ; from study, and perturbation of the brain : I have read the cause of his effects in Galen : it is a kind of deafness.

CHIEF JUSTICE.—I think you are fallen into the disease ; for you hear not what I say to you.

SIR JOHN FALSTAFF.—Very well, my lord, very well : rather, an't please you, it is the disease of not listening, the malady of not marking, that I am troubled withal.

CHIEF JUSTICE.—To punish you by the heels would amend the attention of your ears ; and I care not, if I do become your physician.

SIR JOHN FALSTAFF.—I am as poor as Job, my lord, but not so patient ; your lordship may minister the potion of imprisonment to me, in respect of poverty ; but how I should be your patient to follow your prescriptions, the wise may make some dram of a scruple, or, indeed, a scruple itself.

CHIEF JUSTICE.—I sent for you, when there were matters against you for your life, to come speak with me.

SIR JOHN FALSTAFF.—As I was then advised by my learned counsel in the laws of this land-service, I did not come.

CHIEF JUSTICE.—Well, the truth is, Sir John, you live in great infamy.

SIR JOHN FALSTAFF.—He that buckles him in my belt cannot live in less.

CHIEF JUSTICE.—Your means are very slender, and your waste great.

SIR JOHN FALSTAFF.—I would it were otherwise ; I would my means were greater, and my waist slenderer.

CHIEF JUSTICE.—You have misled the youthful prince.

SIR JOHN FALSTAFF.—The young prince hath misled me : I am the fellow with the great belly, and he my dog.

" Henry IV." (Part II.) Act I. Sc. 2.

CHIEF JUSTICE. — Well, I am loath to gall a new-healed wound : your day's service at Shrewsbury hath a little gilded over your night's exploit on Gads-hill : you may thank the unquiet time for your quiet o'er-posting that action.

SIR JOHN FALSTAFF. — My lord ? ——

CHIEF JUSTICE. — But since all is well, keep it so : wake not a sleeping wolf.

SIR JOHN FALSTAFF. — To wake a wolf is as bad as to smell a fox.

CHIEF JUSTICE. — What ! you are as a candle, the better part burnt out.

SIR JOHN FALSTAFF. — A wassel candle, my lord: all tallow: if I did say of wax, my growth would approve the truth.

CHIEF JUSTICE. — There is not a white hair on your face, but should have his effect of gravity.

SIR JOHN FALSTAFF. — His effect of gravy, gravy, gravy.

CHIEF JUSTICE. — You follow the young prince up and down, like his ill angel.

SIR JOHN FALSTAFF. — Not so, my lord ; your ill angel is light ; but, I hope, he that looks upon me will take me without weighing: and yet, in some respects, I grant, I cannot go, I cannot tell. Virtue is of so little regard in these coster-monger times, that true valour is turned bearherd. Pregnancy is made a tapster, and hath his quick wit wasted in giving reckonings: all the other gifts appertinent to man, as the malice of this age shapes them, are not worth a gooseberry. You, that are old, consider not the capacities of us that are young: you measure the heat of our livers with the bitterness of your galls ; and we that are in the vaward of our youth, I must confess, are wags too.

CHIEF JUSTICE. — Do you set down your name in the scroll of youth, that are written down old with all the characters of age ? Have you not a moist eye ? a dry hand ? a yellow cheek ? a white beard ? a decreasing leg ? an increasing belly ? Is not your voice broken ? your wind short ? your chin double ? your wit single ? and every part about you blasted with antiquity ? and will you yet call yourself young ? Fie, fie, fie, Sir John !

SIR JOHN FALSTAFF. — My lord, I was born about three of the clock in the afternoon, with a white head, and something a round belly. For my voice,—I have lost it with hollaing, and singing of anthems. To approve my youth farther, I will not: the truth is, I am only old in judgment and understanding; and he that will caper with me for a thousand marks, let him lend me the money, and have at him. For the box o' the ear that the Prince gave you, he gave it like a rude prince, and you took it like a sensible lord. I have checked him for it, and the young lion repents; marry, not in ashes and sackcloth, but in new silk, and old sack.

CHIEF JUSTICE.—Well, God send the Prince a better companion !

SIR JOHN FALSTAFF.—God send the companion a better prince! I cannot rid my hands of him.

CHIEF JUSTICE.—Well, the King hath severed you and Prince Harry. I hear you are going with Lord John of Lancaster against the Archbishop and the Earl of Northumberland.

SIR JOHN FALSTAFF.—Yea; I thank your pretty sweet wit for it. But look you pray, all you that kiss my lady peace at home, that our armies join not in a hot day; for, by the Lord, I take but two shirts out with me, and I mean not to sweat extraordinarily: if it be a hot day, an I brandish any thing but my bottle, I would I might never spit white again. There is not a dangerous action can peep out his head, but I am thrust upon it: well, I cannot last ever. [But it was always yet the trick of our English nation, if they have a good thing, to make it too common. If you will needs say I am an old man, you should give me rest. I would to God, my name were not so terrible to the enemy as it is: I were better to be eaten to death with rust, than to be scoured to nothing with perpetual motion.]

CHIEF JUSTICE.—Well, be honest, be honest; and God bless your expedition !

SIR JOHN FALSTAFF.—Will your lordship lend me a thousand pound to furnish me forth?

CHIEF JUSTICE.—Not a penny, not a penny: you are too impatient to bear crosses. Fare you well: commend me to my cousin Westmoreland.

I consider this utter defeat of my Lord Chief Justice Gascoigne one of the most brilliant triumphs of Sir John Falstaff's victorious life.

" If I do, fillip me with a three-man beetle," said Jack, looking after the retreating form of his defeated adversary with ineffable contempt. " Boy !"

" Sir ?" said the small page.

" What money is in my purse ?"

" Seven groats and twopence."

" I can get no remedy against this consumption of the purse: borrowing " only lingers it out, but the disease is incurable. Go, bear this letter to my " Lord of Lancaster; this to the Prince; this to the Earl of Westmoreland; " and this to old Mistress Ursula, whom I have weekly sworn to marry since " I perceived the first white hair on my chin. About it; you know where " to find me.' "

And pray, who was old Mistress Ursula ? We may chance to hear of her by and bye.

II.

THE SAME SUBJECT CONTINUED : DEFENCE OF THE CHARACTER OF THE LORD CHIEF JUSTICE GASCOIGNE : CHARITABLE CONSTRUCTION OF HIS CONDUCT IN THE CELEBRATED ACTION OF QUICKLY *v.* FALSTAFF.

I WOULD that full justice to the greatness, wisdom, and magnanimity of my much calumniated hero could be accomplished without the painful task of censuring and exposing the conduct of those enemies to whose machinations he owed penury, neglect, and persecution in his lifetime—obloquy and misrepresentation after death. To censure at any time is a disagreeable task; more especially when the object of your strictures is a personage whose memory successive generations have held in reverential esteem. It is a thankless office to be the first to call attention to a stain on a reputation hitherto deemed spotless—as it is to be the first to tell your sleeping neighbour that his roof is burning. The raven is an honest bird and croaks the approach of bad weather with unerring truthfulness; but the raven is universally hated. I am aware that there are certain writers who have a taste for this kind of discovery, whose minds' eyes may be compared to a solar telescope, finding out an unsightly mass of blots, blurs, and creases, when the world at large can see nothing but uniform, cheering light. These gentlemen —who, supposing the mind to have a nose as well as an eye, may be called the carrion crows of literary judgment—so keen is their scent for a decomposing reputation, and so intense their enjoyment of dead excellence that has turned bad—are not desirable models for imitation. Neither are their antipodes—the *couleur de rose* critics, who deaden their mental nostrils to any " fly-blown " indications in a character they are compelled to digest; preferring to swallow the whole with hopeful self-persuasion that all has been good, wholesome, and nutritious. The conscientious and impartial writer will endeavour to observe a medium course between these two. But that course, how difficult to discover and observe! The soundest human judgment, like the strongest eyesight, is fallible. What we think are spots on the sun may but be the dazzling effect of more pure light than our imperfect optic nerves can sustain. We may think we are about to strip a masquerading daw, and at our first rude grip a heartrending cry will tell us that we have ruined the jewelled train of a majestic peacock !

The above I admit to be a specimen of that logical process known as " beating about the bush," a proof that I am staggering, like the pencil-leg of a knock-kneed compass, round a point which I have much hesitation in coming to. The case of the obscure youth who acquired immortality by burning Diana's temple, is a stale illustration, but I am fain to use it for want of better. It might be thought that I am aspiring to a renown like that of Erostratus, if the arguments of this chapter should result—as I hope and trust they will not—in a balance of probability to the effect that the venerated name of Sir William Gascoigne was really that of one of the most contemptible scoundrels that ever occupied his wrong place in a court of justice. I repeat that I hope my patient pursuit of truth in this very trying matter will not bring me to a standstill at so awkward a point. Nay, so terrified am I at the bare possibility of doing irreparable injustice to a great man's memory, that I will lose no time in admitting that very probably Sir William Gascoigne was a ten times greater, wiser, and more immaculate being than even his eulogists have represented him, and that, in a still greater likelihood, I myself am an obtuse purblind personage, with no soul to appreciate the more exalted virtues, and with a deplorable squint in my critical vision. Having admitted this as a possibility—without asserting it as a fact—of myself, I may be surely allowed the same speculative margin *quoad* the hypothesis of the Lord Chief Justice now under discussion, not having been, to use the mildest expression, the man he has been taken for. At the same time the reader will understand that I do not wish him to attach to my opinion (should I succeed in forming one on this most trying subject) more weight than is due to the honest expression of a private individual's most impartial judgment, the result of patient, untiring investigation of the most copious and incontrovertible facts, aided by a paramount thirst for truth and an intellect habituated to moral analysis.

Drawn & Etched by George Cruikshank.

Pub.d by Mess.rs Longman & C.o Paternoster Row.

Sir John Falstaff arrested...at the Suit of M.rs Quickly!

I trust that it will now be felt I am prepared to do Sir William Gascoigne the amplest justice; and will lose no more time in enumerating the moral enormities whereof I am so anxious to prove he could not possibly have been guilty. The decision I have already been reluctantly brought to—explained in the last chapter—that his Lordship's character was not free from a strong taint of envy, which only induces me to be the more careful. Let us shun prejudice above all things. Envy, as we all know, if not kept in check by the worthier attributes of our nature, will lead to the commission of every earthly crime, especially of offences such as those which I think—yes, I think—I am about to show you Sir William Gascoigne was incapable of meditating, or, at any rate, of putting into execution.

And now I have worked myself up into a perfectly sanguine condition. I am sure I shall be able to clear the Justice's reputation from the last lingering blemish of suspicion. If I do not succeed I shall be very much disappointed.

In the first place it is improbable that any close degree of intimacy should have existed between a man of Sir William's exalted position and an obscure person like Mistress Helen Quickly, widow and licensed victualler, proprietress of the Old Boar's Head Tavern, Eastcheap.

It is true that the great legal functionaries of that period—as of many much later—were usually men of obscure birth, raised, in most cases (unquestionably in that of Gascoigno), to power and distinction by the exercise of their own talents and virtues; allowing for this, it is not unlikely that Sir William, in early life, may have been acquainted with, and even befriended by, Mrs. Quickly. There is even reason to believe that they were blood relations. A statement from Sir John Falstaff that the lady was in the habit of going about London asserting—with pardonable arrogance—that her eldest son bore a striking physical resemblance to the Chief Justice would lend some probability to this theory. A suspicion on Sir John's part that this boast might have originated in mental hallucination may, or may not, be considered to weaken the evidence. We will pass this over, and confine ourselves to the supposition that Sir William Gascoigne, when a struggling law-student, was possibly greatly indebted to the maternal or sisterly hospitality of Mrs. Quickly. There would be no harm in his accepting gratuitous board—nay, even in his borrowing money—at her hands. Well! as a just man and a grateful, he would, of course, not forget his old benefactress in the days of his prosperity. Duty to his high position would not enable him to avow the acquaintance publicly (more especially if the by no means disproved relationship really existed). Still, it is not unreasonable to suppose that Sir William may have occasionally looked in at the Boar's Head, for a quiet flagon and a confidential chat with his friend the hostess, to whom as a lone woman and a

M

confiding innkeeper, his sage counsels — more especially on questions connected with the debtor and creditor laws of the period — would be in the highest degree serviceable.   The fact of an illustrious legal dignitary having a marked predilection for tap-rooms and bar-parlours is by no means without parallel in English history.   The great Judge Jeffries was given to that species of amusement.   So was a celebrated Speaker of the House of Commons, in the reign of George the Second, whose name I read the other day in a penny morning newspaper, but which I am quite sure I have now forgotten.

Mind, I am very far from asserting that Sir William Gascoigne ever saw the inside of a tavern.   The only positive record of a personal meeting between him and Mrs. Quickly represents them as utter strangers to each other.   But to assume this attitude — supposing the idle suggestions I have propounded (with a view to their ultimate refutation) to have the slightest foundation in probability — would be their most obvious policy.   Let that pass : I merely think it remarkable that on *the very day after the conversation recorded in the last chapter*, good, kind-hearted Mrs. Quickly, who had known Sir John Falstaff "twenty-nine years come peascod time," who, as we have seen, was one of our knight's most devoted admirers, and to whose nature an act of voluntary severity was a moral impossibility, should, at the moment when Sir John was husbanding all his resources for his second campaign against the northern rebels (a position indicated in the conversation just alluded to), from which he might never come back alive, suddenly belie the purport of her whole existence by arresting her ever-honoured guest for a pitiful sum of a hundred marks.   Mrs. Quickly did this; and the act would be incomprehensible, but for a light thrown on its motives by the unerring luminary of Sir John Falstaff's intellect.   He explained it in eight syllables:

" I know thou wast set on to this."

I do not state that Mrs. Quickly was "set on" by Sir William Gascoigne. But I should very much like to know who else could possibly have been her instigator in the transaction ?   I do not suppose Mrs. Quickly would have known where to find Messrs. Fang and Snare — representatives of the Sheriff of London — without some legal advice on the subject.   And allow me to ask, without prejudice, *What was Sir William Gascoigne doing, hanging about the neighbourhood with a strong posse of retainers at the moment of Sir John Falstaff's attempted arrest, unless to promote, and exult in, the discomfiture of his victor of the preceding day ?*   Perhaps the learned judge's personal biographers can clear up this matter on honourable grounds.   Nothing would give me greater satisfaction.   But, till something of the kind be really done, the thing certainly wears an unfavourable aspect.

Leaving the motives of the case an open question, and wishing to give them the most charitable construction, I will confine myself to the facts. Sir John Falstaff, returning from the city, where he had been making purchases for the coming campaign, was waylaid by Messrs. Fang and Snare aforesaid, who attempted to arrest him at the suit of Quickly, that lady being present in person. The terror of Sir John's name had been almost enough to keep the myrmidons of an oppressive law from entering upon their dangerous mission. That of the knight's presence spread a panic amongst their craven forces. Sir John Falstaff was not alone. He was accompanied by the formidable Bardolph—more than a match for any bailiff, as countless well-contested actions had proved—and the less terrible personality of little Robin, the page, before whom Master Fang's boy quailed abjectly. After a brief engagement, the troops of the Sheriff were routed. Victory, as usual, declared herself on the side of Sir John Falstaff—when, also as usual, invidious destiny interfered to deprive him of the fruits of conquest in the shape of the Lord Chief Justice, who suddenly made his appearance, "attended," (observe the precaution) from round the corner—quite by accident, of course!

The Lord Chief Justice, after a brief show of wishing to keep the peace (I wonder if Lord Chief Justices then, any more than now, were in the habit of doing duty as *common policemen,* unless for some private purpose), enquired the grounds of dispute. He certainly said or did nothing to prove that he had any previous knowledge of them; but he fell to abusing Sir John Falstaff, for being then detained in London instead of being on his way to York with his troops, with something like indelicate precipitancy — displaying a predisposition to quarrel unpleasantly suggestive to the modern reader of the fable of the wolf and the lamb.

It may have been a fault of the defective judicial science of the period, and no proof of personal bias, that Sir William conducted himself throughout the hearing of this case more as an advocate than as a judge. At any rate he sided with Mrs. Quickly from the outset, and "summed up" dead against Sir John Falstaff before he had heard a word of the evidence.

Mrs. Quickly stated her complaint in a rambling, disconnected speech, in which I do not say she was absolutely prompted by her learned friend (there is no offence in the designation ; if Gascoigne were really what he pretended to be, to call him the friend of the poor, the widowed and the oppressed, is surely a compliment), but which—from the looseness of the speaker's diction —was clearly a got-by-rote affair, and in no instance an expression of the heart's feelings. The first count in the verbal indictment was a matter of money lent, and debt incurred for board and lodging. The second was one of breach of promise of marriage.

Falstaff appealed to the *Justice*, in words, the purport of which I have already quoted.

"My lord, this is a poor mad soul: and she says up and down the town "that her eldest son is like you: she hath been in good case, and the truth is "poverty hath distracted her."

I have said that I decline giving an opinion as to the foundation of this report. I will only say, now, that the Lord Chief Justice had no better reply to make to it than a quibble. *He did not contradict it. Moreover, he suddenly became civil to Sir John Falstaff, and recommended a friendly compromise.* Curious, was it not?

Sir John Falstaff took Mrs. Quickly aside. The result of their *tête-à-tête* was an almost momentary reconciliation, proving the shallowness of the artificial soil on which the exotic plant of the hostess's animosity had been forced by the subtle devices of her legal adviser, *whoever that may have been.* Scarcely fifty seconds had elapsed, and ere the same number of words could have passed between them, the following colloquial fragment was audible:—

SIR JOHN FALSTAFF.—As I am a gentleman.

MISTRESS HELEN QUICKLY.—Nay, you said so before —

SIR JOHN FALSTAFF.—As I am a gentleman ; come, no more words of it.

MISTRESS HELEN QUICKLY.—By this heavenly ground I tread on, I must be fain to pawn both my plate and the tapestry of my dining chambers.

THE KNIGHT.—Glasses, glasses is the only drinking ; and for thy walls,—a pretty slight drollery, or the story of the Prodigal, or the German hunting in water-work is worth a thousand of those bed-hangings and those fly-bitten tapestries. *Let it be ten pound if thou canst.* Come, an it were not for thy humours, there is not a better wench in England. Go, wash thy face, and draw thy action. Come, thou must not be in this humour with me ; dost not know me ? Come, come, I know thou wast set on to this.

THE LADY.—Pray thee, Sir John, let it be but twenty nobles ; i' faith I am loath to pawn my plate in good earnest, la !

THE BRAVE.—Let it alone ; I'll make other shift ; you'll be a fool still.

THE FAIR.—Well, you shall have it, though I pawn my gown. I hope you'll come to supper. You'll pay me altogether ?

THE INVINCIBLE.—Will I live ?

And what was the upshot of this colloquy? Simply that Mrs. Quickly returned placidly to her home, under the friendly convoy of Bardolph and Robin, the former commissioned by his master to look well after the poor lady, and to see that no designing persons should a second time wean her from obeying the dictates of her better nature. It is worthy of remark that Mrs. Quickly did not say so much as "good morning" to the Lord Chief Justice. I suppose there was some motive for this, as for every other impulse of human action. For my part, I will maintain that course of dispassionate reserve I

Designed & Etched by George Cruikshank

Pub.^d by Longman & C.º Paternoster Row

Sir John Falstaff by his extraordinary powers of persuasion, not only induces Mrs Quickly to withdraw her Action: but also to lend him more money !!!~ Henry 4th A^{ct} 2.^d Scene 1st.~

have so scrupulously adhered to throughout this trying inquiry, and offer no opinion whatever on the subject.

Mind, there is one thing I cannot, and will not, and do not intend to, allow anybody else to believe. I will not have it supposed, for a moment even, that Sir William Gascoigne could have been interested in the issue of this action on any grounds so contemptible as pecuniary commission in the event of recovery. Emphatically—No! If personal feeling *had* anything to do with his interference, it must have been a feeling far nobler than that of mere avarice—to wit, revenge! He had been baffled, discomfited, eclipsed by Falstaff, and he was human. That he may have wished to blight the prospects of Falstaff, is, alas! for our fallen nature, but too possible! But I cannot believe that he would even have accepted so much as a clerk's fee from Mrs. Quickly,—in spite of the notorious corruptibility of judges in the Middle Ages, and the absence of any proof of such greatness of character in the subject of these remarks as should have placed him above the besetting weaknesses of his race and order.

And now I trust I have performed the difficult task I proposed to myself of doing the fullest justice to Sir William Gascoigne's character. More; I flatter myself that when mere barren justice has failed to reestablish the memory of that great man in a sufficiently favourable light, I have at times even soared into chivalry. As his champion defender I have fearlessly grappled with all the accusations that could be brought against him in connection with this critical portion of his career. If I have failed in refuting them, the fault is mine.

It may be asked why I have taken all these pains in clearing up the character of a man who forms but a passing accessory to my main subject? In the first place, reader, let justice be done though the heavens fall. In the second place, if I had not satisfactorily proved—(for I have proved it, have I not?)—Sir William Gascoigne's innocence of those charges, of which he might otherwise have been believed guilty, there are certain matters connected with the close of my hero's public career which it would have been impossible for me to explain away, except on grounds which I will here say nothing about, and which I hope it will not be my painful duty to allude to on a future occasion.

III.

LET us turn awhile from the sickening horrors of war, and the scarcely less revolting machinations of statecraft, faction, and personal rivalry, to contemplate Sir John Falstaff under the soothing influences of the arts and the affections.

With the valour and generalship of Hundwulf Falstaff, the necessities of Roger, the thirst of Hengist, the humour and, alas! the ill-luck of Uffa, — our hero inherited the literary tastes of his celebrated ancestor, Peter. A deficiency in that poet's praiseworthy attribute of industry may have been one reason for his not having enriched the literature of his country by any legacy of first-class importance. Moreover, it must be borne in mind that the principle of encouraging authors to composition by adequate pecuniary rewards — defectively understood even in the present day — was, at that time, not even recognised; and the bare idea of aimless labour to a logical intellect like that of Sir John Falstaff would be naturally revolting.

Nevertheless, high rank may be claimed for Sir John as a British author — not so much from his actual achievements in the field of letters, as from the fact of his having been one of the earliest pioneers in the cause. Viewed by this light, he is entitled to classification in the same category with Chaucer, Lydgate, and others. He lacks the learning and polish of the first-mentioned writer, and is deficient in the patient observation of the second; while both surpass him in fecundity. On the other hand, he is vastly superior to the Monk of Bury in richness of imagination and daring boldness of invention; while the charges of gross plagiarism and corruption of the English language by the adoption of foreign idiom, from which the fondest partiality has been unable to clear the memory of the author of the *Canterbury Pilgrimage*, have never been brought against Sir John Falstaff, that I am aware of.

The Falstaff papers — such fragments of the author's composition as have been saved from the wreck of ages (of which a perfect Spanish Armada has gone down, under the heavy fire of Rear-Admiral Time, since Sir John Falstaff trod the deck of earthly existence) — are not voluminous. Cause has been already shown to suppose that they could never, in any case, have attained to any considerable bulk. But on this head we have no accurate means of deciding. It has already been seen that *Sir John Falstaff had powerful enemies.* It would be to the interest of such people to destroy, or cause to be destroyed, any relics of our knight's greatness that might lead to the perpetuation of his glories and their own infamy. But I am getting upon dangerous ground again.

The favourite form of composition adopted by Sir John Falstaff was the epistolary ; and he may be confidently set forth as the first English writer who brought that delightful branch of literature to anything like perfection. I would not have it supposed that Sir John was a mere idle gossip, like Horace Walpole, Cowper, and such latter-day *dilettanti.* He was essentially a practical man — literature was with him a means, not an end. His pen to him was like his sword—a weapon only to be used upon pressing occasion ; but which, once assumed, was seldom laid aside till it had done good service. When he wrote, it was with the view to remedy some glaring want of the age he lived in. Being essentially the man of his age, he always knew, from the unerring test of his own necessities, what the age wanted, and wrote for it accordingly. There were no journals or magazines in those days. When our knight felt that any crying hardship or calamity inflicted upon suffering humanity — typified in the personality of Sir John Falstaff — might be removed by the exercise of a little eloquence, persuasion, or even casuistry, he had no alternative but to address his arguments, prayers, or remonstrances, to private individuals. And trust me, Sir John Falstaff was not the man to write letters for nothing.

The earliest specimen of Sir John Falstaff's correspondence extant (and of any such, I can fearlessly assert, there exists not one in a single antiquarian collection in Europe which the diligent researches of myself and emissaries have failed to discover) is a little schoolboy letter written in a villanous, sprawling attempt at the Gothic character, scarcely legible, owing to the ravages of time and the defective education of a lad of fourteen, at a period when English had barely begun to be a written language. How boys learnt to write at all under a caligraphic *régime* which made it almost as difficult to pen a syllable as to design a cathedral, is to me a marvel, only explained by the unwelcome theory that our ancestors were much cleverer and more persevering fellows than ourselves. However, that young Jack Falstaff, soon after he found himself put in the way of making his fortune, as a reward for stealing poor Sir Simon Ballard's venison (mythical foreshadow of its owner's doom, whom we have seen so cruelly hung and roasted !), was able to build up his groined "m's," "v's," and "n's," to erect the transepts on his "t's," and ornament the façades of his capitals generally, so as to leave them intelligible at this distance of centuries, is to me a proof that that good, kind, blue-eyed Lady Alice Falstaff, — of whom I regret to have so long lost sight, — was, amongst her other social recommendations, an excellent schoolmistress. For Jack's sake, I am inclined to regret that he did not stop at home to finish his education. But in that case, what would have become of this instructive biography — not to mention one or two amusing works on the same subject by a previous writer encouragingly alluded to in these pages ? Here is the letter — at least, such fragments of it as can be interpreted into modern English with any degree of certainty :—

"My good sweet mother, I am very well ; London is a rare place, nothing but houses. I have seen King Edward, he is an old man, ill-favoured, and ever groaning. He laughs pleasant though, and tweaked me by the ear, giving me a gold florence, saying it was to keep me from hurting his deer. I live in a fine rare house, but there are finer houses here, and Sir Thomas not near so fine as the princes are. You never told me there was a Queen. She is the same name as you, and very fair. The princes call her Mistress Perrers — why, I know not, except it be for sport. I saw the Princess of Wales that we call the fair maid of Kent. She is not so fair as the queen. She passed by the queen tossing her head quite disdainful. I asked why that was, and the queen said she had unruly sons who set their wives against her—whereat the king laughed, and the princes. The queen is not so old as you, and Prince John looks nearly as old as my good father. The queen is a merry lady, kissed me, and said I should be Mercury in her next pageant. She gave me a gold florence too, but my good father had it of me, Thursday last, saying *   *   *

*   *   *   *   *   *   *

Master Jehan says he will give me as many skins to write on as I will, so it be to write to you. Which he says good for me. He calls you that sweet, noble gentlewoman, my mother, and ever lifts his cap at your name. He makes sport for the princes with his sayings. I find no mirth in him, save his bad way of speaking English. He is sad enough with me. He lays his hand on my brow, looks at me, and sighs. I would fain please him, for, with all his tristeness, he is kind to me." [Here three lines are carefully effaced ; the words "saved" and "whipping" being alone decipherable.] "When I ply him with questions, he says ever, ' write to my mother, boy, and love her.' Why, see, now I do write, and   *   *   *

*   *   *   *   *   *   *

says he is struck by the falling sickness,—and truly he fell thrice up the pantler's stairs, coming to see me secretly, for Sir Thomas will not have him about the house   *   *   *   his chamber so sorry it would make you weep. The sanctuary is hard by the abbey. I found him much restored, and had got him canary with the gold florence I sent him—for medicine, he said ; but other distressed gentlemen were drinking it with him that seemed not much in need of medicine. He is nigh ragged, and takes it to heart that I should go in brocaded satin. I pray you send me the six shillings—for I would not have Sir Thomas know of the torn doublet. He comes home Wednesday. The Prince of Wales is yet sick in Gascony. My good father would have me borrow him a suit of Sir Thomas's—for one day —that he might visit a nobleman, owes him money, as he says. I was taking it from the house, no one seeing me but Master Jehan, who is ever prying. I was fain to tell him what I was carrying, and where. To see the rage he flew into, shedding tears, and chattering French, and yet not angry with me, for he said French for poor boy, poor child, many times. He bade me take the things back, and said he would go speak to my good father in sanctuary. I learn that he did so, and said bitter words to my good father — who hath not since named dress to me or bringing him aught of Sir Thomas's. Master Jehan is going again into

Hainault, in Flanders, and in truth I grieve not much. * * * * * My lady, Sir Thomas's mother, gave me a shilling, saying I did well to defend our badge against the Ferrers's—their's is the 'Six Horse-shoes,'—but this will not pay the doublet. I said not I beat him for that he said my good father ran from Creçy; and taunted me with my uncle keeping the sign of the 'Fleece,' in Watling Street. I warrant you I shall hear no more of it. Master Pollen, the pantler, tells me it is true my father had the tablecloth cut cross-ways in front of him, in sign of disgrace to his knighthood, which is a sore shame to us. I would thou and he were friends, that I might not hear him say such bitter things of thee—which I know thou dost not merit. I pray thee forget not the six shillings (easterling). Master Pollen knows a skilful tailor, his brother, will repair it for that money, and Sir Thomas never know. I am bound to an archery play on the moor—whereat Prince John says there is none to match me. I would Wat Smith knew of this. I would fain see him and Hob, and you and Mistress Adlyn and Peter. I pray you send me the six shillings.

"Your loving dutiful Son,

"JOHN FALSTAFF."

The above letter * is not dated; but was obviously written towards the autumn of 1365. From this date—to that of our hero's ripest maturity—there is a deplorable gap in the Falstaff correspondence. Indeed, with the exception of the above specimen, the earliest relic or mention of any manuscript in Sir John's handwriting may be traced to the conversation recorded in the first chapter of the present book.

Of the four letters entrusted by Falstaff to his page for delivery—the contents of two only can be known with any degree of certainty. The missing epistles are those addressed respectively to Prince John of Lancaster, and Ralph Nevil, Earl of Westmoreland—nominal leaders of the second Royalist expedition which Sir John Falstaff had pledged himself to conduct (it will be seen how the pledge was redeemed) against the northern rebels. The loss of these letters is scarcely to be regretted. Being written on the eve of the setting forth of the expedition, they were doubtless mere official despatches—containing reasons for the writer's not having taken the field as early as he was expected to—or some other device in warlike stratagem, and therefore of no interest to any but the student of military science. The two remaining epistles—which have been fortunately handed down to us—are of far higher importance, as throwing light upon the author's condition in mind, body, and finances, at this critical period of his career; when, as has been shown, he was about to raise his mailed heel, a second time, to crush the serpent of Rebellion—which reptile had most unaccountably managed to wriggle away from him alive on the field of Shrewsbury.

* Preserved in the Strongate collection, to which valuable depository of antiquarian lore (and the facilities afforded by its enlightened owner for its inspection) the writer cannot sufficiently express his obligations. He has much pleasure in being the first to announce that it is the intention of the fortunate possessor, Mr. Roderick Bolton, F.S.A., of Kemys-Commander, Monmouthshire, to bequeath this priceless collection to the British Museum at his decease. Long may the melancholy event be delayed which shall establish the nation in possession of so inestimable a legacy!

The first of these documents is a brief, playful note addressed to the Prince of Wales — on the return of that Royal Leader from the successful assertion of his claims to the Principality by the destruction of the bulk of its inhabitants. The manuscript has not been preserved; but the loss is immaterial. It existed as late as the time of Shakspeare, by whose care a verbatim copy of it has been transmitted to us. It is worded as follows :—

" Sir John Falstaff, Knight, to the son of the King nearest his father, greeting.

" I will imitate the honorable Romans in brevity. I commend me to thee; I commend thee, and I leave thee. Be not too familiar with Poins, for he misuses thy favours so much, that he swears thou art to marry his sister Nell. Repent at idle times as thou may'st, and so farewell !

> Thine by yea and no (which is as much as to say as thou noest him); *Jack Falstaff* with my familiars ; JOHN with my brothers and sisters ; and SIR JOHN with all Europe."

This epistle (meant as a mere reminder to the Prince, that his old companion is in London and anxious to see him) is conceived and written in a spirit of the purest pleasantry. This is evidenced in the mock stateliness of the exordium and signature, as well as in the allusion to imaginary brothers and sisters (Sir John, as the family annals and this history satisfactorily prove, being an only son). The caution against Poins is, of course, a joke ; but, as will ever happen in the most playful badinage of a true satirist, founded on a subtle perception of the truth. It is more than probable that Mr. Poins — not having wit to perceive the drift of the Prince's assumed easiness of disposition — may have contemplated the advancement of his family by some such device as the matrimonial device alluded to. At any rate, one thing is certain, *Mr. Poins did not relish the joke.*

However, this trifle serves to display Sir John Falstaff, on the eve of a vast military undertaking, light of heart and dauntless of spirit. The second letter is of a very different character and satisfactorily disproves the short-sighted, shallow theory, that our knight was incapable, on fitting occasions, of the loftiest sentiments as well as the most serious reflection. This letter exists in manuscript, carefully preserved in the collection to which I have so frequently expressed my obligations. I have been favoured with a photographic copy — which I hasten to transcribe with the idiomatic and orthographic modifications I have thought fit to observe in all such cases, for the greater ease of the general reader. Here and there a *hiatus* in the text occurs, due to the ravages of time. These I might easily have supplied from imagination ; but have rigorously abstained from yielding to any such temptation : knowing well that the most imperfect ruin is more valuable to the antiquarian student than the most elaborate restoration.

TO DAME URSULA SWINSTEAD, AT THE TRENCHER, COOK'S HOUSE, BY THAMES STREET.*

"MADAM,—You doubtless never thought to hear of me again. Myself never thought to trouble you more with knowledge of my existence. I speak not of paltry money debts. You will do me the kindness (I may not say justice) to believe that I have not injured only to affront you.

"I am an old man, madam—fifty-three in birthdays, and I may not say how much in suffering and wickedness. Nay, I must put wickedness first. You, madam,—I am in no mood for flattery,—are not young. You were a widow with three prattling children—Robin, Davy, and Maudlin (they have ne'er a thought for old Uncle Jack now, I warrant me)— when I first knew you eighteen years ago. Would for your sake that time had never been! No matter! I would say you have approached that calm, sober lifetime—and there is so little left to love or sorrow for in me—that you may hear what I have to say without heart-rending.

"I write, madam, to bid you a last farewell. I am for the wars, from which my chance to return alive is one to a thousand; and *that one I will cast from me.* You will think at my age,— having so well proved my courage,—I might be let to sleep on my laurels. They will not have it so. They will have courage like charity; wherefore a man, to keep his good name, shall not give his groat to one or two beggars and rest niggard ever after. He must be giving to his death. All's one for that. Duty to honour and my sovereign apart, I must to the wars, having naught left to live for save the earning a soldier's grave.

"I will speak the truth as a dying man speaks it, though it be to own himself villain. I have wronged you, but you know not how deeply. For eighteen years have I paid court to you—ever putting off our marriage upon some pretext, or earning your displeasure by some offence—but ever renewing the tie by fresh oaths and blandishments. *All this time, madam, I was a married man.* You knew it not—the world knew it not—but it was so. Blame me as you will, but pity me. As a headstrong youth, I contracted a foolish marriage with one who—well, she is no more; let her faults perish with her.   *   *
This woman has made me what I am : she has been my blight and ruin. I concealed her, like an ugly wound, down on my father's old estate; and like a wound in the flesh did she prey upon my heart and purse; for Lollard, witch, worse, as I knew her to be, was she not my wife? Happily, we had no children.   *   *   *   *
   *   *   *   *   *   *   *   *
Can you wonder then that without hope or aim in life—without a being to love me in the world—debarred from forming domestic ties, that the very hopelessness of my state should

---

* The "Cooks' Quarter," or assemblage of public eating-houses by the River Thames, existed in flourishing vigour as early as the reign of Henry the Second, and is affectionately described by Fitzstephen. A good idea of the barbarity of the times, and the utter ignorance of the first principles of commercial reciprocity, may be gleaned from a fact mentioned by that old writer, namely, that "the public cooks sold no wine, while the taverners dressed no meat." This unnatural state of things existed for more than three centuries, during which time it was impossible to obtain a glass of ale with your ham sandwich, or a chop with your pint of claret. It was not till the reign of Richard the Second that a reform was effected. Then, the great discovery was made, that it was possible to supply all the component parts of a meal, solid as well as fluid, in one establishment. In the simple words of Stowe, "since then the cooks have sold wine, and the taverners dressed meat." Surely this triumph over the habits and prejudices of ages must have originated in a master mind. Who so likely to feel the evil, so powerful to remedy it, as Sir John Falstaff? Assuming him to have been the Man of the Hour (that is, the dinner hour), in addition to his other claims to immortality, the hero of these pages must be ever revered as the inventor of the noble Art and custom of Dining in the City!—*Vide Fitzstephen and Stowe; Annals and Survey.*

make me regard you with your beauty (it is sore faded now ; I flatter not, you see), your loving heart and your tranquil home, as the fallen spirits must regard paradise? What could I do but hover round the celestial gates? And yet bitterly have I striven to be more than myself — more than mortal man. And here, suspect me not of the vanity of hoping to exculpate myself in your eyes, if I tell you things that may make you set down some of my offences to a cause less gross than you have done. Many a time, even when I have felt raised and purified by your love, have I sought to degrade myself in your esteem: that you might cast me from your heart. It has been at such times I have brought my riotous comrades to your house — have affronted your sober guests — have robbed you of your savings, and shown myself to you a sot, a glutton, a swash-buckler, and a cheat. Had you known the pangs it caused me ! Well, well ! I have omitted duties enough in my life, to be allowed the solace of remembering this one performed at—oh ! how great a cost !   *   *   *

This I must say, that when I first wooed you the woman was ailing, and I had hopes of her death. It has now come too late ; for, even if I should escape the rebels' swords, I cannot hope that you would forgive me so many years' duplicity and frequent ill-treatment, which, after all, I have no right to believe you will set down to its real motives. Moreover, compared to me, you are still young. To my eyes, you would be ever fair ; but that is nothing. You are wealthy, and what should I have to offer you but an old man's love, backed only by a noble name and a soldier's renown ?   *   *   *   *

    *   *   *   *   *   *

Even were it a gift, I would ask it fearlessly for our old friendship's sake. She must have a tomb becoming my rank, and I am penniless. A careless soldier, who is no courtier, cannot force kings to gratitude, or even to justice. The ring, I warn you, is of no great money value —as a jewel it would fetch little—let me say nothing. But to me it is priceless as an heirloom (you see it bears the letters of my ancestor, Keingelt Falstaff, with the hand grasping a staff), and should death fly me, as he will those who willingly pursue him, I would redeem it with — but this is idle. Only one thing could make me forego my resolution, which is a forgiveness I will not even ask for. I make but one stipulation ; that if I fall (as I shall do) you will say you received the ring as a gift in token of our betrothal. The story of my secret marriage will be then publicly known, and it will be no shame for you to own that you once thought to be a poor knight's lady.

"I have said enough. Farewell ! That pardon which I do not beg for alive I know will be freely given after my death. I have but one merit to set against my faults—I love thee. It is said. Farewell !

" JOHN FALSTAFF."

"The boy may be trusted with the money, and will call for it any time in the morning not later than eleven of the o'clock, when we start westward."

The story of Sir John's unfortunate marriage, alluded to in the above, is too apocryphal to be entitled to a moment's discussion. It may, indeed, be unhesitatingly set down as a pure fiction, invented from combined motives of policy and humanity — the former requiring no explanation ; the latter originating in a good-natured desire that Mistress Ursula should at least have the comfort of believing that she had bestowed her heart's affections and substantial friendship for a period of so many years upon a deserving object.

It is well known that Sir John Falstaff never married. "A soldier," as the sage Bardolph once observed in answer to an inquiry upon this very subject, "is better accommodated than with a wife." Sir John appears also to have considerately felt that a wife might be better accommodated than with a soldier; and though, doubtless, in his desire to please the fair sex, he frequently gave rise to dreams of happiness in numerous sensitive imaginations by *promising* the honour of his matrimonial alliance, he was never so cruel as to dispel such visions by the harsh realities that must have ensued upon performance. There is no happiness like that of anticipation. Sir John delighted in making people happy — ladies especially — and the more at a time the better.

It would betray an ignorance of the times to suppose that our knight belonged to any of those chivalric orders who were bound to celibacy. Such institutions — as far as concerns England at any rate — had been long obsolete at his birth. Nevertheless, a lingering trace of their spirit may be found in the contemplation of Sir John Falstaff viewed as a man of gallantry. The knights of old, instead of seeking to advance themselves by matrimonial alliance or to sink their renown in the peaceful joys of domesticity, were accustomed to give vent to their superabundant affections in Platonic attachments. This would seem to have been the case with our hero; who, at the period of his history now under consideration, entertained a chaste regard for a gentlewoman of good family, named Mistress Dorothea Tearsheet, between whom and Sir John no engagement of any kind appears to have existed. I regret that this lady's reputation should have been the subject of much calumny and misunderstanding, chiefly owing to some ribald expressions on the part of those ill-regulated young men, the Prince of Wales and his friend Poins. It is also brought forward in evidence against her, that she committed the impropriety of accepting an invitation to supper with Sir John, at the Old Boar's Head, on the night of the day on which the letter just quoted was written, and then and there indulged in certain conduct and expressions by no means compatible with the bearing of a reproachless damsel. To these charges I can only answer: that, in the first place, it has been asserted[*] that Mistress Dorothea was connected with Sir John Falstaff by the ties of relationship — an assertion which has never been refuted except by a sneer from the Prince of Wales, of whose veracity we know sufficient by this time — and there could be surely nothing wrong in a lady partaking of a farewell repast with a respected kinsman about to depart on a perilous enterprise, and who must have been more than double her age. Besides, it must

---

[*] PRINCE HENRY.—Sup any women with him?
PAGE.—None, my lord, but old Mistress Quickly and Mistress Doll Tearsheet.
PRINCE HENRY.—What pagan may that be?
PAGE.—A proper gentlewoman, sir, and a kinswoman of my master's. *Henry IV. Part II. Act* ii. *Sc.* 2.

not be forgotten that any suspicion of impropriety on the occasion was more than guarded against by the matronly presence of Mrs. Quickly. With regard to the freedom of Mistress Tearsheet's conduct and language, I need merely appeal to the manners of the age. The chaste Queen Elizabeth herself, more than two centuries later, is known to have taken part in the discussion of topics which would not be considered admissible within the circle of a modern drawing-room. That the lady was entitled to the highest respect is proved by the jealous care taken by Sir John Falstaff that she should be treated with such by all comers, manifested in the fact, that when, on the night of the supper alluded to, Ancient Pistol, having entered the room in a state of intoxication, applied some injurious epithets to the lady, Sir John was so far roused from his habitual forbearance — and from the comfortable process of digestion — as to administer to the tipsy officer one of the soundest drubbings he ever received in the course of his well-pummelled existence. Which incident you may read in the Second Part of King Henry the Fourth, or view depicted in Mr. Cruikshank's engraving.

Other specimens of the Falstaff correspondence will be introduced, and duly commented on, in chronological order.

IV.

WARLIKE STRATEGY OF SIR JOHN FALSTAFF: HOW THE KNIGHT ASSISTED THE YORKSHIRE REBELS AGAINST THE KING'S FORCES. — REAPPEARANCE OF MASTER ROBERT SHALLOW.

COMPARISONS have already been made between the hero of these pages and Julius Cæsar, Henry Percy, the great Earl of Warwick, the First Napoleon, and other heroes of ancient, mediæval, and modern history. The resemblance to all or any of them would be incomplete could we not prove that on some one occasion, at least, our hero suffered a sense of personal wrong or interest to withdraw him from a cause whereunto he had sworn allegiance, and induce him to throw the vast weight of his valour and influence into the opposite scale. This is as common and natural a proceeding with the rulers of kingdoms and armies, as it is with vulgar persons to withdraw their custom from a shop, when they have been offended or ill-served — in favour of another where they expect greater civility or better bargains. It is true that the lives of thousands, and the welfare of entire communities, may be

Drawn & Etched by George Cruikshank

Sir John Falstaff driving Pistol from his presence —

Hen.y 4th part 2d Scene 4th —

Pubd by Messrs Longman & Co Paternoster Row —

sacrificed by such conduct on the part of great leaders. But these com-
modities, to such people, are merely what shillings and pence are to the
retail purchasers—the base counters by which the value of their connection
is to be estimated.

Sir John Falstaff, as I have shown, had been slighted by the King,
outraged by the King's Chief Justiciary, and trifled with by the King's son,
(I have not thought fit to call attention to His Highness's last practical joke
attempted on our hero, on the occasion of the supper alluded to at the close
of the last chapter; in which, by consulting the chronicle, it will be seen the
Prince came off no better than usual in such matches). And in the face of
this treatment, it was expected that Sir John would, at a moment's notice
and without a word of apology, come forward with his original loyalty
unshaken to annihilate the King's enemies—now assembled in large numbers
in Yorkshire under the leadership of the Earl of Northumberland, the Archbishop of York, and Thomas Mowbray, Earl of Nottingham and Lord
Marshal of England—(son and successor to Sir John's old lord and tutor—
many years since exiled and cut to pieces by Saracen scimitars, in default
of the privilege of having his ribs poked, his skull cleft, or his neck severed,
comfortably, in his native land—the natural destiny and laudable ambition
of every English nobleman of the period!) Briefly, Sir John resolved that
he would do nothing of the kind.

It might be urged that Sir John—being in the main a good fellow, with a
sense of justice lying somewhere or other at the bottom of his heart, and only
a bit of a rogue upon expediency—in coming to such a resolution might have
been actuated by other motives than such as we have suggested; that he
might have thought the demands of the rebels were rather reasonable than
otherwise (which they were), and that it might have gone against his conscience to aid and abet an intolerable crowned ruffian like Henry the Fourth
—an assassin, an usurper, a kidnapper, a widow and orphan spoiler; and, to
crown all, the man who enjoyed the distinguished honour of having introduced the practice of burning religious reformers (to which order he himself
had once professed to belong) in this country—in his designs against better
men and truer patriots than himself. To accept this theory would be a confession of weakness on Sir John Falstaff's part, classing him among mere contemptible well-meaning persons—wholly destructive to those claims to the
GREAT SOULED or HEROIC CHARACTER which it has been my aim to establish
for him from the very commencement of these pages. So I will follow the
invariable custom of gentlemen of my calling, and adopt the view that best
suits me.

It must not be supposed that Sir John Falstaff went, at once, over with all his forces to the enemy's ranks. This would have been difficult, because, in the first place (which may forestal all further considerations), he had no forces. His general orders from head-quarters were that "he was to take up soldiers in the counties as he went." Upon this Sir John built a most effective stratagem.

The reader who has not been lately at school (the remark will apply equally to the reader who has not yet gone there) is requested to cast his eye over a work, not so well-known in this country as it might be,—the map of England. Let him there study the relative positions of London and York-shire. If gifted with an intellect never so little logical, he will divine from his observations that the shortest way from the metropolis to the great northern county would *not* lie through Gloucestershire ; and that the journey performed *viâ* that part of England would necessitate some considerable loss of time. Yorkshire being the centre of warlike operations, and the necessity for giving immediate battle to the rebels being imminent, it will be credited that reinforcements arriving *viâ* Gloucestershire would not be of material service to the Royalist cause—which, through having been relied on, their non-appearance, in time, might indeed be calculated to injure. Accordingly Sir John Falstaff, to whom a *carte blanche* of counties for his recruiting had been somewhat rashly given, decided that he would go round by Glouces-tershire.

And Sir John did go round by Gloucestershire. That is certain. Also is it that he lost considerable time by so doing. This is proved by the fact that he did not come up with the King's troops in Yorkshire till just at the close of the battle of Gualtree Forest (in which the rebels had been un-accountably routed without his assistance), and that in a "travel-tainted" condition. As we can only judge of men's motives by their acts, we have a right to assume (as I have done) that Sir John Falstaff delayed his arrival purposely—to give advantage to the enemy, with whom he secretly sympa-thised—by withholding his terrible presence.

And yet there may have been another motive. Let us look at all possible sides of the question. Let us assume, for the sake of argument, that Sir John's feelings towards the cause of Henry were not those of hostility but of mere indifference ; and that he felt a not uncharacteristic preference for indulging in the gratification of his own pleasure and advantage, to swelling the victo-ries of an ungrateful monarch. Let us suppose that he bent his northern course a little westward, for the purpose of touching at his favourite Coventry. *Why* his favourite Coventry? Because he once marched through that city with a disgraceful retinue ? Reader, I am surprised at your ignorance. Do you not know that near to the city of Coventry stood the manor of Cheylesford, the private residence of Prince Hal, appertaining (Heaven knows why) to the Duchy of Cornwall, where the Prince and his comrades performed the wildest of their mad pranks ; that it was "thither," according to the chronicler Walsingham, "resorted all the young nobility as to a king's court, while that of Henry the Fourth was deserted ; that it was here the Prince and some of his comrades (of course, Falstaff among them) were laid by the heels by John Hornesby, the Mayor of Coventry, for raising a riot ?" If you do not know all this, reader, let me tell you that *I* do ; and it is of no consequence to you when I came by the information — whether years before I commenced this elaborate historical study, or only the day before yesterday.

Who then so likely to be a popular man in Coventry as Sir John Falstaff—the master, *par excellence*, of the Princely Revels ? What town in the kingdom so likely to be endeared to Sir John's affections as Coventry? Why, the knight's repugnance to run the gauntlet of the gibes of his familiars, admirers, and butts, when at the head of his ragged regiment, is at once explained ! What a joke for the pages and courtiers hanging about the inn-doors ! What giggling from the tavern wenches ! What grim chuckling and rubbing of hands from the long-account-keeping tradesmen ! Above all, what triumph for the malignant soul of John Hornesby, Mayor of Coventry !

As I reflect on this view of the case, I find myself imperceptibly framing a new theory which tempts me to reject my former one. Yes, I have decided. I will assert an Englishman's privilege of doing what he likes with his own, and throw it over altogether.

I am disposed, then, to maintain that, on this occasion, Sir John Falstaff entered Coventry more scantily, but more creditably attended than on the last ; and took up his quarters at his favourite inn (the one where his bill was the shortest) with no intention of moving until the urgencies of war should absolutely compel him. Here he would be surrounded by old Cheylesford cronies —hangers-on to the palace — with their hangers-on and *their* hangers-on — with the hangers-on of the latter—and so on dwindling into indefinite perspective. I can fancy Sir John, the true master of the situation — dispensing the last court scandal—retailing the last town jests—disposing of the rebellion, the King's state of health, the Queen's avarice and last rumoured act of sorcery, the Prince's designs ; in a word, laying down the law generally.

I can conceive him fighting the battle of Shrewsbury over again,—killing Percy by the cruellest of deaths, after the most protracted of sanguinary encounters,—and inflicting upon the absent Earl of Douglas what that gallant warrior, throughout his life, had never been accustomed to receive—

N

wounds aimed at him from behind his back.   The rare honours Sir John
found awaiting him on his return to London — the feasts prepared for him —
and the precious gifts of gold, jewels, and costly raiment, showered upon him
— all these would doubtless be displayed to the minds' eyes of an admiring
audience ; their original value multiplied an hundredfold by the compound-
interest afforded by the exhaustless bank of Sir John Falstaff's golden imagination — in the mint attached to which establishment most of them had,
indeed, been fabricated.   How he would strike envy to the souls of exiles
from the court — palace intendants, stewards, gentlemen-at-arms, and the
like, sent to Coventry, and kept there, by duty or difficulties, — men stag-
nating for lack of news, and fain to follow the fashions " afar off like spies,"
— how would he overwhelm them with glowing accounts of the last Venetian
sleeve, the newest Saracenic hood, (for our Crusading fathers robbed the
Paynims not merely of their heads but also of their turbans !) and the last
Ferrarese device in armour — many costly specimens of which he would care-
lessly allude to as following him at leisure, with the bulk of his baggage, to
be worn when the wars should be concluded — rough homespun, tough
leather, and British iron being good enough for blood-stains and battle-smoke !
How would he silence Detraction — wishing to know whereby Sir John
Falstaff, after all his brilliant achievements, had escaped court preferment —
by frowns and sighs, and mysterious inuendoes !   Who knows but that the
name of Queen Joanna of Brittany — a comely dame, scarce past her middle
age, still capable of inspiring the tender passion — may have been covertly
mentioned in connection with this delicate subject ?   Was not the king old,
ailing, and jealous ?   Had not Duke Edward of York been already consigned,
a hopeless captive, to the dungeons of Pevensey, for no greater offence than
the inditing a not very brilliant copy of verses to her Breton and Britannic
Majesty ?   Had not the bilious monarch, moreover, shown his mistrust of all
persons favoured by his attractive (but supposed demon-leagued) consort —
by the wholesale exile of " all French persons, Bretons, Lombards, Italians
and Navarrese, whatsoever"* attached to the Queen's establishment, with
the exception of a cook, a few chambermaids, two knights, and their esquires
(doubtless elderly and ill-favoured), and a strong body of Breton washer-
women ?   Is it improbable that the presence, about the court, of a personable
and renowned warrior like Sir John Falstaff, — one who, even to the limits of
maturity, retained so many of the graces of his youth, — should have been
looked upon by the suspicious king as perilous to his conjugal felicity ?   At
any rate, is it improbable that Sir John Falstaff should have thought so — or,

* Parliamentary Rolls, 5 Henry IV., p. 572.

whether he thought so or not, that he should have striven to impress his Coventry audience with a conviction that such was the case? Sir John may or may not have submitted such probabilities as these to the consideration of his hearers. Be this as it may, there is one topic he could not possibly, being situated as I have imagined him, have failed to enlarge upon. Depend upon it, the recent conduct of the Lord Chief Justice would be held up to such public scorn and indignation as to render that official's next assize-visit to Warwickshire a somewhat perilous excursion!

Let me consider what kind of an adventure would have been likely to happen to Sir John Falstaff at such a time. I have one.

I can imagine a quiet, cheery-looking old man, in a long, sober-coloured gown, of comfortable well-to-do aspect, with a shrewd wrinkled face, elbowing his way imperceptibly to a place at the table near Sir John (the guests making room for him with some respect), and taking advantage of a lull in the conversation to say, with a twinkling eye and a somewhat admiring smile,—

"We should know each other, Sir John—we have been friends ere now."

"Aye, aye, sir? 'Tis possible. There are more men see Paul's church than the Beadle wots of. But you have the best of me."

"Will you share my tankard while I make myself known. Nay!—'tis a choice Rochelle that mine host broaches only for me on my monthly visits to Coventry. You will not match it in the town vintry.

"Now you speak, sir, I should know your voice. Save you, sir. Nectar, by all the Pagans!"

"It is long since we met, Sir John."

"Do you tell me that, sir? Twenty years at the least; if not nigher thirty. In Brittany, was it not?"

"Not so—not so."

"In Flanders then, or Spain?* I have seen both countries."

"Nay, sir—no further off than Clements' Inn. I was reading the law when you were page to Sir Thomas Mowbray—father to——"

"Him whose father's son I now march against. The chances of war have so willed it. By our Lady, I know the trick of your face—well.—Nay, if you will an' it be another of the same.—'Tis excellent, i' faith. And you have thriven well in your calling, Master ——?"

"Doit—Thomas Doit, to serve you, Sir John."

* Observe that I merely *imagine* Sir John Falstaff to have said he had visited Spain. The annals of that country afford no trace of his presence at any period of history.

"The name was at my tongue's end. Of Oxford, as I think ?"

"Of Stafford, sir."

"Stafford, I would have said. A new health to you, Master Doit. Why we are boys again. I would I needed a lawyer for your sake. But a trusty knave (no offence to the calling, sir) cares well for my estate—and to displace an old servant——"

"Nay, sir. I have enough—enough, sir. The world has dealt kindly by me. I have a snug home, with a crust and flagon for a friend. My boys and maidens are well cared for. I labour now but for pastime."

"Say you so, Master—Joit. We must be better acquainted. And yet that can hardly be with old friends like us."

"You have grown great since then, Sir John."

"An old man, sir, and still plain Sir John! Those were brave times, Master Quoit."

"Will you recall them with me, Sir John, over a supper ? I have a more potent voice in the kitchen here than many of the Prince's gentlemen."

"I would have asked you, Master—ahem ?—Thomas. But, be it as you will, sir, so that we part not company. We have seen nights together, sir ! "

"And days, Sir John ! It is a boast of mine that I witnessed your first great feat of arms."

"Aye, indeed ? Which call you that ?"

"Have you forgotten cudgelling Skogan, the rhymer, at the Court Gate ?"

"Skogan ! To be sure. Why now I have it all ! You were the brave fellow that fought the fishmonger on the same day ! or a tanner's man — which was it ? Talk not of my deeds after that, Master Thomas. I think I see him now with his skull cleft. Why John of Gaunt, Gloucester, and the old King himself, all lauded your prowess, sir. I rose in court esteem through knowing you."

At this, I can conjecture Master Thomas Doit would throw himself back in his chair and laugh till the tears streamed down his merry, wrinkled cheeks.

"Ha ! ha ! ha ! Why this is most excellent ! See how well you know me, Sir John, with all your friendship and remembrance. I thought not to live sixty-nine years to be taken for such a gull as lean Bob Shallow ! "

"Shallow ! "

Having made this exclamation, we may suppose that Sir John Falstaff would repair his not very flattering mistake by a plausible apology, or turn it off with a timely jest —— either being always at his command at a moment's notice. Having pacified the by no means implacable Doit, he would muse upon old times — old forms and deeds growing into shape and colour through the fog of years on the dead level of an old man's memory—like cows and windmills through the morning mist on a Flemish landscape.

"Shallow! to be sure!"—this to himself—sighing and putting his hand to his pocket. "He was the man to know! He paid all! He was a very oyster that would grow fat on the shell again, with a string of pearls round his neck directly you had swallowed him." Then, aloud, with a deeper sigh —"I would he were living now, Master Lawyer!"

"Why he lives, Sir John."

"Say you so?—where?"

"Hard by, in Gloucestershire, scarce a day's ride from hence."

"In good health and case, I trust?"

"The best. For his bodily health, he is of those men whose backs will never break under the weight of their brains. It is long ere the dock withers or the ass dies. For his outward case, Heaven, in its mercy to helpless creatures, hath sent two kinds of crawling things into the world with good houses to cover them—the snails and the fools, Sir John. Master Shallow is in the Peace: he hath his father's broad lands and some twenty thousand marks in money."

"You rejoice me! Master Shallow alive and prospering! Well! Master David Shallow was it not?"

"Robert."

"True. You called him Bob a while ago. From that you have let fall, it would seem he hath not grown in wisdom as in years and possessions?"

"He! Can you make silk purse out of swine's ear, Sir John; or wash blackamoors white? A greater gull than ever!"

"Bardolph."

"Sir John."

"Leave tippling, sirrah, and see to the horses. We'll ride into Gloucestershire before daybreak. 'Tis the county of lusty soldiers—and the rebels chafe for their beating. Another health, Master Doit."

I am convinced that it was some such accident as this that induced Sir John Falstaff to turn aside, temporarily, from his designs against the northern rebels in the King's interest, and direct his forces to the immediate subjugation of Mr. Justice Shallow on his own account. And, indeed, in deciding upon this course, he can scarcely be said to have exceeded or departed from his duty. For in those times of primitive warfare, (especially in the reign of Henry the Fourth, who, in spite of his numerous successful robberies, was not always able to pay his bootmaker, let alone his generals,) the right of private plunder and forage formed in a manner a portion of the soldier's payment. And it was surely excusable that Sir John Falstaff should have

o

been drawn a little from the track of the public game he was pursuing by so tempting a cross scent as that of his former acquaintance Shallow.

Sir John did not at once march on the Shallow stronghold, on the principle of the "hook-nosed fellow of Rome," as he pleasantly described his illustrious prototype of antiquity, merely "to come, to see, and to conquer." No. His first visit was one of mere reconnoitre, rather founded on the policy of another great man whom he resembled — William Duke of Normandy — who, it will be remembered, having made up his mind to conquer England, if he should find it worth his while, paid a friendly visit to the monarch of this country, by whom he was most hospitably received, in order to form his opinions on the subject; parted on the most amicable terms with his entertainer; and promised to look in again the next time he happened to be passing — which he did, taking the liberty of bringing a few friends with him. The parallel will be found striking.

The Shallows were a very ancient county family, tracing their descent almost as far back as the Falstaffs themselves. Common politeness to a great name suggests, at this stage of our researches, the propriety of a retrospective glance at the origin, achievements, social position, and distinguishing traits of a line so illustrious. In order to induce a perfect appreciation of the subject, the historian must (for once in a way, and contrary to his habit) avail himself of one of the most sacred privileges of his order — the right of digression. We of this age and country are too apt to ridicule the stringent and, as it seems on the surface, unnatural regulation of the Egyptians, Peruvians, and other nations of antiquity, and observed by certain Asiatic peoples even to the present day, which forbade a man to engage in any other pursuit, occupation, or calling, than that of his fathers. This was only recognising and enforcing by law the observance of an inherent principle in human society which we see voluntarily obeyed in all communities. Thus, we all acknowledge the claims of certain families who are obviously sent into the world for the purpose of ruling their fellow creatures, and living comfortably on the emoluments arising from that lucrative occupation. In proof of the definite and exclusive mission of such people, it need only be observed, that when, through some exceptional hitch or convulsion in the natural course of things, any one of their order happens to be thrown out of his legitimate employment, he can by no effort reconcile himself to becoming a useful or pacific member of society in a humbler sphere. On the contrary he will move heaven and earth to regain his forfeited position, which he will feel to be so indisputably his right, as to consider no sacrifice of the lives and treasures of other people too great for its recovery; and there will always be found a large portion of the population to abet and justify him by cheerfully making for him the sacrifices he requires. These he will accept without thanks or emotion, just as a spider accepts flies, or a pike titlebats. They are his right—that is sufficient. Leave such beings in the quiet possession of their birthright, and you may hardly be aware of their existence—so little noise or exertion they care to make while all goes on smoothly—and you may be apt to underrate their importance to the social machine. But once dislodge the most insignificant of them from his proper place, and a terrific crash, explosion, loss of life, and utter suspension of progress, will convince you that you had much better have left him where he was, and had better lose no time in putting him back again. We are told that a sacred Brahmin, though permitted, in cases of emergency, to engage in warlike or mercantile pursuits, must, on no account, descend to manual labour. For the Brahmin so descending, and for the inferior castes permitting or necessitating him to do so, it is pronounced by the sacred Vedas perdition in this world and the next. Therefore is the rule never infringed. The inferior *castes*, no matter what the scarcity of seasons or the extortions of their rulers, are careful for their own sakes that the sacred Brahmin shall not be tempted by necessity to the commission of the unpardonable crime of work. In civilisations of more modern fabric this principle of *caste* is equally recognised — none the less thoroughly that its recognition is the result of spontaneous obedience to a great natural law, rather than abject submission to the terrorism of a degrading superstition. We Europeans need no sacred Vedas to threaten us with torments if, in the event of a Kaiser or King having more sons than he can provide with kingdoms or principalities (their common necessaries of life), we decline to shed our blood in quarrels, the object of which is to supply the deficiency. We meet such claims upon us with the same matter of course cheerfulness as that with which the hunter scales the perilous cliff, or the fisherman launches his frail boat in stormy weather, to provide food for a helpless family. We recognise the principle in its widest ramifications—to its remotest edges. In Peru (anterior to the intrusion of that highly objectionable Reform Association of which Pizarro was the President) every descendant of an Inca, in the remotest degree, was as much an Inca as his greatest ancestor ; and every Inca was entitled to a certain share of command, and gold and silver, of which luxuries it need scarcely be hinted their order enjoyed an exclusive monopoly of possession. Let not the irreverent simile of the sow with a litter of too many pigs to correspond with her number of teats, be incautiously hazarded. The increase of Incas caused no difficulty whatever. The people knew the favoured class must be provided for, and in what manner. All *they* had to do was to acquire more territory—that new vice-realms and governorships might be established — and to find out fresh mines of gold and silver. We in Europe do much the same thing. When there is a little unwonted increase in the castes of Princeps, Dux, Comes, Markgraf, Landgraf, Law-ward, Armiger or Hidalgo, what do we do ? Do we insist that such valu-able materials shall be utilised for base purposes ? Do we tell Meinherr Herzog, Monsieur le Marquis, or the noble Earl, that we have already as many of their progeny as we can provide for in the regular way, and that the residue must be absorbed into the community as philosophers, artists, writers, traders, handicraftsmen, and husbandmen ? As readily would we think of cutting up armorial banners and brocaded tapestries for door-mats and ploughboys' inexpressibles, merely because we had happened to accumulate a greater stock of those dignifying treasures than our ancestral walls would accommodate. In such an emergency, all our thoughts and energies would be directed to the one mighty object of extending our premises, that we might have a sufficiency of rooms for the display of our priceless hangings. Such an enlargement might subject us to some inconvenience at the time—neces-sitating much straitening, a little chicanery perhaps, and a trifling matter of bankruptcy. But we would not be deterred by such ignoble considera-tions. We would extend our premises — honestly if we could—but we would extend them. I suppose it was a rule in ancient Egypt, that since certain men came into the world expressly and exclusively to be shoemakers and feather-dressers, the community to which they belonged was bound to wear out a sufficiency of shoes, and spoil a sufficiency of feathers, to keep them in profitable employment. It would have been very unfair otherwise. Just so when, by common consent, we declare that a certain branch of the community shall do nothing but govern empires, kingdoms, princi-palities, provinces, or departments, we are bound, at whatever cost, to pro-vide them with a sufficiency of empires, kingdoms, principalities, &c., to govern. It may be expensive ; but it is only commonly just. If we have decided that our pet spaniel shall eat nothing but nightingales' tongues, why, in justice to the poor dog, we must go out and shoot enough nightingales to keep him in condition — even though we neglect our business, and live ourselves, while hunting, upon pig-nuts.

As there are families born to command, so are there families born to serve. I know the representatives of one or two highly respectable lines (they are not very fond of me by the way, and never invite me unless some better-bred person has disappointed them—which I also generally manage to do in my turn, one way or another), who can point to splendid galleries of ancestral portraits, each one the counterfeit presentment of an individual who has dis-tinguished himself as the faithful and devoted servant of some royal or otherwise illustrious personage. One will have been Gold Shaving Pot in Waiting to such a monarch—another Groom of the Dirty Clothes Bag to such another—and so forth. All have worn livery of some kind or another, with pride to themselves and satisfaction to their employers. I honour these men, not as the unthinking do, for the reflected glories cast upon them by the great names with which theirs have been associated, but for their own merits as honest flunkies, who accepted their earthly mission and fulfilled it with diligence and civility; and who, having completed their time of servitude in this down-stairs world, have gone to better themselves elsewhere, provided with the best of characters. There have been great men in these lines—warriors who have won difficult battles as the subservient aides-de-camp to incapable princes; statesmen who have saved or ruined empires, as part of their professional duties, for the immortalization of their honoured employers; gifted authors who have lived to see statues erected to their patrons, due to the fame of books which they themselves had written ungrudgingly for a secretary's wages or a toady's perquisites. The offshoots and collaterals of these illustrious houses have doubtless included, in their number, artists of the highest ability, who have passed their lives cheerfully on small salaries, painting backgrounds and draperies, for such of the governing *castes* as may have drifted into the field of fashionable portraiture and are naturally fitted for command there as elsewhere; mute inglorious Mozarts and Beethovens who have retired contentedly to workhouses, when they have completed their life-labour of preparing some operatic automaton for opulence and fame; and so on, down through grades innumerable, to poor old Figaro, who weeps tears of joy when he hears that the wig his skill has prepared has been mistaken for the natural growth of the Count Almaviva's bald and wrinkled pate, and Betty, who is reconciled to short commons and irregular wages, when she listens stealthily at the half-opened ball-room door to hear Belinda praised and envied for taste that was Betty's own. My Lord Gold Stick in Waiting, the Grand Duke's hereditary Bootjack, Mr. Boswell the biographer, Mr. Wagg the dining-room jester, Mr. Wenham the confidential secretary, faithful Caleb Balderston, and supercilious John Thomas—they are all of the same race. The prosperous may repudiate the unsuccessful members—as Jocelyn Fitzmyth of Belgravia ignores John Smith of Deptford, or as Sir Morris Leveson the city millionaire cuts the acquaintance of poor Moses Levi of Petticoat Lane,—a kind of meanness which, *en passant*, would be effectually prevented by the adoption of the old Egyptian principle—whereby the cobbler was bound, as with the stoutest of thongs and waxed-ends, to stick to his last. Under that dispensation Fitzmyth would be kept to his cabbage garden, and Sir Morris would have to wear a Jewish gaberdine—just as Mr. Wagg would be sentenced to perpetual cap and bells, and my Lord Goldstick, Bootjack, Wenham, and all the rest of them, to wear plush and powder, whether they liked it or not. But the sumptuary distinction is unnecessary. They are all born footmen, let them disguise themselves as they will. You have only to ring a bell within their hearing —seeing that it be of gold, silver, or baser metal, according to their relative grades of servitude—and they will speedily jump up to answer it ; betraying their natural propensities like the cat in the fairy tale, who had been changed into a beautiful princess, when she caught sight of a stray mouse on the palace floor. So much for the *caste* of servants.

I have shown early in this work that the Falstaff family were a race of courtiers, with a tendency to one or two other callings not necessary here to particularise. My hero was—alas ! that I should have to say it—the last of his line. Did any descendant of Sir John's happen to be living in the present day, no doubt he would be found hanging about the aristocratic clubs, in debt to the very waiters, "tabooed" by strait-laced members for his frequent scrapes, chronic dissipation, and irreverent jests, never respectable and never prosperous, given dreadfully to low life, but always sure of some countenance and protection as the boon companion of some influential personage, and careful to keep within the pale of good repute, so far as to retain his *entrée* to St. James's Palace —preserving through all difficulties a handsome court suit and stock of court behaviour for state occasions. Supposing any descendants of our old acquaintance Wat Smith, the Maldyke demagogue, to be living (and the prevalence of the family name renders the supposition more than probable), they are, doubtless, to be found among the radical iron-workers of the Midland Counties, or those turbulent Sheffield knife-grinders, whom nothing short of a Royal Duke's presence can awe into loyalty and respect. There are families of actors, who have been histrios from a date earlier than Gammer Gurton's Needle, and who stick to the family calling, whether on the stage, in the cabinet, the senate, the mart, or the pulpit. There are born farmers, born authors, born warriors, born sailors, born jewellers, born publicans, and born hangmen. I have known even hereditary grocers and undertakers. But perhaps there is no instance in which we so thoroughly recognise the sacredness of *caste* as in the case of the born labourer. The contentment with which people of that class will submit to the most incredible hardships rather than make an effort to emancipate themselves from their normal sphere, added to the indignant opposition with which any rare effort of the kind on their part is invariably met by the classes above them, is surely a convincing proof that they were brought into the world for the purpose of remaining exactly where they are.

We have also born beggars — in various stages of society — who pursue their traditional calling —

> " Some in rags
> And some in bags,
> And some in velvet gowns,"

but who are all beggars alike, and could under no circumstances exist, except by the charity of the industrious and productive portions of the community. We have also hereditary thieves, who are protected in their various guilds and corporations, and enjoy innumerable legal privileges.

I have now traced the various defined strata of our social geology almost to the lowest formation. My philosophical excavations have occupied some time, but not a stroke of the moral pickaxe has been unnecessary. It was absolutely indispensable that I should get to the very bottom of the pit. I have now all but reached it. Having cut my way through the beggars and thieves, there is but one step lower I can take. I will accordingly proceed to the consideration of country justices.

The family of the Shallows had been in the commission of the peace from time immemorial. I have not such authorities at my elbow as can inform me under what honorary title the earlier Shallows — at the time when Keingelt Felstaf was getting into squabbles with Ceorles and Welshmen, and pecuniary difficulties with his Sodalitium — exercised their judicial functions. It is of little consequence whether a judicial assembly be called a Wittenagemote or a Petty Sessions — so that the spirit of its justice be the same. Suffice it that the hereditary vocation of the family, in all ages, has been to supply the ranks of that inestimable and truly British body — the unpaid magistracy. Of the advantages to the community of such a class of public officials it would be idle to speak; so obvious is it that a judge whose services are gratuitously rendered, and are therefore protected by the common rules of politeness from impertinent investigation as to their quality and value, must be enabled to administer justice in a far more independent and manly fashion than the hireling who is amenable to public criticism, and bound to interpret the law according to the opinions of others; whereas, the unfettered volunteer need only consult his own conscience and enforce such a construction of the statutes AS HE MAY DETERMINE TO BE THE RIGHT ONE. One great result of this system is the preservation, in a state of vital activity, of many fine old laws, which the apathy or sycophancy to the public approval of less disinterested but more immediately responsible magistrates might suffer to fall into disuse. The Shallows, from the remotest period, have distinguished themselves as conservators of the law in this respect. In the time of the Anglo-Saxons, members of the race had been remarkable for their diligence in the conviction of malefactors by the process of red-hot ploughshares, the ordeals of hot and cold water, and similar unerring and time-honoured tests of criminality. Long after these cherished features in the national juris-prudence had been formally abolished, through the vexatious meddling of effeminate Norman legislators, and nominally superseded by moveable Courts of Assize, the Shallows of Gloucestershire had the hardihood and patriotism to adhere to their practice in the teeth of all Royal Commissions of Inquiry and threats of suspension whatsoever. It was one Simon Shallow who, early in the reign of Edward the First, had the honour of executing the last assassin ever convicted in an English Court of Justice, by the flowing of blood from the body after death on its being touched by human fingers. The event was long remembered in the county, and its records are still preserved with excusable pride by the descendants of the Shallow family. It was, indeed, a masterly expression of the great English spirit of resistance. A murder had been committed — at least a dead body had been found at the foot of a precipice with the skull shattered. The reigning Shallow proceeded to try the case according to the immemorial custom of his ancestors. He at once caused all suspicious characters in the neighbourhood to be arrested. This he effected by ordering his own keepers to seize upon all persons suspected of poaching and other practices dangerous to the stability of the community, and by soliciting all adjacent landowners in the commission to come to the rescue of law and order, by causing to be arrested all similarly disaffected persons within their jurisdiction. Master Shallow's keepers did their duty, and the neighbouring justices responded to the appeal. A goodly array of prisoners were brought into the presence of the body, which was laid on a table, tilted at a proper angle. The county justices assembled in strong force, in order to witness the vindication of the majesty of Old English law, threatened with undermining by divers royal messages. Two or three of the suspected criminals (against whom there was nothing particular beyond a pheasant's nest or so, and who had been considerately warned not to lay too violent a hand on the body, lest they should cause a movement of the head which might be fatal) had passed triumphantly through the ordeal. A hardened malefactor was about to be tried, upon whom the gravest suspicion rested. He was the most accomplished deer-stealer in the neighbour-hood. There was not a justice present through whose preserves the cause of law and order had not suffered by his depredations. It was in vain that this fellow pleaded with tears in his eyes that he had loved the deceased as a brother, and called witnesses to prove that he had parted with him amicably at the door of an alehouse; that they had taken different directions, and that the prisoner had spoken to divers persons at a distance of five miles from the scene of the supposed murder at the very moment when, if at all, it must have been committed. He was smartly reprimanded, with a counsel to remember what presence he stood in, and bidden to "lay on firm, and not touch the clothes * instead of the flesh, as their worships wotted well of that device." The man raised his hand fearlessly, and was about to lay it on the body when a breathless messenger rushed into the justice hall, announcing that a troop of King's officers were riding fast from Oxford with a view of putting a stop to the proceedings, tidings of which had reached that city, where His Majesty then held his court; and threatening the terrors of the law to any magistrate who should be convicted of participation in the illegal course of procedure now in progress. The justices rose in mingled wrath and fear, and in so doing managed to shake the table. Simultaneously with their movement the hand of the accused fell mechanically upon the body, the head of which rolled from its supports, causing an effusion of blood. "Lo, he is guilty!" cried the justices, triumphant in the moment of their apparent defeat. "Men of England!" said one of them (whose park had suffered dreadfully within the past month), "will ye see the laws of your fathers trampled on by a set of evil advisers — chiefly Frenchmen — who have falsely obtained the ear of His Majesty, whom heaven preserve! Will ye have your sons and brothers murdered in cold blood? Ten minutes more and the murderer will be rescued from justice by a set of French lawyers, who will set him free by quirks and quibbles. Now or never is your time to assert your rights. To the nearest oak with him, ere yet the blood is dry, according to the custom of your fathers!" The mob murmured approval: a superstition a thousand years old was dear to them. The keepers and constables clamoured — not one of them but had known the taste of the prisoner's cudgel. The prisoner himself protested, appealed to the King's justice, finally lost his temper and called the justices a pack of murderous noodles. The prisoner had his friends; but they were a disreputable minority of poachers and sheep-stealers. The bulk of the auditory were tenants or retainers of the justices. The approach of horsemen galloping at top speed was announced from a neighbouring hill. If ever a blow could be struck in defence of the old English laws, now was the time. Then, as now, it was a recognised principle that Britons never, never would be slaves, and where is the personal freedom in a country where you cannot hang a man in your own most approved fashion? Briefly, the prisoner was hanged on the nearest oak; and the Royal Commission

---

* A common expedient resorted to by the consciously guilty in the Trial of Ordeal by Touch; similar to that practised by the ignorant of the present day, who think that by "kissing the thumb" instead of the book in a court of justice they evade the legal and sacred responsibilities of an oath.

appointed to investigate the matter, arrived just in time to cut him down and bury him with his lamented friend.   Master Shallow was a timorous but by no means an inhuman or an unjust man.   He had proposed sparing the culprit—whose guilt could scarcely be considered established, seeing that the body had been shaken by the rising of the court, and the flow of blood might have been accidental—provided he (the culprit) would make an ample confession of his crime and express his obligation to the magistrates who had tried him, before the King's Commissioners.   But this suggestion was overruled by the majority, who declared that there was no time for the consideration of trifling personal interests when they had a great principle to establish.   So the convicted murderer was hanged with Master Shallow's full warrant and approval.

It turned out—on the evidence of two cowboys, who had witnessed the event, but apparently not thought worth alluding to it until questioned—that the supposed murdered man, being under the obvious influence of malt liquor, had himself staggered over the precipice at the foot of which he had found his death.   Master Shallow as chief of the sitting justices (what we should call Chairman of Sessions) was tried by the Royal Commission, and found guilty of murder for putting a man to death by a process long since declared illegal by royal edict.   Master Shallow was himself sentenced to suffer the extreme penalty of the law, but King Edward happening to be in one of his periodical money difficulties, the sentence was commuted to a heavy fine —which, to the honour of magisterial loyalty and good-fellowship, be it stated, the Gloucestershire justices nobly subscribed to meet.   Master Shallow retained his judicial appointment, with a caution to abstain from the trial of criminals by exploded Saxon ordeals for the future, which he care-fully observed.   Nevertheless he earned lasting renown in the county, as the man who at the imminent risk of his own life had stood up for the maintenance of a great national institution.   The Shallows, on the establish-ment of coat armour by Edward the Third, assumed in honour of this event the device of a man pendant on an oak branch, salient, in a field of green, proper.   But some misconception arising in the public mind as to this being meant to represent an episode in the personal history of one of the family, the design was abandoned, and the traditional "dozen white luces," (the origin of which is enveloped in mystery,) by which the house is still identified at the Heralds' College, adopted in its place.   It may not be irrelevant to state that the two over-officious cowboys were speedily selected, on the press-warrant of Master Shallow, to supply a deficiency in King Edward's army — and perished nobly, fighting their country's battles, in one of that monarch's numerous expeditions against the disaffected Scots.

The Shallows continued to merit renown by their resistance on all possible occasions to anything like innovation in the administration of justice. Our own Robert Shallow, at an advanced period of life, was only induced by serious remonstrances from King Henry the Fifth (for whom he was wont to express the strongest regard, having been very intimate with his grandfather) to desist from the ancient practice of trying aged women for the crime of witchcraft by launching them in deep water upon sieves, — when, if they went to the bottom and proved their earthly nature by remaining there for five or ten minutes, they were pronounced innocent and permitted to come to the surface and return to their homes at their earliest convenience : on the other hand, if they did not immediately sink, they were considered to be in league with the powers of darkness and taken out to be burnt. Throughout subsequent reigns the Shallows were remarkable for their indefatigable enforcement of the Game Laws, and of the measures enacted for the punishment of "masterless men," that is, of persons wandering in search of employment—an offence which even in the present day is treated by their descendants with greater rigour than any other.

Representatives of the house of Shallow — with the name variously modified — abound in our own time. They are to a man somehow connected with the amateur administration of justice. They are to be found in the country digging up obsolete enactments for the committal to imprisonment and hard labour of agricultural journeymen who may be disposed to treat themselves to a day's holiday. They are the terror of itinerant showmen, unemployed mechanics and poachers, by whom they are hated. On the other hand they have the enthusiastic support of the genuine criminal population, to whose professional exertions they are by no means obstructive. They are learned in the rights of rabbits — and know a greater variety of legal torture for avenging the unlicensed death of one of that favoured species than a French cook could invent receipts for disguising its carcase. You will find them trying strange experiments with pet convicts in model prisons, and actively throwing impediments in the way of government inquiries into the conduct of brutal governors of those institutions — too often the hot ploughshares and ordeals by touch of modern criminal jurisprudence. Little opportunities of serving a friend like this are of course due to the country Shallows as an offset to their gratuitous services. As one of the earliest of the family counsellors has expressed it, " Heaven save but a knave should have some countenance at his friend's request ; an honest man, Sir, is able to speak for himself, when a knave cannot." Their worships are further privileged to carry out this principle by limiting, within their jurisdiction, the knavery of keeping open houses for the sale of injurious tipples at exorbitant prices, to such knaves, only, as they may consider "entitled to some countenance at their friends' request." In London — where some of the fraternity are permitted to exercise their functions within certain limits — their most conspicuous public achievements are an annual out-door masquerade of obsolete meaning, strongly reminding us of their ancestor Robert's appearance as "Sir Dagonet in Arthur's Show" — and certain frantic but hitherto unsuccessful attempts to put down pitch-and-toss, polkas, and suicide — practices which still continue prevalent in the British metropolis.

Of the personal character of Master Robert Shallow, the worthy representative of this race and order in Sir John Falstaff's time, some glimpse has possibly been obtained from an early chapter of this work. Sir John at the advanced period of life to which I have now brought him, remembered the justice "at Clement's Inn, like a man made after supper of a cheese paring; when he was naked he was, for all the world, like a forked radish, with a head fantastically carved upon it with a knife: he was so forlorn" (I am quoting Sir John's own words) "that his dimensions to any thick sight were invisible; he was the very genius of famine; he came ever in the rearward of the fashion, and sung those tunes to the over-scutched huswives that he had heard the carmen whistle, and sware they were his fancies or his good-nights. And now is this Vice's dagger become a squire; and talks as familiarly of John of Gaunt as if he had been sworn brother to him; and I'll be sworn he never saw him but once in the Tilt-yard; and then he burst his head for crowding amongst the marshal's men. I saw it, and told John of Gaunt he beat his own name; for you might have trussed him and all his apparel into an eel skin; the case of a treble hautboy was a mansion for him, a court, and now he hath land and beeves!"

Considering that, when Sir John Falstaff made these reflections upon the past and present of Master Robert Shallow, nearly fifty years had elapsed since the events alluded to, it will be admitted that our knight's recollection of the passage in the Tilt-yard (with which my readers are familiar) and the substance of the witticism it evoked from him at the time, prove his memory to have been at least unimpaired. It is strange that Sir John should marvel at Master Shallow's possession of land and beeves. It will be found through all ages that the Shallows have had an eye to the main-chance, which it is very rarely indeed you find a fool neglecting. A mole may have very small eyes, but he is not quite blind. He is dazzled by pure daylight, it is true, and may never see a flower. But he is an excellent judge of dirt, which is to him the great necessary of life, and he will never lose sight of the importance of keeping a sufficient heap of it about him.

V.

VISIT TO JUSTICE SHALLOW'S.

My supposition that Sir John Falstaff was indebted for his knowledge of Mr. Shallow's existence, whereabouts, and prosperous condition, to some such accidental renewal of his acquaintance with Mr. Doit, of Staffordshire, as I have imagined, is strengthened in probability by the certainty that our knight really did meet with the latter-named gentleman, and at Coventry, within a few days anterior to the date which my historical calculations have decided me in assigning to the battle of Gualtree Forest. This is proved by a letter from Mr. Doit, discovered among the Falstaff papers on the knight's decease, apparently one of a numerous series, in which the writer somewhat sharply requests payment of a certain "obligacion" which he has held for some time in acknowledgment of monies advanced by him to Sir John on the occasion of their happy "reknitting of their old fellowship" at Coventry, "which honour," Master Doit sarcastically observes, "albeit of great price, is one I had not been so prodigal as to purchase with fore-knowledge that it would cost me the sum it is like to," to wit, fifteen pounds eight shillings, the amount of the said "obligacion," which is mentioned as bearing the date of the 7th of June, 1410.

Be the origin of the event as it may, Sir John's visit to the domain of Justice Shallow is matter of public history. The Falstaff troops marched from Coventry to Stratford-on-Avon, between which town and Evesham the justiciary seat of the Shallows was situate, — and there halted.

It may be thought that an event so suggestive as a visit from Sir John Falstaff to Stratford-on-Avon—the future birthplace of his greatest historian, but for whose genius it is possible that the name and achievements of our knight would have lapsed into an oblivion from which not even these affectionate pages (which, of course, would have been written under any circumstances) could have rescued them — might be made the text for much instructive and entertaining reflection. But *cui bono?* It is to be hoped that the character and objects of this work are now sufficiently understood to acquit the writer of any suspicion of a tendency to digress from the iron road of facts into the flowery groves of fanciful speculation. The fact, that Sir John Falstaff passed through Stratford-on-Avon, more than a hundred years before the birth of William Shakspeare, can scarcely have had any influence upon the dramatist's after labours in connection with the warrior's history. It is true, that Sir

John Falstaff was in the habit of leaving his mark wherever he went; and in any town where he may have sojourned, if only for the space of a day or two, there would be no likelihood of his being speedily forgotten. But a century is a long time. And I am disposed to think that any interest or value attached to such Inn Memoriams of Sir John's progress through Stratford as that city might be expected to possess at the date of his departure, would cease with the announcement of the knight's death without heirs or estate. On the whole, I have decided to dismiss the question and resume my narrative.

It was no part of our hero's plan to take Mr. Shallow by surprise. His designs upon that rural potentate were not of a nature to be carried by a *coup de main*. He prepared for his appearance in Gloucestershire by sending on an *avant courier*, with the following dispatch.*

"*Unto the right worshipful my good friend Master Robert Shallow, be this delivered in haste.*

"Right trusty and well-beloved Master Shallow, I commend me to you by our ancient friendship ; and please you to wete that being armed with the King's press for the raising of soldiers in the counties, I shall require at your hands the pick of half-a-dozen good and sufficient men. Thus much for business. Being sore pressed for time, and our General, the Prince of Lancaster, crying out for me, I would fain depute the choosing of the men to one of my lieutenants or ancients, — had it not reached me that the justice with whom I have to deal is no other than mine old friend Master Shallow. Knowing this, I cannot but play traitor to my duty and forfeit a day of the King's service, to ride over in my own person, that I may once more say I have taken Master Shallow by the hand.

"I pray you detain me not, and betray me not—that I give up to friendship that time which is the King's. But I have no fear, as we have stood by each other ere now. Disturb not your household to make us welcome, as we may not unsaddle, and I bring none with me but a simple following befitting my rank as the King's poor officer. The main force of my army I leave here, in camp, hard by Stratford, and I must back in haste lest the knaves run riot, and embroil me with the townsfolk.

"Pick me good men, I pray, for the rebels wax insolent. Have them of the better class of

---

* The preservation of this important document is probably due to the hereditary vanity of the race of Shallows — who from the time of John of Gaunt down to the last presentation of the Freedom of the City of London to a foreign prince, — have never been known to lose an opportunity of claiming acquaintance with persons of rank and celebrity. The letter was preserved for many years in the family. The original Gloucestershire branch becoming extinct, it passed into the hands of some collateral descendants (through the Slenders and Aguecheeks, both nearly allied by blood and marriage to the Shallows), domiciled in the vicinity of Chepstow, in whose possession it remained *perdu* until the early part of the present century, when the head of the family having providentially taken to drinking, and his goods being sold by auction, the treasure was discovered by his county neighbour, Mr. Roderick Bolton, F. S. A., and by him purchased for incorporation with the Strongate Collection.

yeomen if it may be — men whose lives are worth fighting for the care of. Your starveling hinds and villains are rank naught for march or battle-field.

"Written at Stratford-on-the-Avon, the 8th day of June, in the year of Grace 1410.

"JOHN FALSTAFF (Knight)."*

The receipt of this letter threw Master Shallow into an ecstasy of excitement.

Here was the renowned courtier, Sir John Falstaff, the "friend of the mad prince and Poins," the conqueror of Shrewsbury, the great wit, traveller, and leader of the fashion, writing to him, plain Robert Shallow, Esquire, in terms of familiarity, and promising a speedy visit. There was only one drawback to the justice's delight. There was no time to make adequate preparations for so important an event, or to ensure such an attendance of influential neighbours as Master Shallow would have wished to overwhelm with the sight of his distinguished guest. The worthy Justice would have liked triumpha arches, rustic festivities, and bands of music. He would have gladly kept open house to all the gentry of the county for the occasion. Not that he was in the least degree a liberal man, or that he cared two pins for Sir John Falstaff personally. He was rather niggardly than otherwise; and fifty intervening years had not one whit blunted his recollection of one or two sound drubbings and many slights and sarcasms inflicted on him in youth by our knight. But, to compare lesser things with great, it is not to be supposed that noblemen and gentlemen who impoverish their exchequers and turn their

---

* The biographer — or, as he perhaps ought to be styled in connection with this department of his labours, the editor, is again called on to defend the course he has adopted with reference to such ancient manuscripts as he has found necessary to transfer to his pages. Objections have been made — which the periodical form of publication adopted in this work affords an opportunity of meeting—to the plan of modernising the orthography, and in some cases the phraseology, of these compositions, whereby it is asserted their interest is materially weakened. There can be no defence so adequate to the emergency as the plea of an illustrious example. Sir John Fenn, the learned and ingenious editor of the *Paston letters*, vindicates a similar line of conduct with regard to his treatment of that inestimable collection, in the following language; —

"The thought of transcribing (or rather translating) each letter according to the rules of modern orthography and punctuation arose from a hint which the editor received from an antiquary, respectable for his knowledge and publications; whose opinion was, that many would be induced to read these letters for the sake of the various matters they contain, for their style, and for their curiosity, who not having paid attention to ancient modes of writing and abbreviations, would be deterred from attempting such a task by their uncouth appearance in their original garb."

The present editor has not, like Sir John Fenn, enjoyed the advantage of a special hint from any antiquary, "respectable for his knowledge and publications" or otherwise. But he trusts that the learned baronet's own valuable precedent will be sufficient excuse for his conduct under similar circumstances. If not, he can only say that if the letters relating to the history of Sir John Falstaff, quoted in the course of this biography, had not appeared in their present form, *it would have been a matter of downright impossibility for the British public to have read them at all.*

country seats topsy-turvy for the reception of royal and princely visitors, on their triumphal progresses through a land, are actuated by a mere spirit of loyalty. A year's rent-roll of the Carabas estates is not consumed in decorating the state chamber that His gracious Majesty or Her Serene Highness may enjoy a comfortable night's rest ; but that the satin hangings, the golden cornices, the encrusted bed-posts and the jewelled coal-scuttles, may be enumerated in the fashionable journals, and engraved in the Illustrated News ; and remain in their integrity, to prove, to the envy of contemporaries and the admiration of posterity, that king or prince once honoured Carabas Castle by going to bed in it. The great Baron Reginald de Bœuf does not marshal his eight hundred retainers in new scarlet surcoats with enormous badges displaying the ancestral device of the calf's head richly embroidered in gold on the left arm, merely that King Richard Cœur de Lion (who happens to be passing Torquilstone Castle on his way to York to negotiate a national loan with the great commercial house of Isaacs Brothers) shall be flattered by a delicate attention from a faithful subject. This consideration may have entered into the baron's calculations ; his lordship having daughters growing up whom he would like to place in posts of distinction about the person of Queen Berengaria, and a son in the church who can hardly aspire to a mitred abbacy without his majesty's countenance. But the real and paramount motive is that Cedric the wealthy thane of Rotherwood, the haughty Templar Sir Brian de Bois Guilbert, (that conceited eastern traveller who is stopping at the Castle, and turns up his nose at all its primitive arrangements), Sir Philip de Malvoisin, the very reverend Prior Aymer, and indeed all the baron's acquaintances and neighbours, down to the very woodland ragamuffins of Barnsdale and Sherwood, shall be impressed with the fact that the Torquilstone estates can muster an array of eight hundred men, and afford to clothe them in new scarlet and gold lace. If a man were to propose to present me with a piece of plate in consideration of my distinguished services to literature, I should accept the plate of course, and immediately turn it to some useful purpose. But my gratitude,—which I would be careful to express in the most glowing terms at my command,—would never blind me to the fact that my friend had been actuated less by a sense of my great merits as poet, historian and moral philosopher, than by a wish to see his name at the head of a subscription list, and to take the chair at a public dinner, ostensibly in my honour. Much as I hate digression, I will illustrate my meaning by a personal anecdote. I once found myself — Heaven knows how I got there ! — in a little out-of-the-way Flemish village, which had been thrown into a state of commotion by the prospective opening of a partially completed line of railway, the first train of which was expected to stop at a little toy station in the vicinity. A peer of the realm, one of the directors of the company, and representative of a noble line of great antiquity, dating, in fact, from the very foundation of the Belgian monarchy, had signified his intention of assisting at the inaugural ceremony. The inhabitants of Tiddliwinckx resolved to greet him with an appropriate address. This was prepared by the Vicaire (with the kind permission of the Curé, who was himself, nevertheless, opposed to railways in the abstract as somewhat smacking of Protestantism), and carefully studied for delivery by the Bourgmestre. The station was tastefully decorated with flags, and the inhabitants mustered in large numbers in the stiffest of dark blue blouses and the snowiest of caps. The thrilling moment approached. The Bourgmestre paper in hand, was all trepidation, where indeed he was not trousers and shirt collar. The train signal was awaited with breathless anxiety. It was not given. A quarter of an hour — a second — another elapsed, and no train made its appearance. At length a pedestrian messenger arrived at an easy pace up the line, with the unwelcome tidings that an accident to the rails, some six miles distant, had brought the engine to a standstill, and the distinguished visitors had been compelled to retrace their way to Brussels. The Bourgmestre and his colleagues were in despair. The suspension of railway traffic was a matter of utter indifference to them : but they had missed the pleasure of talking to a count, and an eloquent address had been composed, and the difficulties of its orthography mastered, for nothing. The friends of the heartbroken Bourgmestre attempted to lead him away from the scene of his disappointment. But he refused to be moved or comforted. He had come there to read the address, and read it to somebody he would. I think rather than have gone home without delivering it he would have read it to the gend'arme on duty, or to the one Flemish railway porter who did not understand a word of the French language, in which the oration was supposed to be written. In a fortunate moment his eye fell upon me. A ray of hope illumined the previously sad bourgmestral countenance. After a brief conference with his colleagues, he approached me politely and inquired if " Monsieur was connected with the Railway Interest ? " I replied that I had not that advantage. He expressed his regret that I should have been implicated in the common disappointment, and suggested, as some compensation, that I would perhaps like to hear the address which it had been his intention to deliver, had not unforeseen circumstances prevented. I declared that nothing would give me greater pleasure. The address was accordingly *read to me.* I replied in a neat speech, setting forth the advantages of railway communication, and the high position which, through its means, the enlightened community of Tiddliwinckx was destined to occupy in the civilised world ; concluding by a compliment to the magistrate on his eloquence, and expressing my high sense of the honour he had done me in selecting me for its recipient. The bourgmestre was perfectly satisfied, and invited me to dinner.

To return to Master Shallow. Immediately on the receipt of Sir John Falstaff's letter, he sent messengers to his most influential neighbours, praying them on various pretexts to visit him in the morning. But he was singularly unfortunate. Justice Aguecheek (related to the Shallows through the Slender family) was gone to London on law business. Justice Greedye was invited to a great dinner on the following day, and was preparing for the event in the hands of his apothecary. Justice Trulliber was gone to attend the hog market at Taunton, and would be three days absent. Masters Woodcock and Westerne were on ill terms with each other, and with Master Shallow, on some business of litigation. It would be useless to invite either, especially the latter, who would be certain to receive any civil message with foul language and possible ill treatment of the bearer. It seemed likely that Sir John Falstaff's visit would be wasted, like a rare dish prepared for an honoured guest who does not arrive, and which the family are fain to consume in dudgeon. Utter disappointment was prevented by the arrival of one Justice Silence — Master Shallow's own cousin by marriage, who made his appearance punctually, at the hour appointed on the eventful morning. Master Silence was a dull man, and not given to converse or tale-bearing. But he would serve as a witness to his kinsman's familiarity with the coming man. And while he would be able to confirm the heads of any narrative Master Shallow might choose to frame on the subject, his natural taciturnity would prevent him from contradicting any superadded details which his imaginative relation might choose to furnish for its embellishment.

Sir John Falstaff arrived attended by that "simple following" he had spoken of ; which, it is needless to say, consisted of his entire army — properly bribed and instructed to declare that they were backed by countless legions in camp at Stratford. Master Shallow received our knight with the joy with which an ambitious spider of small dimensions may be supposed to regard the approach to his web of a gigantic blue-bottle. Master Shallow — simple man — imagined that he was going to turn Sir John Falstaff to his advantage. "Friend at court" was the justice's maxim, "is better than penny in purse." Sir John's own feelings, on entering the cosy, well-stocked domain of the ancient race of Shallow, may be compared to those of a majestic fox entering an unprotected poultry yard.

As I have stated that this preliminary visit of the Falstaff forces to the stronghold of Shallow was only one of reconnoitre, to enable the general to

Drawn & etched by George Cruikshank

Published by Longmans & Company

Sir John Falstaff, at Justice Shallows, exercising his wit & his judgement in selecting men to serve the King —

—— Henry 4th — Part 2nd Act 3rd Scene 2nd —

plan his great assault for a future occasion, and as circumstances rendered it necessarily of short duration, I will pass over it briefly. Sir John's treatment of his host was affable, but dignified. He suffered Master Shallow to refer to their past intimacy, and lie to his heart's content on the score of his youthful achievements. Sir John selected such men as he considered desirable for the King's service from the levies provided for him; accepted a brief repast, and departed, having promised Master Shallow to renew their acquaintance on the termination of the wars, in a second visit to that gentleman's hospitable mansion, extracting in return a half-promise from its owner to accompany him to court. It is strange that Justice Shallow, gifted, as we have seen him, with a remarkably retentive memory, should have forgotten how costly a luxury he had found the honour of Sir John Falstaff's patronage in early youth. But it is the constant failing of very foolish old gentlemen to imagine they have grown wiser with age.

In the present day, when so much of the public attention is directed to the question of raising recruits for the British army, a glance at the way in which such matters were regulated in the fifteenth century may not prove uninstructive. It will be seen that the modes of actual levying differed materially from those at present in vogue. But it may silence cavillers to learn that our ancestors—whose wisdom may not be disputed—were fully in accord with the opinion of modern rulers as to the class of men to whom the fighting of their country's battles might be with the greatest propriety entrusted.

I will show you how Sir John Falstaff, with the assistance of Justice Shallow, recruited the diminished armies of King Henry the Fourth.

Sir John on his arrival at the justice's mansion, having exchanged a few hasty civilities and remarks on the weather with his host and the scarcely audible, visible, or tangible Master Silence, proceeded to business.

"Gentlemen," he inquired, "have you provided me here half a dozen of sufficient men?"

Master Shallow replied in the affirmative, and requested his guest to be seated.

Sir John took a chair, and begged that the recruits might be brought before him.

Five miserable-looking individuals were marshalled into the courtyard, officered by the valiant Bardolph. Whether Master Shallow's arithmetic had been at fault, and he had calculated erroneously as to the addition of two and three; whether there was a scarcity of men in the neighbourhood; or whether one of the original number had deserted, is doubtful. However, it is certain that of the half-dozen recruits asserted to be in readiness only five made their appearance.

Master Shallow proceeded to call over the muster roll — not appearing to notice the deficiency.

"Ralph Mouldy — let me see. Where is Ralph Mouldy ? "

" Here, if it please you."

Mr. Mouldy's voice and expression of countenance declared plainly that it didn't please *him*.

Mouldy was in all probability a dangerous poacher, so anxious was the worthy magistrate to recommend him for military service.

"What think you, Sir John ? A good limbed fellow ; young, strong, and of *good friends*."

The last recommendation decided Sir John at once. Mouldy would do.

" Is thy name Mouldy ?"

" Yea, if it please you."

" 'Tis the more time thou wert used."

Master Shallow was in ecstacies. The practical joke of sending a man to the wars against his will had already tickled the excellent justice's sense of humour. But to make a verbal jest on his calamity to his very face, and on his own name, was irresistible.

"Ha ! ha ! ha ! most excellent i' faith ! Things that are mouldy lack use. Very singular, good. Well said, Sir John. Very well said."

" Prick him," said Sir John.

And down went a mark against Mouldy's name, making him as much the King's property as though he had been honestly bought by a sergeant's shilling.

Mouldy grumbled like a malcontent as he was. He thought that he might have been let alone.

" My old dame will be undone now for one to do her husbandry and her drudgery. You need not to have pricked me : there are other men fitter to go than I."

As if that were a reason for your not going ! For shame, Mouldy !

Simon Shadow was the next called.

"Aye, marry, let me have him to sit under," said Sir John, "he's like to be a cold soldier."

Shadow was approved and pricked.

" Thomas Wart ! "

" Where's he ? "

" Here, sir ! "

" Is thy name Wart." (Sir John Falstaff was the questioner.)

" Yes, Sir ? "

" Thou art a very ragged Wart."

" Shall I prick him down, Sir John ? "

"It were superfluous ; for his apparel is built upon his back, and the whole frame stands upon pins. Prick him no more."

Renewed ecstacies of Mr. Justice Shallow. His worship had always considered a ragged man a most laughable object. But the matter had never been represented to him in such a truly ridiculous light as by his facetious guest.

"Ha ! ha ! ha ! You can do it, Sir, you can do it. I commend you well. Francis Feeble."

"Here, Sir."

"What trade art thou, Feeble ? " Sir John asked.

"A woman's tailor, Sir."

"Shall I prick him, Sir ? "

"You may ; but if he had been a man's tailor, he would have pricked you."

Feeble was approved and pricked. He was the only one who appeared to submit to the operation without wincing. Feeble proved the most valiant ninth part of a recruit on record. He appeared delighted with his prospects. The only drawback to his military ardour and satisfaction was a regret that Wart could not be permitted to accompany him. This makes it difficult to decide whether Wart was his bosom friend or his mortal enemy.

"I would Wart might have gone, Sir," quoth Feeble.

"I would thou wert a man's tailor," replied the Captain, "that thou might'st mend him and make him fit to go. I cannot put him to a private soldier that is the leader of so many thousands. Let that suffice, most forcible Feeble."

Feeble was satisfied. So, no doubt, was Wart.

"Peter Bullcalf of the Green," was the next called.

"Trust me, a likely fellow," said the Knight : "prick me Bullcalf till he roar again."

"Oh good my lord Captain ——" Bullcalf roared without waiting for the operation.

"What, dost thou roar before thou art pricked ? "

"Oh ! Sir, I am a diseased man." Bullcalf bellowed, proving that his lungs were at all events not yet affected.

"What disease hast thou ? "

"A villainous cold, Sir — a cough, Sir — which I caught with ringing in the King's affairs on his coronation day, Sir."

"Come, thou shalt go to the wars in a gown ; we will have away thy cold ; and I will take such order that thy friends shall ring for thee."

It was fortunate that with this sally Sir John Falstaff desisted for the present, or he would in all probability have been the death of Master

Robert Shallow. That gentleman repeated the words, " And I will take such order that thy friends shall ring for thee," to himself, many times over, that he might be able to retail the jest to his admiring friends. He circulated it at first as one of the many brilliant things Sir John Falstaff had said on the occasion of his first visit to Shallow Hall. But in the course of time the worthy magistrate appropriated it to his own service, and never missed an opportunity of bringing it forward (with the point carefully omitted) as an original witticism from the inexhaustible *repertoire* of himself, Master Robert Shallow.

Bullcalf was pricked. The justices and their military friend withdrew to luncheon.

" Good Master Corporate Bardolph," said Bullcalf when the troops were left alone with that warlike personage, " stand my friend, and here is four Harry ten shillings in French crowns for you."

Bullcalf urged his plea by further arguments. They were unnecessary. The first was more than sufficient.

" Go to : stand aside," said Bardolph, pocketing the money.

Mouldy quitted the ranks and motioned his superior to grant him also a private conference.

" And good Master Corporal Captain, for my old dame's sake, stand my friend : she has nobody to do anything about her, when I am gone : and she is old and cannot help herself. You shall have forty, Sir."

Chink ! Chink !

" Go to : stand aside."

" Sir, a word with you," said Bardolph when his Captain reappeared with the two justices. " I have *three* pound to free Mouldy and Bullcalf."

It should be observed that four ten shilling pieces added to forty shillings at that period, as now, made a total of *four* pounds sterling. Bardolph's education had been neglected — and let us hope that his miscalculation was merely the result of a total ignorance of the rules of compound addition.

A word to the wise is sufficient for them. Sir John Falstaff at once decided that Mouldy should stay at home until past service, and Bullcalf be left to grow till he should be fit for it. Sir John would have none of them.

" Sir John, Sir John," urged Master Shallow. " Do not yourself wrong : they are your likeliest men, and I would have you served with the best."

It is not improbable that Bullcalf was a poacher too.

Sir John Falstaff was indignant.

" Will you tell me, Master Shallow, how to choose a man ? Care I for the limb, the thewes, the stature, bulk and big assemblance of a man ? Give me the spirit, Master Shallow. Here's Wart. You see what a ragged appearance it is. He shall charge you and discharge you with the motion of a pewterer's hammer : come off and on swifter than he that gibbets on the brewer's bucket. And this same half-faced fellow Shadow, give me this man —he presents no mark to the enemy; the foeman may with as great aim level at the edge of a penknife. And for a retreat—how swiftly will this Feeble, the woman's tailor, run off ? "

Briefly, Feeble, Wart, and Shadow were enrolled among the king's soldiers serving under Sir John Falstaff. Bullcalf and Mouldy were allowed to go about their business.

It will be seen from the above that the ancient manner of choosing soldiers differed not materially from the modern one. The better class of men were rejected, and the ranks supplied from the dregs of the population. Any charge of venality against Sir John Falstaff and his lieutenant for suffering Mouldy and Bullcalf to buy off their services, I hope I can meet, by calling attention to the fact that there are even now certain favoured persons — whole regiments in fact — ostensibly in her Majesty's service, who are invariably privileged to stop at home in times of danger. Or I can dispose of the matter more simply by stating that Sir John Falstaff merely gave permission to the two warriors elect, Mouldy and Bullcalf — to return to their homes on urgent private affairs.

It may be objected that Sir John Falstaff observed an unjustifiable tone of levity in transacting a business of such gravity as the forcible abduction of poor men from their homes — to risk their lives in a quarrel, the issue of which could not personally interest them. But Sir John's jests on the names, wardrobes, and personal appearance of his recruits, were at all events harmless. I have heard of much more practical jokes being passed on the British soldier by the authorities engaging him in my time ; such as promising him certain sums of money for his services, and deducting nearly the whole amount for the expenses of his outfit ; sending him to fight under a broiling sun, weighted with half a horse load of useless accoutrements ; supplying him with firelocks that burst in his hands ; shipping him on board crazy old vessels that go to pieces in still water ; and a thousand others.

VI.

ON THE MAGNANIMITY OF SIR JOHN FALSTAFF IN ABSTAINING FROM PARTI-
CIPATION IN A DISGRACEFUL ACTION. — EPISODE OF COLEVILE OF THE
GRANGE.

IN estimating the characters of great men, it is recognised as a principle that
we should give them almost the same credit for the mischief they abstain from
doing as for the positive good they effect. Abstention from evil, under
circumstances of great temptation to its performance, is unquestionably a
virtue of the highest order. In proof of the high esteem habitually awarded
by mankind to this rare although negative excellence, I will refer merely to
the celebrated letting-alone case of the Roman Scipio, and the well-known
parallel to it afforded by the conduct of Sir John Falstaff himself, who (at
a later period of his career than the one at present under notice), having
occasion, for professional reasons, to break open a gentleman's lodge, kill the
gentleman's deer, and maltreat the gentleman's servants, was yet, in the very
height and impetuosity of action, enabled to put a sufficient curb on his
impulses to resist the temptation of kissing a keeper's daughter!

The little incident of self-denial just alluded to, though in every way deserving of the highest eulogy, has, as it seems to me, been dwelt on by the commentators with undue stress, rather implying a suspicion that it might have been an
exceptional case in the character and conduct of our knight, and remarkable
only on that account. So far from this being the truth, I could establish precedents for the occurrence by a thousand proofs of glaring offences which Sir John
Falstaff did *not* commit, while otherwise occupied in the way of his business.
I will content myself, however, with a single example, couched in an incident,
which here falls naturally into its place, by which it will be seen that the
hero of these pages could, on occasion, abstain from taking part in even the
greatest acts of rascality of his time; moreover, when the greatest facilities,
and even inducements, existed for his participating in such means of glory.

The following passage from Hollinshed will facilitate comprehension of
the incident.

" Raufe Nevill, Earl of Westmoreland, that was not far off, together with
" the Lord John of Lancaster, the King's son, being informed of this
" rebellious attempt*, assembled together such powers as they might make,

---

* *i.e.* That of Northumberland, Hastings, Mowbray and Archbishop Scroop—with a view
to the suppression of which Falstaff and others were now marching into Yorkshire.

" and coming into a plain within the forest of Galtree, caused their standards
" to be pight down in the like sort as the Archbishop had pight his, over
" against them, being far stronger of people than the other; for (as some
" write) there were of the rebels, at the least, eleven thousand men. When the
" Earl of Westmoreland perceived the force of adversaries, and that they lay
" still and attempted not to come forward upon him, he subtilely devised how
" to quail their purpose, and forthwith despatched messengers unto the Arch-
" bishop to understand the cause, as it were, of that great assemble, and for what
" cause, contrary to the King's peace, they came so in armour. The Archbishop
" answered that he took nothing in hand against the King's peace; but that
" whatever he did, tended rather to advance the peace and quiet of the Com-
" monwealth than otherwise; and when he and his company were in arms, it
" was for fear of the King, to whom he could have no free access by reason
" of such a multitude of flatterers as were about him; and therefore he main-
" tained that his purpose was good and profitable, as well for the King himself
" as for the realm, if men were willing to understand a truth; and herewith
" he showed forth a scroll, in which the articles were written whereof before
" ye have heard. The Messengers returning unto the Earl of Westmoreland,
" showed him what they had heard and brought from the Archbishop. When
" he had read the articles, he showed in word and countenance, outwardly, that
" he liked of the Archbishop's holy and virtuous intent and purpose; that he
" and his would prosecute the same in assisting the Archbishop, who,
" rejoicing at that, gave credit to the Earl, and persuaded the Earl Marshall
" against his will, as it were, to go with him to a place appointed for them
" to commune together. Then, when they were met with like number on either
" part, the articles were read over; and, without any more ado, the Earl of
" Westmoreland and those that were with him agreed to do their best to see
" that a reformation might be had according to the same. The Earl of West-
" moreland using more policy than the rest: 'Well (said he), then our travail is
" come to the wished end; and whereas our people have been long in armour,
" let them depart home to their wonted trades and occupations: in the mean
" time let us drink together in sign of agreement, that the people on both
" sides may see it, and know that it is true that we be light at a point.'
" They had no sooner shaked hands together, but a knight was sent straight-
" ways from the Archbishop to bring word to the people that there was a
" Peace concluded, commanding each man to lay aside arms, and resort home
" to their homes. The people beholding such tokens of peace as shaking of
" hands, and drinking together of the Lords in loving manner, brake up their
" field and returned homewards: but in the mean time, while the people of
" the Archbishop's side drew away, the number of the contrary part increased,

" according to order given by the Earl of Westmoreland. And yet the
" Archbishop perceived not he was deceived till the Earl of Westmoreland
" arrested him and the Earl Marshall, with divers other. Their troops being
" pursued, many were taken, many slain, and many spoiled of that they had
" about them, and so permitted to go their ways."

Now, I am happy to say, that with all his faults, Sir John Falstaff was
guiltless of participation in this infamous transaction. From the Shakspearian account of the occurrence (which does not materially differ from that
of the elder and more prosaic chronicles), it is clear that Falstaff and his troops
were not among those who treacherously " increased," according to orders
from the Earl of Westmoreland, while the people of the Archbishop's side
" drew away." Sir John did not make his appearance on the shameful field
till the heat of action was past and the disgraceful pursuit abandoned.

It is true that the fact is on record, that on our hero's reaching the
skirts of Gaultree Forest, he met with a runaway rebel, by name Colevile
of the Dale, whom he immediately challenged, and who, as quickly sur-
rendered himself prisoner, on the mere suspicion that his challenger was
no other than the redoubted Sir John Falstaff. This circumstance, whilst
adding another to the thousand existing proofs that our knight was a man of
acknowledged bravery and martial renown — at the same time, seems a little
to weaken my theory, that Sir John is entitled to credit for having withheld
his countenance and assistance from the treacherous " subtiltie " of Westmoreland and Lancaster. It looks rather as though he had come a little late for
the scramble, and was anxious to make up for lost time in the pursuit and
plunder of stragglers. Colevile, however, seems to have fallen in his way
most temptingly, and from the alacrity with which he gave himself into custody, he would seem to have been an individual ambitious for the distinction
of being led captive at the wheels of Sir John Falstaff's car of triumph.

The following conversation explains the circumstances of the capture * : —

SIR JOHN FALSTAFF. What is your name, sir? Of what condition are you; and of
what place, I pray ?

COLEVILE. I am a knight, sir, and my name is, Colevile of the Dale.

FALSTAFF. Well then, Colevile, is your name ; a knight, is your degree ; and your place,
the dale. Colevile, shall still be your name ; a traitor, your degree ; and the dungeon, your
place — a place deep enough. So shall you be still Colevile of the Dale.

COLEVILE. Are you not Sir John Falstaff ?

FALSTAFF. As good a man as he, sir, whoe'er I am.

　•　　　*　　　*　　　*　　　*　　　•　　　*　　　•　　　*　　　*

COLEVILE. I think you are Sir John Falstaff, and I yield me.

Henry IV. Part II., act iv. scene 2.

This capture of Colevile (which, considering Colevile's alacrity to be caught, I don't well see how Sir John could have avoided), is, I am happy to say, the only evidence on record, of our knight's having been in the slightest degree mixed up with this most rascally transaction in the most rascally age of English history : perpetrated in the name, and by the son and officers, of a distinguished rascal, who, by his own vast demerits, had raised himself to the exalted position of the King of all the Rascals in England. Sir John's remarkable abnegation of self in this affair, almost induces me to recon-sider my by no means hastily formed estimate of his entire character. I begin to doubt seriously that Sir John Falstaff was one bit of a courtier after all. Had he been a person of that description, he would certainly have toadied King Henry the Fourth much better than he did, by aping (as is the fashion with people of a courtly turn) the most salient points of that lugubrious, and especially infamous, monarch's character and conduct. This is a new light on the mystery of our knight's repeated failures in the attempt to rise in court favour. He was not half a rogue — that is the long and short of the matter. And King Henry the Fourth, of unblessed memory, who had mur-dered his first cousin, who had stolen his first cousin's wife's jewels and em-broidered petticoats, — who was capable of every crime, from pitch and toss with loaded farthings to manslaughter with arsenicated preparations, — felt for him much of that contempt which a six-bottle squire of the old school cannot bnt feel for a modern milksop, detected in the effeminate act of putting water in his tumbler of sherry.

VII.

DOUBTS ON THE GENIUS AND TESTIMONY OF SHAKSPEARE. — LETTER FROM
MASTER RICHARD WHITTINGTON. — AND OTHER MATTERS.

WHETHER or not it is that I have been taking an overdose of that familiarity which is said to produce contempt, I will not pretend to say, but one thing is very certain — namely, that I by no means feel that exalted respect for the late William Shakspeare as an historical authority, which on my setting forth on the present biographical pilgrimage formed so prominent an ingre-dient in my wallet of provisions for the journey. Candidly, Shakspeare turns out to be, by no means, the man I had taken him for. An able dramatist, undoubtedly — endowed with considerable power of insight into the secret springs of human emotion, with an aptness for a rugged forcible kind of versification, and an unquestionable turn for humour—he must, nevertheless, be pronounced lamentably deficient in those higher attributes of the historical writer, by which it is the laudable ambition of the present scribe (for instance), to know himself distinguished—and of which the most scrupulous correctness as to dates and localities, is by no means the least essential. And, indeed, as I reflect on the subject and turn over a variety of precedents in my mind, I am reluctantly brought much nearer than I ever expected to come to the by no means uncommon opinion that Shakspeare is an over-rated personage in literature.

I am led to this admission—most distasteful to my feelings and predilections—by the irresistible fact that nearly all of his commentators and critics, for the most part persons of vast erudition and acumen, by whose exalted standard the present humble recruit in the army of letters would shrink from offering himself for measurement; who, commencing (like their unpretending junior) with the most enthusiastic faith in, not to say idolatrous admiration for, the subject of their investigations, will seldom be found to have proceeded to any depth in their labours ere they agree in making out Shakspeare a most ridiculous, not to say contemptible personage. The late Mr. Thomas Campbell, who, notwithstanding the unavoidable accident of his birthplace, may be considered a tolerably competent and impartial judge of English literature, being employed by certain publishers to prepare an edition of the works of the Immortal Bard, as he is termed (I am not fond of this slavish kind of nomenclature myself, considering that, as a rule, one man is nearly as good as another), and plunging into his task with great ardour and alacrity, and in the most reverential spirit imaginable, nevertheless speedily got sick of the service of adulation—I would say "puffery," were the epithet consistent with the dignity of history—on which he had been engaged, and even complained, in a letter to a friend, of the kind of stuff he was compelled, by the necessities of his position and the terms of his contract, to "write about Old Shakey." Now from such high-flown designations as the Immortal Bard, the Sweet Swan, &c.,—to which Mr. Campbell, at the outset of his editorial career, had been addicted, like other people,—"Old Shakey" (in the forcible words of a modern art-critic) is "not fall—it is catastrophe;" and, depend upon it, the learned gentleman had found out some weak points in the poet's character to justify the familiarity. I may be answered, I am aware, with the stale proverb that no man is a hero in the eyes of his own valet, the abstract wisdom of which, as well as its partial application to the case in point, I cheerfully admit. An editor or commentator of a great man's writings unquestionably occupies, to the great man, the position of a valet or groom of the chambers, having to perform for him the most menial offices, such as looking out his new readings for him, polishing his sentences, trimming his periods, and throwing away his slip-slop. These irksome and even degrading duties may excite in the bosom of the overworked official a feeling of disgust for his situation, which no liberality or punctuality in the matter of wages and perquisites can alto-gether annihilate; and the constant absorption of his attention by such ignoble matters of external detail, can scarcely fail to blind him to the inner greatnesses of the demi-god whose wig and whiskers, so to speak, he is eternally occupied in brushing and oiling. I would, therefore, guard against too hastily accepting the opinion of such persons upon the great men whom they are employed, as it were, to render presentable to society, just as I would hesitate to base my estimate of the soldierly and statesmanlike qualities of the first Cæsar on the representations of the ingenious artist in laurel who was engaged to conceal the baldness of the great Roman by the " gentleman's real wreath of glory" of the period; or, were I a sculptor (which it may be a fortunate thing for the British metropolis I am not, seeing that I have influential friends who would undoubtedly employ me in adding to the public monuments), as I should decline modelling a statue of England's last, greatest, and most symmetrical George upon the one-sided views of the tailor who measured him for his last padded and frogged surtout, or of the hosier who was in the secret of the royal calves, during the decadence of the first — whatever you like to call him — of Europe. Nevertheless, there is no withstanding overwhelming masses of evidence, let them emanate from sources never so obscure or prejudiced. And when we find that the commentators upon Shakspeare, almost without exception, when they have taken hold of what are vulgarly considered the finest passages in that author's writings,— when they have carefully held up those passages against every possible kind of light, turned them inside out, pulled and tugged at them, this way and that, ripped open their seams, scratched off their nap or surfaces, and, in fact, submitted them to every conceivable test, — when, I say, we find that the com-mentators, having made these searching experiments, almost invariably decide that what to the superficial observer has appeared something of exquisite goodness and beauty must be accepted as nothing more or less than the rankest nonsense — why, then, the dispassionate judge is bound to shake his head in common deprecation with the scrutineers, and admit that very possibly the Sweet Swan, &c., may be nothing more than " Old Shakey " after all. Nay, some of the most laborious and indefatigable of the class alluded to have so carefully sifted the matter, and so thoroughly have con-vinced themselves of the utter flimsiness and impalpability of the supposed Mr. Shakspeare's claims to literary distinction, as to have been irresistibly led

to the conviction that no such person ever could have existed ; but that the
rather ingenious and plausible-looking phantasms in the forms of plays and
poems, bearing his name, must be considered as mere spontaneous exhala-
tions or *fungi* produced from a kind of intellectual chaos—much as primroses,
oak-trees, horses, beautiful women, poets, and philosophers are held to have
sprung into existence, by the tenets of certain kindred thinkers on subjects
connected with theology.

The last is a culminating phase of Shakspearian free-thinking, to which, I
confess, I have not yet been able to bring myself. I am still young, and
possibly hampered by nursery traditions on the subject. But I hope it will
be admitted that I am gradually emancipating myself from the unpopular
trammels of Shakspearian superstition, when I venture so far as to affirm
that the Swan of Avon (I must be understood now to make use of the
designation in an ironical sense) was, in some respects, a —— Yes! I have
lashed myself up to the necessary pitch of defiant resolution — a HUMBUG !
I fearlessly assert that there is a prevalent looseness in his chronology, for
which I defy his most slavish admirers to prove that the correctness of his
grammar is at all of a quality to compensate. Why, he actually leads us to
infer that within a few weeks, at the outside, of the treacherously won field
of Gualtree, Sir John Falstaff, being then on his second visit to the domain
of Mr. Justice Shallow, in Gloucestershire (having just returned from the
inglorious campaign), did receive, through the officious instrumentality of
Ancient Pistol, tidings of the death of King Henry the Fourth. Now I hope
I have, by this time, proved, to the satisfaction of the most captious, that the
battle of Gualtree must have been fought (bought, or stolen, whichever the
reader pleases) in the summer of 1410. The lamented death of Henry
the Fourth—lamentable because it did not take place some forty-seven years
earlier — occurred on Saint Cuthbert's Day, otherwise the 19th of March,
1413. Assuming then, as we are led to, from the representations of the
Shakspearian chronicle, that Sir John Falstaff, on the disbanding of the
Royalist army under Prince John of Lancaster and the Earl of Westmoreland, betook himself, at once, to the hospitable mansion of Mr. Robert Shallow,
and there remained until the Sovereign's demise, this would give to our
knight's visit a duration of something like two years and three-quarters. Now,
though I freely admit that we find nothing in the antecedents of Sir John to
make it improbable that he should have extended a gratuitous residence in
comfortable quarters to that, or even a longer period, in the event of impunity
having been granted to him to do so, it is in the wildest degree incredible that
even a greater fool than Mr. Robert Shallow—did history present us with such
a personage—would tamely have submitted to the infliction of guests so ex-

pensive as our knight and his retainers, for even one-twentieth part of that term. No country gentleman's revenues could have stood it. The unaided exertions of the insatiable Bardolph alone would have exhausted the family cellar and exchequer in a fortnight.

It is therefore undeniable that in this particular instance, if in no other, Shakspeare has not only violated historical truth—either wilfully or through negligence — but has also shown an imperfect appreciation of the probabilities. That Falstaff and his retinue could not possibly have lived on the Shallow estate for the space of two years and three quarters, is as self-evident as that an able-bodied man could not subsist for the same period on a single leg of mutton. The supposition that Master Shallow would have continued glad to see them, up to the end of a residence so protracted, is too insanely preposterous to be entertained for a single moment.

Having carefully balanced the matter, I am inclined to decide that the second visit of Sir John Falstaff to Master Shallow's, as described in the Shakspearian chronicle — the account of which offers strong internal evidence of a basis on authentic information — took place precisely as exhibited by the dramatist, who chose, however, for his own convenience of composition, and with the reckless indifference to the higher canons of criticism by which many really able writers of *that* period were unfortunately characterised, to anticipate the course of events to the culpable extent I have alluded to. It could not be otherwise. It has been made clear, from documentary evidence recently laid before the reader*, that the Falstaff expedition to Yorkshire deviated into Gloucestershire in the month of June, 1410. The unqualified statement that Henry Plantagenet, surnamed Bolingbroke, and fourth English king of his baptismal appellation, breathed his last on the 19th of March (in the old style), otherwise the festival day of St. Cuthbert†, in the year 1413, was by no means incautiously hazarded. The writer will stake his reputation on its accuracy, which, if called into question for a moment, he is prepared to corroborate by the undeniable evidence of Hollinshed, Hardyng, Stowe, Speed, White Kennet, Mangnall, Pinnock, and other writers of antiquity. You see there is no getting over facts. They are things of such matchless stubbornness that none but a donkey would venture to cope with them in the exhibition of that valuable attribute.

We must consider, then, that there is a period of two years and probably

---

* Vide Epistle from Sir John Falstaff, Knight, to Master Robert Shallow, Cust. Rot., &c., in the Strongate Collection; or (for greater convenience of reference) in pp. 134, 135, of the present biography.

† Vide Romish Calendar.

seven or eight months in the life of Sir John Falstaff unaccounted for in the
Shakspeare Chronicles. In what manner were those years and odd months employed by the hero of these pages ? For once in a way, the biographer is driven
to supply an extensive gap in his narrative by mere conjecture. It is reasonable to suppose that the time was passed by Sir John in his native country,
as I find no evidence, in the records of continental nations, of the influence of
a master spirit of our knight's calibre on the dynastic, social, or religious
struggles of the period. It is also to be feared that Sir John continued to live
in comparative obscurity, and certainly in exclusion from court favour. The
latter hypothesis is, indeed, based on something more than conjecture, and
may be considered proved by certain important omissions in the chronicles
of the time. On the 23rd of January, 1411, Sir John Falstaff would have
completed his fifty-ninth year. A moment's reflective calculation will convince the most inconsiderate that on the same date in the following year our
knight would have attained the reverend age of threescore. Extend this
line of inductive reasoning to another twelve months, and a result of sixty-
one is obtained. Now, it would be reasonable to suppose that had Sir John
Falstaff, at these times, been in the enjoyment of that royal esteem to which
his merits and services undoubtedly entitled him, any one of the three anni-
versaries indicated would have been made the occasion of court festivities.
I defy the most laborious investigation to produce the slightest authentic
evidence, from the writings of the time, of any such recognition of our
knight's importance and public services having been made at any of the royal
residences. It will be found, it is true, by consulting Hollinshed, the Cotton
MSS., Stowe and other authorities, that London, in the commencement of
1413, was the scene of great military and naval pageantry; that numbers of
the king's forces were mustered in the metropolis, and that there was such a
display of ships and galleys on the river Thames as had not been seen since the
magnificent days of Edward the Third. From the same and contemporary
writings, it will be found that towards the close of the Christmas holidays—
which King Henry the Fourth, in consequence of the mortal illness wherewith
he was already smitten, had kept in strict seclusion with his Queen Joanna, at
the Palace of Eltham—His Majesty, in spite of grievous bodily suffering, made
shift to return to London, in order to be present at certain rejoicings ordained
to be held at his chief palace of Westminster, at a time closely coincident
with the anniversary of our hero's birth. I am inclined to think, however,
that it will prove, on careful investigation, that the mustering of troops and
display of naval armaments had been commanded, not, as would superficially
appear, to celebrate the day of Falstaff's nativity by tournaments, sham
fights, water quintains, and the like, but with the more serious design of

carrying out a project, long entertained by the king, of proceeding with a powerful army to Palestine, there to assist in the attempt to recover the holy sepulchre from the hands of the Paynim followers of Mahomet *—a kind of moral Insolvent or Bankruptcy Court of the period, to which very great rascals indeed were accustomed to apply for protection against the prosecutions of conscience, and by which (if enabled to do things on a liberal scale as to expenses in other people's lives and property), they were supposed to whitewash themselves of all liabilities in this world and the next. The rejoicings at Westminster may be partially explained by the fact that King Henry's birthday happened to fall within a few days of that of Sir John Falstaff. And, keeping in view the habitual and ineradicable selfishness of Henry's character, it is more than probable that His Majesty had decreed the festivities in question on his own account, and not on that of our more meritorious hero. As a proof that, in spite of the numerous embarrassments of the royal family, the glaring and systematic manner in which the priceless services of Falstaff were ignored by the court could not have been attributable to any absolute scarcity of means, it may be mentioned that about this time Queen Joanna presented one Thomas Chaucer, an individual whose only claims to personal distinction lay in the fact that he was, as it were, the half-brother of English Poetry—being the son of its reputed father—with the manors of Wotten and Stantesfield for life: the hospitalities of which, there can be no question or doubt, would have been dispensed with much greater dignity and liberality by Sir John Falstaff. As a further proof that the favours heaped upon this mere Son of a Somebody were only conferred with a view to the humiliation and discomfiture of Sir John Falstaff, it may be mentioned that Mr. Thomas Chaucer—a man of the slenderest physical and mental dimensions—was shortly afterwards appointed to fill the Speaker's Chair of the House of Commons—a seat which, had the appointment of the Right Man to the Right Place been a recognised principle in those days any more than it is at the present time, Sir John Falstaff was, most obviously, *the* man to fill. But, as has been repeatedly urged, our knight had powerful enemies. I name no names, as a rule, and have an abhorrence of malicious insinuations. I will content myself with the statement that the dignity of Lord Chief Justice of England, *with all its influence for good and evil,* continued to be represented by a distinguished personage, with whom we are already acquainted in that capacity, until some years after the demise of Sir John Falstaff.

---

* Vide the writings of Froissart, G. P. R. James, and others. The Italian poet Torquato Tasso has an able work not wholly disconnected with the interesting subject of the Crusades as these expeditions were termed.

Sir John lived in London—there can be no doubt of that. Had his name been John Dory instead of John Falstaff, the sea could not have been a more indispensable element to his existence than was the metropolitan atmosphere to him, surnamed and organised as he actually was. Where else could there have been found a Boar's Head, with its accommodating hostess, its inexhaustible cellars, and still more (if the adjective can be said to admit of a comparative degree) inexhaustible credit? What other English city, district, or province, has ever, at any time of the world's history, produced a hero-worshipping class so willing to pay liberal terms for the honour of even an ex-great man's society. Where else in England have there ever been known such good dinners, such boon companions, and such accommodating tradespeople?

Talking of tradespeople (a subject to which I am by no means greatly addicted, suggesting, as it does, such painful memories and still more disagreeable possibilities) there is a document extant, the faithful transcript of an earlier document, no longer in existence, which will serve to throw some light on the position of Sir John Falstaff during this most obscure, and consequently most interesting, portion of his biography. It is a letter from Master Richard Whittington, mercer, some time Lord Mayor of London, addressed to Sir John Falstaff, in answer to a communication from that great man, which has unfortunately not been preserved. The epistle, as will be seen, is not dated; but the unmistakable allusion contained in it to King Henry the Fourth's intended expedition to the Holy Land leaves no doubt that it must have been written in the winter of 1412–13. The shrewd, sarcastic tone of the letter (the orthography whereof in the following transcript has been modified for the convenience of the modern reader, in obedience to the rule invariably observed throughout this work) will, it is hoped, be found sufficiently characteristic of its distinguished writer, to dispense with any necessity for the production, as evidence, of the original manuscript, which was unfortunately destroyed in the ever-lamentable burning of the famous Whittington library, in Arundel Street, Strand, some two or three years since.

"TO MINE EXCELLENT FRIEND SIR JOHN FALSTAFF, KNIGHT, BE THESE DELIVERED.

"RIGHT WORSHIPFUL SIR JOHN,

"Methinks, in future, I shall call you my cat. For as there be those who insist that I owe my standing as a good citizen and man of wealth to a certain cat which I took with me to Barbarie (where, Heaven be praised! I never was), who did there earn for me large sums in money, slaves, and jewels, by freeing the king's chamber of mice and rats; so will you have it that I have risen to be alderman and mayor, to buy lands and endow churches, alone through having ridden on your crupper from Blackheath to the Southwark side of London Bridge, in the year of grace, 1364, when we were both lads, little wotting we should live to know each the other as old men. Now I call my patron to witness that I had never a cat that did aught for me beyond skimming the milk in my kitchen. I took with me to Flanders, and thence through France and Germany to the ignorant estates of the East, a certain Thrift or Judgment, which the witless have fabled into a cat, whereby I was enabled to point out to many foolish peoples the way to clear themselves of grievous pests and torments in government and common life, which might well be likened to rats and mice, for the which good services I was so well rewarded by the thankful rulers of those countries as to return to mine own with the means for large and honourable trading. But the vulgar will have it that it was not I myself, but the cat, effected all this. So would you have it, Sir John, that because I came to London a barefoot, ragged, herring-bodied scarecrow, and am now a man of substance (not in the flesh, Sir John; there you have still the best of me), I owe my advancement to you, who brought me half a dozen miles on the way. It was a pleasant ride,—I mind it well,—and a timely, for I was heartsore and footsore when you took me up. But I am a trader, Sir John, and keep books. And when I look over our account, I cannot but think that I have long ago paid for that ride at a rate of posting far beyond what my travels to Germany and the Asiatic countries (which the blockheads will have Barbarie) cost me altogether. Let us cast the sum. There was two shillings (out of the first four of my earning), soon after our coming to London, to replace your torn doublet, which you declared you dared not write to your lady mother about.* There was five marks on your coming of age, when you had bidden certain young noblemen of the court to meet you at the tavern, which I was fain to lend you, as you had lost the money set aside for their entertainment, the night before, at play. You wept so bitterly, and so feared me with threatening self-destruction, that I must needs do this though it forced me to put off my first slender venture with the Flemings. Then, when they knighted you, there was forty other marks, that you might present yourself becomingly at court. Ten marks on my being made mayor, that it might not be said I forgot an old friend who had helped me to my rise in life. Since then, at divers times, in silks, velvets, and moneys lent, eight hundred and forty-three pounds nine and elevenpence. Now, all this I have been told, time after time, I have owed you for bringing me to London, and putting me in the way of fortune. It hath been a dear ride to me, Sir John. Blackheath to London is, let us say, six miles. A hundred and forty-one pounds eight shillings seven pence and a fraction is costly posting for times like these, Sir John. Methinks it is time I should hold myself quit of your debt, or that if any be still due you should forgive me the remainder. A truce to jesting, old friend Jack. I will lend thee no more money, and that is the plain truth of the matter. It is of no more use to thee than pearls to a pig. Thou art no more going to the Holy Land with King Henry than I am going thither behind thee on thy crupper (which Heaven forefend, considering the costliness of that mode of travel). Come thou hither to dine, sup, and sleep as often as may list thee, and thou art welcome to the best my roof can afford. But I am a trader, Sir Jack, and a keen one,—I give naught for naught. Sell us thy company, good-fellowship, merry jests and gentleness, and I will pay thee in kind (saving the jests and merry tales, wherein I am the bankrupt and thou the niggard miser). Show us thy jolly face and we will reflect it in endless bowls of as many wines as thou mayest name, like to a face in a chamber lined with tinted mirrors, till thou seest thyself million-fold, and of all colours. Mine honest wife and thy little playfellows, whom thou hast deserted, have been trained in my school. They join the outer world in calling thee foul names, since thou withholdest from them that familiarity which is their due. Dame Alice calls thee downright rogue,—that thou wilt not pay her the long arrears of society and converse thou owest her,—and for which she says she has a mind to pursue thee up and down every law court in Christendom. The little Jews have long arrears of caresses against thee, and are prone to insist on their bargain to the letter. Pay these debts, thou hardened prodigal, and we will see what can be effected for the future. As for money, thou shalt none of it, for it only serves to keep thee from us,

---

* See *antè*, p. 108.

wasting that of thy company which is our lawful right, as thine oldest friends, on thankless tavern roysterers who love thee not. I am now too old a merchant to repeat that kind of unprofitable venture.

"I have again fallen into jesting, mine old friend, which methinks between aged men who love each other, on grave matters, should not be. If thou art in serious strait I will help thee as heretofore and while I live, and no man save ourselves the wiser; but the spirit of a weakly man, born to poverty and grown up in the need of turning all around him to his selfish advantage, will assert itself within me; and I cannot bear to serve thee that I may lose thee. When thou lackest naught (it is the shopman who states his debt) thou dost never think of the poor shambling youth of Blackheath, whom thou didst lift, not only into horseback, but out of despair and heart-sickness by the contagion of thy health, courage, and kindliness; and to whom at the turning point of his fortunes (for despair was then setting in) thou didst give a ride worth far more than many hundreds of pounds a mile. Whereas, when thy purse is empty, thou art ever prompt to remember Master Richard Whittington, some time lord mayor of London and always a rich merchant and housekeeper. This is the only charge thou wilt ever hear me bring against thee; for it is the only thing in which thou hast ever wronged me —and I meddle not with other men's debts or claims; but when one justly owes me that which I deem he can pay, I will ever urge it, though he were my brother.

"Dear, beloved, and, whatever the world may of thee (for I have the conceit that I look deeper into men's natures than the thoughtless commonalty), honoured Sir John Falstaff, if money could win thee to be near me and mine—who love thee deservedly, and to whom thou hast never been aught but what is just and pure — thou shouldst have it from my well-stored coffers poured untold into thy pockets. But I have ever found it act as a spell that parts us. Remedy this if thou canst. Come and dwell with us — with all thine extravagancies and all thy retinue if thou wilt. Our cellars may perchance even hold out a year's siege against the redoubtable Master Bardolph. All I stipulate is that thou shalt give me thy stalwart Jacka-napes, Robin, to save from perdition, by placing him in the new school I am building; this for his own sake and more for that of two sober little kitchen-maidens of Mistress Alice's, whom I should be loath to grow familiar with the kind of conversation I fear he must have picked up ere this in thine erratic progress.

"Briefly, Jack, I will not send thee the money thou demandest. Come and ask for it, and Dame Alice and I (with the bantlings to hold on by thy skirts) will do our best to keep thee from going away till thou gettest it.

"Thy friend,
"Richard Whittington."

It is scarcely probable that Sir John Falstaff being in, even for him, unusually embarrassed circumstances, could have withstood the temptation of indefinite hospitality, at the expense of a wealthy and sympathetic friend. It may, therefore, be taken for granted that the winter of 1413–14 was passed by our knight and his retainers under the genial roof of the renowned citizen, mercer, traveller and philanthropist, Master Richard Whittington. I use the term "Master," being inclined to think that the distinguished Londoner in question had not yet attained to the dignity of knighthood. My memory fails me on the subject, and the question is not one of sufficient importance to demand reference to authorities. Certain indications in the above letter lead me to believe that it was written by a plain undubbed citizen: for though Whittington himself, as a cosmopolitan philosopher, may have held all titular distinctions in contempt, and considered himself no better man after knighthood than before it, yet it would be in the highest degree unreasonable to suppose that the wife of his bosom could have participated in his apathy on the question. The above letter was, most obviously, written under the immediate supervision of the excellent Dame Alice Whittington — obviously from the terms of reverential decorum in which that lady is spoken of in it. *Is* it likely, that a city gentlewoman of the period, whose husband had successfully aspired to chivalric honours, would allow that husband to speak of her in a letter to another knight of real noble birth, as mere "Mistress Alice," or that the writer would have been permitted by her to sign his epistle without the affix of "eques"? Certainly not. This, however, is irrelevant. The present work purports to be the history of Sir John Falstaff. That of Richard Whittington has been already written, and published in a neat and commodious form, profusely illustrated, and to be had of all booksellers.

A.D. 1413. Assuming that Sir John Falstaff actually spent his Christmas with the Whittington family, surrounded by the, to him, unwonted luxuries of a refined, pure-minded matron (who, if, as I have supposed, she *had* been inclined to look over her husband's letters and insist on his asserting, on his and her behalf, any dignities which his honourable exertions might have earned for the pair of them, need be none the worse for that); the innocent prattling of an honest man's young children; and, above all, the enduring friendship and protection of the honest man himself — an old warrior with the world, who had passed through many fires, and who could be lenient to the failures of combatants in more trying, if less honourable fields, only thanking his stars that he himself was alive, sitting by his fireside, and with all his scars in front!—a thoughtful friend who could perceive good, where the world only saw bad; who could remember the beauteous promise of spring in the very depths of winter!—why should Sir John Falstaff have torn himself away from such a peaceful haven — old creaky hulk as he was, with every timber starting, and not sea-worthy for a two years' voyage — to be again buffeted about on the turbulent waters of uncertainty and dissipation? Alas! alas! Why does the poisoned cup kill? Why does the broken leg limp? Why does the bent bough grow downwards, and trail its meagre fruit among the worms and mud? Why does the old maimed hound hunt in dreams? Why do the ruined gamesters in the German demon stories, gamble away, first their doublets, then their vests, then their hose, then their shirts, and ultimately, their souls?

I can fancy Sir John Falstaff for a few days leading a life of marvellous peace, and even happiness, in the orderly household of sage Master Whittington, who loved our friend for the strong latent good that was in him, and to whom the doubly errant knight's vices and irregularities were mere

hateful excrescences, to be abhorred, as we abhor the consumption that kills
our favourite sister, but which makes us love herself the more in our indignation at its rapacious cruelty.   I can fancy a few pleasant evenings by the
big fireside, Sir John telling innumerable pleasant stories from the vast
resources of his sixty years' experience, tempering them, with that sagacity
of his which no excess or reverses could blind, to the innocence and capacity
of his hearers.   Dame Alice embroidering, or sitting sedately with her hands
crossed upon her straight-cut mediæval skirt, as we see the ladies in the old
illuminations; Master Richard, in an arm-chair like a young cathedral,
playing with a big gold chain, of bulk and substance to suggest the idea of a
watch-guard with which a fine-grown Titan, particularly anxious to be up
to the time of day, might have carried Big Ben in his waistcoat pocket;
and the little people, crawling lovingly over the knight's round knees, and
looking up into his bloated, purple, damaged, handsome face, with a by no
means misplaced confidence in, and admiration for, their amusing instructor.
For — come! — where do you find a single instance on record of Sir John
Falstaff having by word or deed — expressed, performed, or omitted — contri-
buted to the corruption of a single innocent creature?   You may tell me of
little Robin the page, whom Sir John dragged mercilessly after him through
the various moral sloughs and slums he himself was destined to wade through.
To this I can only answer, that Robin was corrupt as St. Giles's when Sir
John found him; and that I do not pretend to set up my poor scapegrace old
knight as a social reformer.   He was merely a reprehensible, cynical, *laisser
aller* philosopher.   He took things as he found them, and could no more
mend them than he could mend himself.   He could no more have made a
good boy of Robin than he could have forced Bardolph to sign the temperance pledge, or than he could have spared sufficient money from his own
daily expenses to found a Magdalen hospital for the especial reformation of
Mistress Dorothea Tearsheet—assuming the prevalent aspersions on that lady's
reputation to have been based on anything but the most malicious calumny.

But those pleasant evenings in the Whittington household could not have
lasted.   The first flush of pleasure derived from comfortable quarters,
abundant and luxurious provisions, and the security from legal interference
being over, the very respectability of the thing would become irksome.   Let
Whittington try never so hard to place his guest on a footing of equality
with himself, the unconscious patronage of the man who had fought and won,
over the man who had merely skirmished and lost, would, in the long run,
become intolerable.   And then there is the great force of habit.   There is
undoubted fascination in " the desolate freedom of the wild ass."   Unlimited
sand, with an occasional root of cactus or prickly pear, would, I presume,
be far more acceptable to a quadruped of that species than a daily bran-

mash, turnips, and warm straw bedding, where there would be harness and padlocks withal. I can fancy Falstaff beginning to find the early hours and decorous regulations of the Whittington establishment considerably too much for him. Respectable members of the Mercers' Company would doubtless look in, and gaze upon him as a curious monster. He would yearn for the naughtinesses of the Boar's Head, with its limed sack, sanded floor, and obsequious retainers. And then there would be the ever-present and dreadful consciousness of Master Whittington himself, to whom no weak point in the character of Sir John Falstaff was a mystery; who would help Sir John liberally to sack, knowing it was not good for him; who would lend Sir John money, knowing he would bestow it in bad uses; who would let Sir John talk himself breathless, and smilingly count all Sir John's lies on his fingers! Depend upon it, there is nothing so intolerable to a sensible man who has made a fool of himself through life as the silent criticism of another sensible man, who is aware of the fact, and who himself has done nothing of the kind.

Therefore I am inclined to think that Sir John Falstaff and his old friend Richard Whittington must have come to a one-sided quarrel within a month, at the utmost, of Sir John's more than probable residence in the Whittingtonian household. It may have been a question of stopping out late, or of introducing an unbecoming companion (let us say Ancient Pistol, whom Sir John, in a moment of vinous aberration, may have been so inconsiderate as to present to Dame Alice Whittington as a model member of mass-going society). At any rate, it is very certain that, in the month of March, 1413, Sir John Falstaff was no longer, if he had recently been, a guest of Master Richard Whittington, or even a resident in the British metropolis.

Sir John Falstaff, on the 21st of March, 1413, was again the honoured visitor of Master Robert Shallow, in the Commission of the Peace for the county of Gloucester.

VIII.

MILDNESS OF THE SPRING SEASON IN 1413.—DITTO OF THOMAS CHAUCER'S POETRY AT THE SAME EPOCH.—DEATH OF KING HENRY THE FOURTH, AND OTHER INDICATIONS OF NATIONAL PROSPERITY.

THE spring of 1413 was one of extraordinary mildness. It is a matter of deep regret (to us) that there were no newspapers at that period; otherwise we should undoubtedly have had handed down to us many valuable records of enormous primroses, wonderful thorn-blossoms, and forty-belled cowslips, which might not impossibly have equalled in interest the statistics of parallel phenomena in the present day. It is true that parliament was sitting at the time, and the reporters (had such an objectionable class then existed) might have evaded the important duty of chronicling these matters, on the pitiful and unusual plea that they had something better to write about. They do so now-a-days; and often give us nine columns of a parliamentary speech, the valuable substance of which we had all much rather see condensed in a short paragraph surmounted by the heading of " Enormous Cabbage."

Thomas Chaucer, the son of the immortal Geoffry, already alluded to in these pages, has feebly attempted to immortalise the phenomena of this remarkable season in verses which, it will be admitted, at all events, prove his inferiority to his father as a poet.*

" 𝔜𝔢 𝔉𝔞𝔶𝔯𝔢 𝔖𝔢𝔞𝔰𝔬𝔫 𝔬𝔣 𝔐𝔞𝔯𝔠𝔥, 1413.

" VERSES IN MEMORY THEREOF BY THOMAS CHAUFCIRE † ARMIG.

" OF yᵉ year fourteen hundredde and thirteen,
    Yᵉ month of Mars can never be forgotten;
So fayre a season eyne had never seen,
    And I came into myne estayte of Wotten,
    Which till yᵉ globis hystorye bee rotten
Yᵉ race of man will proudlyk bear in mynde
    (Mote I become a salted herring shotten
    If I another rime save this can fynde),
All nature sang with joy that Fortune proved soe kynde.

" Yᵉ lyttel birdis on yᵉ twiggis hopped
    As and it were yᵉ smylynge month of June,
And forth their merrie roundelaes y-popped,
    Like minstrels lacking one to start yᵉ tune,
    Each pypynge forthe his own—ne in commune.
Yᵉ brookys that were frozen stiff before,
    Like heathen runagates did very soon
Betake themselves from Isis unto Thor
(A sorry clench methynks I sholde bee sorry for).

---

* In refutation of this proposition, there is but one theory that can be considered as carrying the slightest weight, namely, that Thomas Chaucer *did not* write the poem here quoted *in extenso*. There is doubtless much that might be said on both sides of the question, which had therefore better be left open.

† English poetry would seem to have had an official descent — the family name of its reputed father being derived from the office of Chauf-cire or Chaff-wax (a dignity still in existence, with, it is said, real functions and an undeniably real salary attached to it) doubt-less held by one of his not very remote ancestors. The vanity of restoring the name to its original orthography, instead of adhering to the form it had assumed in the time of the illustrious Geoffry, is another proof of the weakness of Thomas Chaucer's intellect, if the quality of the above verses were such as to leave the slightest necessity for anything of the kind.

" Yᵉ primeroses and cowslippis were shedde,
   Like golden buttons upon jerkyn green,
Or bits of butter upon cabbitch spread
    (Good eatynge wyth ane hande of pork, I weene
    Yᵉ salted kind, with pease y-boiled, I meane).
Yᵉ honeysucklis buddys gan unclose,
   And fine spring onions were in market seen ;
Whyles Mistress Chaufcire casts her winter hose,
And forth along yᵉ lanes withouten cloggis goes.

" I wot it was a comelyk syght to see
   Yᵉ earlye birdis pyckynge up yᵉ wormes ;
And earlye radyshes in bunchys three
    For yᵉ halfe-farthynge — reasonable terms !
    Albeit there is one who round affirmes
He hathe knowne cheper in yᵉ Southerne clime. —
   'Tis playne I have of poesie yᵉ germes
Within me ; but to spinne for ever rime
I lack my father's gust, and soothe have not yᵉ time."

It certainly says little for the justice and intelligence of the age that the writer of the above verses* should have been appointed to the Speakership of the House of Commons, and other equally honourable and far more lucrative dignities, at a time when a man of Sir John Falstaff's merit was going about the kingdom, if not absolutely begging, certainly reduced to one, if not both, of the other two proverbial alternatives, in order to obtain the means of livelihood. However, suppose we put Thomas Chaucer back into that comfortable niche of obscurity from whence he should, perhaps, never have been dragged, and confine our attention to the main subject in hand — the genial summer spring of 1413, as bearing on the adventures of Sir John Falstaff.

I have said that on the 19th of March, in this year, Sir John Falstaff was a second time the honoured guest of Master Robert Shallow at the worthy justice's family seat in Gloucestershire. It hath been urged to me, for certain reasons not altogether contemptible, and which will be mentioned presently, that such could not have been the case; but that Sir John and his retinue could not have arrived at Master Shallow's until the 20th of March, on which day they also took their departure for London. I prefer adhering to my original statement, and for three reasons. Firstly, because it is scarcely credible that I could have made it without having thoroughly satisfied myself that at least the balance of probability was in its favour. Secondly, the practice of eating his own words is one of the most baneful into which the historical writer can possibly fall — leading to habits of pusillanimity and indecision which must ultimately destroy the independence of character so

---

* Assuming their authenticity as established — if only for the sake of argument.

indispensable to his pursuits, and leave the neatly-arranged flower-beds of his work at the mercy of all such of the swinish multitude of critics or ob- jectors as may choose to thrust their ringed noses into the matter. Thirdly, the portion of my manuscript containing the statement alluded to hath been some weeks in the hands of the printers, and (as I am led to believe, from the relentless assiduity with which those estimable citizens, but austere and implacable task-masters, have, by their emissaries, persecuted me within the last fortnight for further supplies of written matter) hath been long ago sent to the press, and is now beyond all possibility of correction until such time as a second edition of the entire work shall be called for. So that, in short, I was right.

I am aware that, in order to make good my position, I shall be required to prove that Ancient Pistol — a warrior not habitually remarkable for his excellence in any manly or athletic pursuits — did, in the course of a single day, accomplish a very rapid and daring act of horsemanship, calculated to tax the endurance of stronger thews and sinews than the worthy Ancient's; being nothing less than the conveying to Master Shallow's Gloucestershire residence in the evening, tidings of an event that had taken place in London in the morning. But I trust I have sufficient powers of special pleading and aptitude for the historical business generally, to be enabled to get over far greater obstacles than are presented by this emergency. Pistol need not have ridden the whole distance himself. He might have been lying in wait for the expected tidings, which he was the means of conveying to Sir John Falstaff — let us say, somewhere between London and Oxford — whither the news of the event in question, namely, the death of the king, who expired on the 20th, would assuredly be conveyed post, immediately on its occur- rence. A well-authenticated episode in the life of Ancient Pistol makes it more than probable that London, at about this time, was scarcely a safe residence for him. The gallant subaltern was in a temporary difficulty for having, with other warlike spirits, "beaten a man," who would seem to have been left at the termination of the encounter in a precarious condition, inas- much as, within a day or two of the occurrences immediately under notice, we find he had breathed his last in consequence of injuries he received on the occasion.* The provocation was doubtless great; in all probability, nothing less than an unpardonable insult to Mrs. Dorothea Tearsheet, in the presence of whom and of Mrs. Quickly the punishment appears to have been inflicted. When we remember that Pistol himself had been known (under the influence of vinous aberration, it is true) to speak slightingly of the former lady, and

---

* _Beadle._—Come, I charge you both go with me; for the man is dead that you and Pistol beat among you. — Henry IV. Part II. Act iv. Scene 5.

that he was by no means a man of strait-laced notions in the matter of respect for the sex generally, the outrage upon his patron's friend and kins-woman* must have been great indeed to impel him to so terrible an act of vengeance. But the law is not accustomed to take cognizance of such honourably extenuating circumstances in cases of murderous assault, and it can scarcely be doubted that Pistol was, at this time, "keeping out of the way,"—by no means an unaccustomed manœuvre to that distinguished professor of military stratagem. Whither could he fly for protection except to the sheltering wing of Sir John Falstaff? What tidings so likely to be anxiously awaited by him as those that would assure him of his patron's greatness, with dispensing power over the laws of England? Depend upon it, Ancient Pistol, at the time of King Henry the Fourth's death, was as far from London, and as near to Falstaff, as his circumstances would permit, and keenly on the watch. The thing is as clear as day. Or, assuming that it is not, and that I must admit that Pistol actually *did* himself accomplish the journey from London to Gloucestershire in a single day. Why not? Of all tactics in the art of war, there was none which this veteran soldier had so deeply studied, and so frequently practised, as that of successfully managing a retreat. There was no possible amount or speed of running away, on pressing emergency, of which he could have been reasonably pronounced incapable.

I am now enabled to resume my narrative with the most perfect composure; and I really wish the captious and fastidious would not compel me to do violence to my predilections by such frequent digressions.

It must have been then—in short, it *was*—the evening of the nineteenth of this much-talked-of month of March, which Sir John Falstaff, with Master Robert Shallow, his entertainer, and Master Silence, the latter gentleman's unobtrusive kinsman, found of such unseasonably tempting mildness as to induce them to get up from the supper table, whereat Davy, Master Shallow's factotum, had deftly served them with the choicest efforts of William Cook's genius ("some pigeons," "a couple of short-legged hens," "a joint of mutton," and "pretty little tiny kickshaws," *ad libitum*, are indicated by the chronicler as having, in all probability, formed the staple articles of the bill of fare), to partake of dessert in the open air, in a snug arbour of the justice's orchard. Sir John, with his retinue, consisting of Bardolph, Robin, and possibly some half dozen supernumeraries, had arrived just in time for supper—ostensibly *à l'improviste*, and with no intention of staying for a longer time than might serve them to repose and refresh themselves.

---

* For arguments on this subject see *antè*, p. 113.

"By cock and pye, Sir," Master Shallow had said on our knight's arrival, "you shall not away to-night."

To which Sir John had replied that he must be excused.

But Master Shallow would not excuse him : he should not be excused. There was no excuse should serve : Sir John should not be excused. And Master Shallow had immediately ordered supper, and bidden Sir John to off with his boots.

It is needless to say that Sir John had no wish to be excused, but that he had come intentionally to stop. He had long had Master Robert Shallow "tempering between his finger and thumb," and had now come to "seal with him." He had, years ago, seen to the bottom of Justice Shallow. He knew that ornament to the magistracy to be nothing better than a time-serving humbug, and he had come, as I think most justifiably, to take any possible advantage of him. It was a breach of hospitality, if you will; but remember we are treating of great men and their motives. My only regret is that I am compelled to exhibit my hero, towards the end of his career, engaged in the pursuit of "such small deer" as a pitiful country justice. When I compare John Falstaff, in his sixty-seventh year, on this particular evening, stretching his limbs under Master Shallow's oak (as yet the mahogany tree was an un-naturalised exotic), picking the short legs of Master Shallow's roasted hens, and washing down as much of Master Shallow's garrulous mendacity as limitless draughts of Master Shallow's sack and Bordeaux might enable him —all the while meditating through what particular chink in Master Shallow's vanity he could best get at the same gentleman's purse-strings ;—when I compare this with another picture presented on the preceding evening, by another great man of imperfect notions of *meum* and *teum*, frequently mentioned in these pages, younger in years, but centuries older in depravity than Sir John, and with both feet already in the grave—legs, body, and all rapidly sliding in after them—Henry Bolingbroke on his death-bed, in short —counselling his young son and successor—

> "to busy giddy minds
> With foreign quarrels: that action hence borne out
> May waste the memory of the former days;"—

(that is, the days of his early rascality, the fruits of which he would have his son preserve by the fomentation of fresh villanies)—when I compare the conduct of these two waning celebrities, the one within half a dozen hours of death, the other with good two years and a quarter of life in him, (alas! no more,) I am more forcibly than ever reminded of my reluctantly formed suspicion, that the character of Sir John Falstaff may have been really deficient in the heroic element after all, and am made to feel that he comes out, by comparison with the more wholesale practitioner, in a pitifully moral and respectable light.

I am getting so near the end of my poor old knight, (I call him mine, though I have but the sorriest stepfather's claim to him, and doubtless deserve to have him removed from my charge for ill-treating him as I have done,) and am so closely in sight of the overthrow of his last hopes and energies, that I have scarcely the heart any longer to make light of his rogueries. I will try and explain how I feel with regard to Sir John Falstaff. Consider me a street urchin in a town where a very fat old gentleman has been in the habit of misconducting himself, and so publishing his irregularities in the public thoroughfares, as to have forfeited the respect of well-behaved citizens, and make himself the target for all kinds of pleasantry from the lowest and most thoughtless. I have had my jeer, and my pebble, and perhaps my rotten egg, at the poor old man, with the rest of the *gamins*, and rare fun we have considered it. But a day arrives when I see the old gentleman paler than usual. The red of his cheeks has become an unwholesome purple. He no longer walks jauntily, but totters. The stick, that he used to shake in merry defiance at his tatterdemalion critics, is now necessary to support his steps. There is a tear in his eye. He is suffering — failing — and I (being, perhaps, a sensitive, well-meaning ragamuffin) beat my breast, and am ashamed of my conduct. I feel inclined to go whimpering for pardon to him, and ask him to let me serve him in some menial but comforting capacity. But the stronger boys are not of my way of thinking. To them he is more ridiculous than ever in his weakness and decay. They pelt him the more, and laugh at him the louder. He falls. I run to try and help him. I look in his face, and wonder that I could ever have seen there anything to laugh at. It is to me all sadness and bitter suffering. I forget the stories I have heard against him. I am conscious of nothing but an old man, fallen in the mud, who cannot raise himself. I would do anything to express to him my contrition and sympathy. I feel an absurd inclination to offer him my tops and marbles — nay, my very slice of bread and butter itself. At least, I would treat him respectfully. But ——— the other boys jeer at me, and I am ashamed of my passing weakness; and, like a mean-spirited young sneak as I am, I turn round, and make game of the poor old gentleman more mercilessly than ever, with a strong sensation that I deserve to be flayed alive for doing so.

At any rate, I am glad that the spring of 1413 *was* a genial one—seeing that Sir John had but two more springs of any kind between him and the grave; and was doomed to bask in but little more sunshine, either of the actual or of the figurative kind. It pleases me to dwell on such little pleasures and comforts I may find proof of his having enjoyed from this time forth. I am delighted to feel confident that the supper provided for him by the anxious care of Master Shallow was good and abundant. I take comfort in believing that William Cook had done his spiriting with zeal and ability: that the short-legged hens were roasted to a turn; that the joint of mutton was a small brown haunch, which had walked, when capable of pedestrian exercise, towards Gloucestershire, in a south-easterly direction—from the Welsh mountains in fact (a hope, not without foundation in presumptive evidence — seeing that Master Shallow had, at any rate, one kindly friend from that hospitable district—Hugh Evans, by name, a gentleman in holy orders, at this time established in the neighbouring county of Berkshire); that the pigeons were plump and tender victims, either served up on an altar of the crispest toast, or brought to the sacrifice in a sarcophagus of melting crust; and that the "pretty little tiny kickshaws" embraced every available delicacy of the early season.

At all events, it is certain that Sir John had had something he liked, and plenty of it. There is no record in his life that displays him in a more thorough state of serenity and genial goodfellowship with all mankind than the passages in the chronicle of Henry the Fourth*, referring to the evening in question. There we find Sir John " unbuttoning himself after supper," lounging " upon benches after noon " in Master Shallow's orchard, inhaling the soft breeze of the premature summer, listening to the carols of the birds immortalised (through the medium of these pages) by the poet Thomas Chaucer†, and partaking of a " last year's pippin " of the worthy justice's " own graffing," with the addition of a "dish of carraways and so forth." The "so forth " is not particularised in the chronicler's page; but from the conduct of Master Shallow himself and of his kinsman, Silence, on the festive occasion, it would seem to have been a long time in bottle, and furnished forth with no niggard hand.

Let us follow the scene, as described in the chronicle, for its termination sounds the key-note to the great crisis in the history of our hero's declining fortunes.

Master Shallow had drunk too much sack at supper. He said so, though there was not the slightest necessity for the confession. Master Silence had similarly committed himself, but to such an extent as to make any confession

---

* Part II. Act v. Scene 3.

† Nicholas Chaucer, kinsman of the above, was at about this time a distinguished memoer of the Grocers' Company, in the city of London. Assuming that he combined with his aromatic calling the congenial one of butterman, the preservation of Thomas Chaucer's manuscript—doubtless submitted to his relative's approval in the regular way of business— is at once accounted for.

on his part a matter of some difficulty. We hear of men being blind drunk, crying drunk, roaring drunk. Master Silence was singing drunk. He could only express himself in snatches of old songs, which he poured forth with a volubility which nothing could stop.

> " Do nothing but eat and make good cheer,
> And praise Heaven for the merry year
> When food is cheap and females dear,
> And lusty lads roam here and there.
> So merrily.
> And ever among so merrily ! "

I confess to a warm affection for Master Silence. He was a stupid old gentleman, and doubtless more tiresome in his taciturnity than even his cousin Shallow in his garrulity. But what there was of Master Silence seems to have been good. Much as has been said against old proverbs and old wine, there yet remains some defence for both. I believe in the truth of the proverb which asserts that there is truth in wine. It is a dangerous and exhaustive kind of manure, I admit. In agricultural phraseology, it " rots the ground" terribly. But, as long as the ground lasts, it develops the latent germs within it marvellously. Master Silence was little, if any, more inebriated than his kinsman. But the same flask (or number of flasks) which had made Justice Shallow only a coarser or an infinitely more vulgar sycophant and timeserver than ever, paying court, not only to Sir John Falstaff, but even to Bardolph and little Robin the scapegrace page, for the sake of the knight's imaginary court influence, merely set Master Silence thinking of the pleasant season, of the bounty of Providence, of the claims of kindliness and goodfellowship. Unable to speak for himself, he searched in the dark, cobwebby, unhinged cupboards of his feeble memory for the most tuneful and thankful expression of his feelings, in other men's words, that would help him to

> " Praise Heaven for the merry year."

I would rather have had his dim chaotic sensations about the fine spring weather and the beauty of earthly existence than Master Shallow's most ambitious dreams of " penny in purse," to be obtained through a " friend at court." I resemble Sir John Falstaff, at all events in this respect, that " I do see the bottom of Mr. Justice Shallow," and there is nothing in the bed of the puddle but mud, and stones, and potsherds. But I do not pretend to penetrate to the mystery of what Master Silence felt as he sat there, intoxicated and reprehensible, in the arbour, breathing in Nature, and mumbling old songs,—any more than I would dare to analyse the feelings of my fat baby, who now sits opposite to me in his mother's arms, eating a pocket-handker-chief, and staring at the fire.

At any rate — as I wish from henceforth to regard none but the best phases in my hero's character — I am glad to know that Sir John Falstaff treated Master Silence in his melodious cups with tolerant kindness and even encouragement. He would have fleeced Master Shallow, I sincerely believe, of every farthing in that dignitary's exchequer — and (as I am upon the candid tack) I confess that my high estimate of his character would not have been materially lowered had he effected that desirable end. But I do sincerely believe that Sir John Falstaff would not have taken advantage of Master Silence's condition to borrow from him so much as a hundred bezants — unless, indeed, provoked to do so by great necessity or temptation.

"There's a merry heart!" said Sir John Falstaff, whom we may picture to ourselves picking his teeth lazily, with his legs stretched on the arbour seat, his head resting on the back of his plump hand, the broad, purple disc of his countenance reflecting the rays of the March sun that, like himself, had risen gloriously, had shone now and then brilliantly, but was now going down early and rapidly, covered with clouds and blotches (having made its appearance on earth, you see, in what was, after all, an unfavourable season). "Good Master Silence, I'll give you a health for that anon."

The sunset was lost on Master Shallow. His appreciation of out-of-door beauties was bounded by "Marry good air!" It gave him an appetite, and he was quits with Nature. He was bent on serving the guests whom he intended to make serve him.

"Give Master Bardolph some wine, Davy," said his worship.

In Sir John Falstaff's own words, "it was a wonderful thing to see the semblable coherence of his (Shallow's) men's spirits and his." As Shallow was to Falstaff so was Davy to Bardolph and Robin. Davy — who also meditated a London season, with introductions to the best society — busied himself with attending to the wants of those subaltern officers.

Master Silence again burst into song, unsolicited —

> "'Tis merry, 'tis merry, my wife's as all ;
> For women are shrews both short and tall,
> 'Tis merry in hall when beards wag all
>   And welcome merry Shrovetide.
> Be merry, be merry, &c."

"I did not think Master Silence had been a man of this mettle," murmured Sir John, who, I think, by this time was beginning to get drowsy.

"Who, I?" said the meek songster. "I have been merry twice and once ere now."

The festivities continued, but with a somewhat languishing spirit. Master Shallow's angular chin began to beat double knocks against his bony chest. He had the greatest difficulty in keeping one eye — the weather one, doubtless — open. Bardolph confined himself to the main business of his consistent life — good, steady drinking. Davy officiated as Ganymede. Robin was silently contemplative. There were spoons and tankards in the orchard, and nobody sober to watch them! Sir John spoke not, except to give a word of encouragement to Master Silence, whose vocal exertions he rather approved of, as calculated to save him the labour of conversation. It is not absolutely recorded, but circumstantial evidence makes it probable, that Sir John Falstaff, having drowsily pledged that inveterate songster in a bumper, fell instantly fast asleep, and was snoring in blissful ignorance of actual circumstances — only to dream of coronets that were never to be worn and coffers that were never to be filled — when he was roused from his nap by a terrific knocking at the outer gate.

Everybody was on the alert. Justice Shallow, in the midst of a dreamy platitude of welcome, breathed into the confidential recesses of his folded arms, started into wide-awakefulness with an echoing knock of chin against chest, which must have been highly detrimental to his remaining dental economy. Davy flew to the gate. Master Silence considered the startling occurrence an excuse for further melody. Bardolph drank. Robin, it may be presumed, took some advantage of the confusion; but as the Shallow spoons were not counted that evening, it is uncertain to what extent.

There was cause for disturbance. In those days an Englishman was obliged to make his house his castle. The meanest homestead — and Master Shallow's was not one answering to that definition — had to be carefully guarded by moat and drawbridge. They kept early hours then. All the family were expected to be in-doors by sunset, for it was not safe to be out after dark. Any vassal, pig, or other retainer, stopping out after the gates were closed, might do so at his own peril. A late visitor — especially one making such formidable announcement of his arrival as that which disturbed Sir John Falstaff from his comfortable after-supper nap, and sent Master Shallow's little dried walnut of a heart leaping into his mouth, like a parched pea from a shovel up the chimney — was not only a source of astonishment but of alarm. It might be a robber at the head of a forest-band come to levy what we should term an execution on the goods and chattels; or a travelling abbot on his way to some ecclesiastical conference, having brought the *élite* of his monks and their appetites with them; or a proscribed nobleman and his suite, to harbour whom would be certain death in the course of a month, and to behave uncivilly to whom would be the same in the course of a minute and a half; or it might be the king who had been kicked off the throne, or the other king who had kicked him off in pursuit of him. In any case, the chances were ninety-nine and nine-tenths to a decimal fraction that the visitor would prove one who, at his departure, would leave the proprietor a sadder and a poorer man than he had been in the morning. The probability of a needy and harmless wight being found sufficiently mad or intoxicated to make a disturbance at a rich man's door (more especially if the rich man happened to be in the commission of the peace), just as the family might be supposed to be retiring to rest, being of the remotest.

The speedy return of Davy to the orchard with the information that the demonstrative visitor was merely "one Pistol, come from the Court with news" for Sir John Falstaff, must have had an immediately soothing and reassuring effect upon the assembly.

At the word "Court" Sir John Falstaff pricked up his ears instinctively. A momentary thrill ran through his system. Had they, at last, "sent for" him? Was he really wanted to guide, counsel, or amuse — at any rate, to be recognised and rewarded?

Pshaw! The very name of the messenger was a proof to the contrary. Pistol was, doubtless, in the neighbourhood; had heard of his patron's whereabouts; and tracked him, as usual, in the hope of a flagon, a supper, and a piece of silver! Sir John was a philosopher, and was engaged in the digestion of his own supper. He would not allow that vital process to be prejudiced by the excitement of possibly fallacious hope. He fell back upon the garden seat, and ordered Pistol to be admitted.

Pistol strode into the orchard, looking daggers around him. Pistol was in the habit of looking daggers, as I might be in the habit of looking fifty pound notes. The process was by no means a proof that he had one about him to make use of when called upon. He said —— But you shall hear what he said, and what was said to, and about, him, in the dramatic chronicler's own words, with such unwritten elucidations, or "stage directions," as your humble servant may consider himself justified in venturing upon.

SIR JOHN FALSTAFF (*indifferently*). — How now, Pistol?

PISTOL (*with gesticulations of extravagant homage*). — Sir John, God save you, sir.

SIR JOHN FALSTAFF *(suspiciously, buttoning his pockets*). — What wind blew you hither, Pistol?

PISTOL. — Not the ill wind which blows no man to good. Sweet knight, th'art now one of the greatest men in the realm.

MASTER SILENCE (*dimly reminded of a forgotten ballad, sings*). — "By'r lady, I think he be, but goodman Puff of Barson."

PISTOL (*at once discerning that Master Silence is a man who may be safely bullied*). — Puff? Puff in thy teeth, most recreant coward base! — Sir John, I am thy Pistol, and thy friend,

Drawn & Etched by George Cruikshank.

Pistol informing Sir John Falstaff of ye Death of Henry ye Fourth —

Henry 4th Part 2d Act V. Scene 3d —

Pub.d by Mess.rs Longman & Company

and helter-skelter have I rode to thee; and tidings do I bring, and lucky joys, and golden times, and happy news of price.

SIR JOHN FALSTAFF. — I pr'ythee now, deliver them like a man of this world.

PISTOL. — A foutra for the world, and worldlings base ! I speak of Africa, and golden joys.*

SIR JOHN FALSTAFF.—O base Assyrian knight ! what is thy news ? Let king Cophetua know the truth thereof.

MASTER SILENCE (*sings seraphically*). — " And Robin Hood, Scarlet, and John."

PISTOL. — Shall dunghill curs confront the Helicons ? And shall good news be baffled ? Then, Pistol, lay thy head in Furies' lap.

MASTER SHALLOW (*rising, with magisterial assumption of sobriety*). — Honest gentleman, I know not your breeding.

PISTOL. — Why then, lament therefore.

MASTER SHALLOW. — Give me pardon, sir :—if, sir, you come with news from the court, I take it, there is but two ways, either to utter them, or to conceal them. I am, sir, under the king, in some authority.

PISTOL (*drawing a rusty rapier*). — Under which king, Bezonian ? speak, or die.

MASTER SHALLOW. — Under King Harry.

PISTOL. — Harry the fourth ? or fifth ?

MASTER SHALLOW. — Harry the fourth.

PISTOL. —A foutra for thine office ! — Sir John, thy tender lambkin now is king : Harry the fifth's the man. I speak the truth : when Pistol lies, do this ; and fig me, like the bragging Spaniard.

SIR JOHN FALSTAFF (*leaping to his feet like a colt*). — What ! is the old king dead ?

PISTOL. — As nail in door : the things I speak are just.

SIR JOHN FALSTAFF (*quivering with excitement*). — Away, Bardolph ! saddle my horse. — Master Robert Shallow, choose what office thou wilt in the land, 'tis thine. — Pistol, I will double-charge thee with dignities.

MASTER BARDOLPH.— O joyful day ! — I would not take a knighthood for my fortune.

(*He drinks and exits.*)

PISTOL (*smiling sardonically*). — What ! I do bring good news ?

SIR JOHN FALSTAFF. — Carry Master Silence to bed. — Master Shallow, my Lord Shallow, be what thou wilt, I am fortune's steward. Get on thy boots : we'll ride all night. — O sweet Pistol ! — Away, Bardolph. — Come, Pistol, utter more to me ; and, withal, devise something to do thyself good. — Boot, boot, Master Shallow : I know, the young king is sick for me. Let us take any man's horses ; the laws of England are at my commandment. Happy are they which have been my friends, and woe unto my lord chief justice !

PISTOL :   Let vultures vile seize on his lungs also !
              Where is the life that late I led say they ;
              Why, here it is ! (*snaps his fingers.*)   Welcome those pleasant days.

Scene closes.]

The time long hoped for had then arrived. There was no more thought of drowsiness or dissipation for that night, — no more of debt or difficulty for

---

* It will be observed that Shakspeare almost invariably makes Pistol speak in a kind of mongrel blank verse — apparently in remote imitation of the masques, pageants, and miracle plays then recently introduced into this country from Italy—fashionable amusements, whereat the worthy ancient (in his capacity of hanger-on of all dirty work to the upper classes) doubtless frequently assisted, in a supernumerary capacity. Sir John Falstaff answers him playfully, from one of the earliest known specimens of this kind of composition — See Payne Collier's *History of Dramatic Poetry*, and other works to be met with in the admirable and compendious catalogue of the British Museum, which will amply repay perusal.

the future.   Henry of Monmouth — Sir John's pet pupil, his "tender lamb-kin"— was king ; and surely, if such feelings as gratitude and goodfellow-ship existed in the hearts of princes, no man had greater right to look forward to emoluments and dignities under the new *régime* than Sir John Falstaff. He himself was incapable of forgetting old friends in his prosperity, and he could not suspect such baseness in others.   We have heard him declare that he would double charge Pistol with dignities, that Master Shallow might choose what office he would in the land—it should be his ! Bardolph, knowing his master's disposition, would not take a knighthood for his fortune. Not one present was omitted from the circle of Sir John Falstaff's compre-hensive benevolence.   Even to poor Master Silence he performed the only kindness which that vocalist was just then capable of benefiting by, — he ordered his inebriated worship to be carried up to bed !

Depend upon it, there was no time lost in booting and saddling for the townward journey.   Be sure that the command to "take any man's horses " was carried out to the letter, and backed by the legal warrant of Justice Shallow — (for were they not on His Majesty's service ? could the govern-ment of the realm possibly go on without the immediate presence in the capital of Sir John Falstaff?)

What a terrible distance was that which separated Sir John from London and the young king ! How he wished for the power to annihilate time and space ! Alas ! he was born in a wrong age for locomotive purposes.   Half-a-dozen centuries earlier, a knight-errant of his vast merit and renown, wishing for a rapid mode of transit, would but have had to summon his guardian fairy, and that obliging genius would have ordered her griffins to be put-to for his accommodation, with a lift in her enchanted car, immediately. In the present day, four hundred and forty years later, the thing would be scarcely more difficult.   A post-chaise to the Tewkesbury station, and a special train thence to London, would settle the matter in three or four hours. But the task of conveying Sir John Falstaff, rapidly, over the vile roads of the fifteenth century, by mere horse-power, would be a difficulty which the mind of a Pickford alone could be qualified to grapple with.

And yet, incredible as it may seem, Sir John Falstaff actually contrived to reach the metropolis on the third day after his departure from Master Shallow's residence.   I am not prepared to say that *no* magic power was employed in effecting this apparently miraculous transit.   On the contrary, the aid of a rather potent magician appears to have been successfully invoked for the occasion — one, at whose bidding, the roughest roads become level, the stoutest doors fly open, the veriest griffins, tigers, crocodiles, and Cerberi of gate-keepers become docile as lambs ; an enchanter, at whose very aspect, or even name, horses saddle themselves, inn-tablès spread themselves, corks fly out of self-pouring wine-bottles, pigs spit themselves, larks, pheasants, and wild duck stop in their mid-air course, and fall, ready-stuffed and roasted, on to eager travellers' plate. Need I say that I allude to the evil, but fascinating necromancer, King Money?

SIR JOHN FALSTAFF BORROWED A THOUSAND POUNDS OF MASTER ROBERT SHALLOW!

I would have it printed in letters of gold, would the arrangements of the printing-office admit of such distinction, for I am proud to chronicle so meritorious an achievement, the glory of which is doubled by the moral certainty that Master Shallow never received a single farthing of the money back again. On one account only can I be brought to regret the transaction: I am sorry the amount was not *two* thousand.

IX.

INAUGURATION OF THE NEW RÉGIME. — MALIGNITY OF THE LORD CHIEF JUSTICE.

THE news of Henry the Fourth's decease was the occasion of a state of public excitement to which we should in vain look for a parallel in any dynastic or ministerial crisis of modern times. Rumour, with all her hundred tongues gabbling at once, flew hither and thither, announcing that the respectabilities were "out," and the reprobates "in." For a few brief hours Sir John Falstaff really ranked, in the popular estimation, as the most influential subject in the realm (and that distinction, however briefly enjoyed, is something for a man to look back to with satisfaction!) The knight's "paper," previously a drug in the money-market, was eagerly bought up by the Jews, calling themselves Lombards *, of the city. Traders, on the fair pages of whose ledgers the name of Sir John Falstaff had long stood as a blot and eyesore, ordered expensive dinners, and made rash presents to their wives and daughters. Others, who had issued writs for the apprehension of the

---

* A precaution necessitated by the rigour of the existing statute law, which excluded the Jewish people from residence on English soil. Two unredeemed "obligacions," in the handwriting of Sir John Falstaff, for considerable sums advanced, — one by Cosmo di Levi, the other by Ichi di Solomoni, — are still in existence, to attest the observance of this rule. — *Vide Strongate MSS.*

knight's person, called in those documents with breathless eagerness. Grave burgesses, lawyers, and even ecclesiastics, who had the day before commented severely on our hero's irregularities, now boasted of his acquaintance, and quoted his witticisms. A spirited hatter in the ward of Chepe displayed, in front of his booth, a new falling hood-shape, labelled with the recommendation, "AS WORNE BY SIR JOHN FALSTAFFE AND YE COURTE," for copies of which he received an incredible number of orders. The "Old Boar's Head" did such a morning's stroke of business as had not been achieved within the memory of the oldest tippler. The principal wine-merchants of the Vintry obsequiously intimated to Mrs. Quickly that unlimited credit would be given to her at their respective establishments, and our worthy hostess's landlord immediately doubled her rent.

The feeling of the Court may be summed up in one word — panic. The favourites of the late king thought of nothing less than packing up their portmanteaus, and making the best of their way to their several country seats. The opinion was universal that Sir John Falstaff would be raised to a rank, at all events, equivalent to what we call prime minister; and it was of course anticipated that our knight would select his companions in office from men of character and habits congenial to his own. It is needless to say that none such could be found amongst the lugubrious familiars of the late monarch. The princes of the blood themselves—the new king's own brothers—were by no means free from the general apprehension. It seems rather odd that they should have believed in the possibility of gratitude existing in the bosom of one of their own blood; but it is nevertheless certain that they agreed to look on Sir John Falstaff in the light of "the coming man," a prospect they regarded with considerable apprehension and alarm. For they were by no means jovial princes, these young fellows. "A man," as Sir John himself had observed of one of them, "could not make them laugh." The individual Prince here referred to was John of Lancaster, afterwards Duke of Bedford, whom we have already seen distinguish himself by treacherously butchering a band of generous foemen, who had trusted themselves unarmed to his honour — an achievement which he followed up later in life by a congenial experiment on the person of one Joan of Arc, at Rouen, in Normandy. A second was the renowned Duke Humphrey, whose social and hospitable qualities have grown into a proverb. These two will serve as examples of the entire stock. Such men could scarcely have felt much sympathy for, or hoped anything from the friendship of, Sir John Falstaff.

As for the Lord Chief Justice Gascoigne, he no sooner heard of the old king's death than he proceeded to make what, in modern colloquial parlance, is termed "a bolt of it." He had been hanging anxiously about the palace during the morning, and on the confirmation of his worst fears took precipitately to his heels. He was detected in that sagacious but undignified act by the Earl of Warwick*, who detained him in conversation.

Gascoigne made no concealment of his terrors; and indeed the noble earl gave him no encouragement whatever to their mitigation. They agreed— with the Princes John, Humphrey, and Thomas, who, accompanied by the Earl of Westmoreland and other nobles of the Court, soon after joined their conference — that the common prospects of the late king's favourites and admirers were decidedly unfavourable. It was the opinion of the Earl of Warwick that many nobles who "*should* hold their places" (meaning himself for one), would have to "strike sail to spirits of vile sort;" as a specimen whereof it is presumed he had the impudence to allude to the hero of these pages. The Chief Justice confessed himself prepared for the worst, admitting that the "condition of the time" could not look "more hideously" upon him than his imagination had pictured to him. It was admitted, on all hands, that his lordship's only safe policy would be to adopt the unpalatable course of "speaking Sir John Falstaff fair." This salutary piece of advice was first offered by the Duke of Clarence. And I am willing to stake my reputation as a historian upon the statement that the Lord Chief Justice *was perfectly prepared to act upon it*, had not things taken a wholly unexpected turn. For he was silent on the subject; and the case was evidently one of those wherein silence is consent.

But the new king made his appearance amongst the group (who were waiting in an antechamber like criminals to hear their sentence), and speedily changed the aspect of things. He threw off the mask at once. He had no intention to alter anything. He had stepped into his father's shoes, and meant to walk in his father's footsteps. *Le roi est mort, vive le roi!* If they had really been taken in by his having falsely represented himself as a jovial good sort of fellow, why, he could only feel flattered by the compliment to his powers of personation. In reality, he had succeeded to the tyrannical and conquering business of his unlamented father, which he intended to carry on with spirit, accepting all the premises, bad-will, and fixtures as he found them. The princes and earls were, of course, delighted, as feeling assured of a lengthened tenure of Court favour and office. But the Lord Chief Justice was still uneasy. He had once committed the present King of England to prison, and monarchs are not in the habit of forgetting personal affronts.

* Immediately after the death of the king, Warwick stops Gascoigne in a "room in the palace," with the questions, "How now my Lord Chief Justice? Whither *away?*" The prevaricating responses of the learned justice betray his nervous anxiety to be off.—*Vide* Henry IV. Part II. Act v. Scene 2.

I have before hinted at a possibility that this event was a matter of private arrangement between the prince and the judge, for purposes of mutual popularity. But to take a liberty with a prince, even at his own request, is always a ticklish business. If you exceed the limit of your instructions, woe betide you! I do not say that such was the case; but it is barely probable that the cell to which the Prince of Wales was confined on the occasion in question, may have proved rather more damp, and less comfortable, than His Royal Highness had intended. At any rate, it is certain that Gascoigne on this, his first meeting with King Henry the Fifth (in the royal capacity), was in a state of great trepidation, and evidently apprehended nothing less than immediate disgrace and suspension from office. Recovering, however, a little courage and composure at the new King's indications of a disposition to carry out his late father's policy—I was about to say principles—he ventured upon a little special pleading in defence of his conduct in the matter of the world-famous police case, which he judiciously mixed up with a little covert flattery—delicately hinting that Henry the Fifth himself might some day have a disreputable son, to whose vagaries a severe administration of the Common Law might prove a wholesome corrective. Acting on the old north-country proverb that "the old woman would never have looked in the oven for her daughter if she hadn't been there herself," His Majesty King Henry the Fifth (a sagacious man at all times) saw the wisdom of this suggestion, and at once confirmed Chief Justice Gascoigne in the permanent enjoyment of his dignities and emoluments.

I grieve to write it—but the deed was done, and it shall be chronicled. The first employment made by the Chief Justice of his new lease of power was to indulge in a dastardly act of vengeance. With indecent haste he rushed from the palace, and issued warrants for the apprehension of Mistress Helen Quickly, licensed victualler, and of Mistress Dorothea Tearsheet, spinster, on a frivolous and untenable charge. For what reason? it will be asked. I can find no better one than that the former was the friend, and the latter the beloved kinswoman, of Sir John Falstaff. Do you suppose the justice had forgotten the setting down he had received at the hands of our hero, the substance of which (transferred from the pages of "Shakespeare"), will be found in the second chapter of the fourth book of this history? And with the petty vindictiveness we have seen him employ on more than one occasion, is it probable that he was at all the sort of man to behave in the hour of his own triumph with magnanimity towards a fallen foe? We will waive the question of Gascoigne being possibly indebted to Mrs. Quickly for early board and lodging, as being, if not irrelevant, at any rate superfluous. The case is quite black enough against him as it stands.

At any rate, it is certain that the two ladies in question were ignominiously arrested by the warrant of the Chief Justice*, and to complete their disgrace (and Sir John Falstaff's) transferred from the custody of the constables to that of the town beadle.

In proof that the arrest had been made under circumstances of extreme injustice and barbarity, it need only be urged that each of the fair captives was so violently provoked by her aggressors, as entirely to forget all her antecedents of good breeding and propriety, and to indulge in positively coarse and abusive language.

Mistress Tearsheet, for instance, was betrayed into the following decidedly unladylike outburst, addressed to a beadle in human form :—

"I'll tell thee what, thou thin man in a censer! I will have you as soundly swinged for this, you *blue-bottle rogue!* you filthy, famished correctioner! if you be not swinged, I'll forswear half kirtles."

I have extracted this passage from the chronicle, not for the vulgar purpose of harrowing the reader's feelings with the spectacle of lovely woman goaded by injustice and violence even to the pitch of unbecoming self-forgetfulness, but from motives purely archæological. The derisive term "blue-bottle" — so frequently heard in the present day, applied to the guardians of the public peace by ladies and gentlemen in circumstances of trial similar to those of Mistress Tearsheet — is thereby proved to have had an origin at all events as early as the commencement of the fifteenth century, — a valuable antiquarian discovery, for which I trust some learned gentleman with capital letters after his name will be just enough to give me credit in the pages of some eminent scientific journal.

Ere the hour of noon had that day sounded Sir John Falstaff's bills were again waste paper. His creditors, who had indulged in costly dinners, and given rash presents to their wives and daughters, countermanded their suppers, and withdrew their names from numerous charitable subscription lists. The writs were re-issued. The hatter in the Ward of Chepe altered his placard to "Yᵉ GASCOIGNE SHAPE," and disposed of his invention more rapidly than before. By half-past three in the afternoon the sheriff's officers were in possession of the "Old Boar's Head" for a pitiful debt to a small ale brewer.

---

* If not by his warrant, by whose? What less dignified functionary would have presumed to put so large a construction on the English laws of the period as that manifested by the arrest in question? I would cheerfully pause for a reply, were not the printer's boy in such an abominable hurry.

T

X.

CORONATION OF HENRY THE FIFTH.—TRIUMPH OF THE LORD CHIEF JUSTICE
GASCOIGNE, AND DISGRACE OF SIR JOHN FALSTAFF.

THE coronation of Henry the Fifth took place immediately on his assumption
of the royal dignity. Authorities differ as to the exact date of this imposing
ceremony. Fleming, in his Chronicle, fixes it as late as the 9th of April, in
which he is supported by Stowe and a host of respectable authorities. Rapin
comes nearer the probable truth in assigning it to the first of the same
month — a date which leaves us not without slight suspicion of a seasonable
pleasantry intended by the lively French historian at the expense of his
readers. The general balance of probabilities, supported by important circumstantial evidence, brought to light in the search after materials for this
history, points out the 22nd of March as the day on which Henry the Fifth
practically succeeded to the crown of his father's cousin. In those days a
king was considered no king until he had worn the crown ; and as it was
never in the least degree clear, even to the most discerning intellect, to whom
the crown really belonged, the important claim of possession was naturally
the first thing thought of by the individual enjoying the nearest prospect of
its appropriation. It is hardly probable that a sagacious prince like Henry
of Monmouth should have postponed the vital ceremony a single day longer
than was absolutely necessary. Pressing necessities of state afforded a decent
excuse for hastening the funeral of Henry the Fourth ; and there can be no
doubt that his successor's publicly announced alacrity to walk in his father's
footsteps induced him to try on the paternal coronation shoes on the earliest
possible occasion.

Should any doubts on this subject exist, they are at once dispelled by reference to the facts already in the possession of the reader — which it may be
as well to recapitulate. Sir John Falstaff received the tidings of the old
king's death on the 19th of March. On the third day after this our knight
was in London. That the day of Sir John's arrival in the metropolis was
also that of Henry's coronation is a matter of history.

The chronicler Fleming, speaking of the auspicious accession of Henry the
Fifth to the throne of England, informs us that—" Such great hope and good
" expectation was had of this man's fortunate successe to follow, that within
" three daies after his father's decease diverse noble men and honorable
" personages did to him homage and sware to him due obedience, which had

Drawn & Etched by George Cruikshank

Pub'd by Longman & Company

Sir John Falstaff receiving a most unexpected rebuke from King Henry the fifth —— Henry IV.th part 2nd Act V, Scene, Vth —

" not beene seene done to any of his predecessors kings of this realme, till " they had beene possessed of the crowne." Differing with the learned and voluminous chronicler as to the absence of precedent in such matter of homage (the worship of the rising sun, on the appearance of his first rays of power, being older in England than Stonehenge), I can only say that there was no noble man or honourable personage whatever in the realm more eager to do to the new king homage, and swear to him due obedience, than Sir John Falstaff, Knight. Only that unfortunately Sir John was, as usual, a little too late with his homage. All the nice pickings of court favour and promotion had been snapped up before his arrival.

The coronation day, in the words of the venerable chronicler last quoted, was " a sore, ruggie and tempestuous day, with wind, snow and sleet, that " men greatlie marvelled thereat, making diverse interpretations what the " same might signifie." To Sir John Falstaff it might have been interpreted to signify the cold blasts of adversity, icy ingratitude, flowery visions blown into the air, fair prospects nipped in the bud, the tree of Hope torn up by the roots and lying prostrate !

The day, however, so inauspiciously commenced would seem to have cleared up, as upon the conclusion of the coronation ceremony (with the details whereof it is not the present writer's business to encumber his pages) the royal party proceeded on foot in solemn procession from the gateway of Westminster Abbey to Richard the Second's great hall, in the neighbouring palace. It is true that the royal party might have got wet in so doing—the umbrella not having been yet invented, and the cab-stand being an institution undreamt of even by the most Utopian imagination. But I am inclined to think that if Henry the Fifth's first public appearance as a crowned head had been made under circumstances so unfavourable to dignity as a pelting shower, some adverse chronicler would have taken care to mention the circumstance. If the newly-placed crown, for instance, had been blown off into the mud, or if the gartered leg of majesty had got over its ankle in a puddle of the period, depend upon it we should have heard of it. There were plenty of literary men present, who would not have failed to report such a circumstance. There was John Lydgate, the monk of Bury, for one, who had come to town expressly to superintend the rehearsal of a coronation anthem (composed, it was whispered, by the king himself), to which the worthy ecclesiastic had adapted words. John, as a faithful courtier and professional laureate, would infallibly have immortalised any such calamity in sympathetic verse. And we should most likely have had the subject treated from a facetious point of view, for the coronation guests of that day had

" A chiel amang them taking notes "

from North Britain; one James Stuart, in fact, a shrewd humorist, an excellent poet, and a man of genius generally, but who having made the mistake of coming into the world some five hundred years before his time, and wishing to force upon an independent Scottish nobility the glaring anachronism of an enlightened government in the fifteenth century, was very properly shown the error of his ways, and duly assassinated at midnight in his own chamber, according to the custom of that country and period. Altogether I prefer adhering to Mr. Cruikshank's pictorially recorded opinion of the weather on the occasion of Henry the Fifth's first emerging a crowned monarch from the portals of Edward the Confessor's venerable minster. The wish is father to the thought, I admit. If only for the sake of the fair spectators in the balcony, I must strive to believe that the day turned out fine. I cannot bear to think that those dainty creatures — many of whose effigies may doubtless be found, at this day, in the neighbouring cloisters, lying on their backs, with crossed hands and chipped noses (attributed, by the vergers of the abbey, as a matter of course, to the iconoclast malice of Oliver Cromwell)—should have had their hoods, kirtles, and day's pleasure spoiled by the "wind, snow, and sleete" of a "ruggie and tempestuous day." Depend upon it that, towards ten o'clock in the morning (the hour at which, according to the early habits of the period, the coronation ceremony would have come to a close), the sky began to clear up.

In a literal and physical sense only, be it understood. Metaphorically, as far as Sir John Falstaff was concerned, the sun was never destined to shine more; for the sun of poor old Jack's existence was Henry Plantagenet, fifth king of England by that name, and the face of that sun Jack Falstaff was never to see but once again. And then — oh, Nemesis, Parcæ, and all unkind heathen deities whatsoever! — with what clouds before it?

Clouds of coldness, of displeasure, of — yes, I will say it, and quite in earnest — of cruelty. Aye, and a yet more impenetrable obstruction to the desired rays than any such clouds — the presence of a powerful enemy! On the brief and only occasion of Sir John Falstaff being brought face to face with King Henry the Fifth (as a crowned monarch) Chief Justice Gascoigne was at His Majesty's elbow, the most favoured servant of the realm. Alas! poor Jack!

Let us particularise the scene.

Sir John Falstaff—with Master Shallow, his friend; Bardolph, his henchman, maître d'hotel, valet, and factotum; Pistol, his indefinite subaltern; and Robin, his page — reached the gates of Westminster Abbey just as the ringing of bells and the harmonious swelling of many hundred voices within the sacred edifice, almost drowned by the shouts of the populace outside, announced that the ceremony was at an end. Sir John had ridden post, his impatience scarcely allowing him to sleep during the whole of his three days' journey. He was untrimmed, draggled, jaded, and travel-stained. He was nervous, breathless, excited. I am not prepared to assert positively that he was quite sober; and, indeed, it may be slightly palliative to the conduct of Henry the Fifth, which I am about to describe in terms of the severest reprehension, that—for a newly-crowned monarch of doubtful antecedents, anxious to stand well with the more respectable portion of the community—to be hailed as a bosom friend, in the presence of kings, princes, and ambassadors, by a group composed of Messrs. Falstaff, Shallow, Bardolph, and Co., under the influence of a three days' journey, having been for the most part performed in bad weather, in the course of which frequent attempts had doubtless been made to replace the important necessity of sleep by recourse to refreshment of a widely different character,—would naturally be rather a trying business. However, let us to the facts.

Of course Sir John Falstaff had sufficient influence with the guards and retainers to force his way through barriers of every description. He was treated with negative respect on all sides; but he certainly did not meet with the enthusiastic reception he had anticipated. As he glanced anxiously round on the many familiar faces present, he noticed an expression of awkwardness and constraint upon each. Many old acquaintances averted their heads. Such as were bound to recognise the knight did so in terms of studied formality. Sir John began to feel the raw March atmosphere absolutely oppressive. He strove to crush his rising misgivings.

"Stand here, by me, Master Robert Shallow," he said, lugging that magistrate through the last layer of the king's Cheshire archers that stood between them and the royal pathway. "I will make the king do you grace. I will leer at him as he comes by, and do but mark the countenance that he will give me."

"Bless thy lungs, good knight!" said the valiant Pistol, who had already shown himself publicly in his ancient haunts, and, indeed, turned a pretty penny by the acceptance of peace-offerings from myrmidons of the law, his former enemies and oppressors.

"Come here, Pistol; stand behind me," said Sir John. Alack, how nervous he was getting! He twirled and plucked at the ends of his beard till he winced with pain. He gnawed his finger nails. He played the old gentleman's tattoo with his mud-stained boot on the steaming rushes beneath him. He twisted buttons off his *just-au-corps*. His breath was short, his under lip drooped, and his teeth chattered.

"Oh, if I had had time to have made new liveries, I would have bestowed the thousand pounds I borrowed of you!"

Master Shallow winced.   He, too, was nervous.

" But 'tis no matter; this poor show doth better ; this doth infer the zeal I had to see him."

" It doth so."   Master Shallow breathed his answer thickly.

" It shows my earnestness in affection."

" It doth so."

" My devotion."

" It doth, it doth, it doth."

(Heavens ! how Master Shallow must have twiddled with his chain or chewed at the cape of his riding hood as he repeated these words in rapid crescendo !)

" As it were, to ride day and night, and not to deliberate, not to remember, not to have patience to shift me."

" It is most certain."

" But to stand stained with travel and sweating with desire to see him ; thinking of nothing else ; putting all affairs else in oblivion, as if there were nothing else to be done but to see him."

" 'Tis *semper idem* for *absque hoc nihil est*," put in Pistol.   " 'Tis all in every part."

" 'Tis so, indeed."   Master Shallow gasped out these words, which were scarcely audible.   He was in a high state of trepidation, and it will be admitted that he had exactly one thousand reasons for feeling so.

The moments seemed hours.   Would the king never come?   Sir John almost dreaded that he should die with his eyes unblessed by the sight of his royal pupil and favourite, clad in the attributes of majesty.   His gaze was riveted on the cathedral door.   He was deaf to all sounds in his eager listening for one well-known footstep.   Pistol vainly attempted to enlist his sympathies by a narrative of the wrongs of the Fair Dorothea.   Sir John mechanically promised to deliver the captive princess from her oppressors, but his words scarcely conveyed a meaning.

The anthem swelled.   The shouts were resumed.   Officious retainers bustled forth to clear the way.   Sir John Falstaff's heart beat almost audibly. He felt sick and giddy as a dazzling vision burst upon his sight—round which all other objects on the scene, animate and inanimate, seemed whirling like weird shapes in a demon dance about a magic fire.   King Henry the Fifth, in all the pride and splendour of newly anointed majesty, stood before him !

I dare be bound Henry of Monmouth never more thoroughly merited Master Stowe's simple panegyric on his personal graces than at that moment. " This prince," says the worthy old Cockney, "exceeded the mean stature of men ; he was beautiful of visage, his neck long, bodye slender and leane, and his bones small ; nevertheless he was of marvellous great strength, and passing swift in running."

I have no doubt that His Majesty, on reaching the open air, would have been but too happy to exercise his skill in the latter accomplishment so as to avoid the compromising recognition of Sir John Falstaff and his friends, had circumstances permitted; but it was an ordeal not to be avoided.

"Save thy grace, King Hal! My royal Hal!" Sir John shouted at the top of his voice.

It is possible that Sir John Falstaff's muddy boots, drenched doublet, three days' linen and all, might have been tolerated on the score of gentle birth and past services. But there was no getting over the bodily presence of Bardolph, Pistol, and a dilapidated, draggle-tailed country justice from the wilds of Gloucestershire.

"The heavens thee guard and keep, most royal imp of fame!" was the salutation of Pistol.

"Save thee, my sweet boy!" added Falstaff.

Henry the Fifth was certainly a great man. The opportunity for exercising his "passing swiftness in running" failing him, he was fain to fall back upon his "marvellous great strength" of moral assurance, and appear to deny all knowledge of his former associates. He drew himself up to his full height, "exceeding the mean stature of men," and, turning to the illustrious dignitary at his side, said coldly —

"My Lord Chief Justice, speak to that vain man."

Which of course my Lord Chief Justice was only too eager to do, in his own chosen terms.

"Have you your wits? know you what 'tis you speak?" his lordship inquired, in his most withering, commit-you-three-months-for-contempt-of-court tones.

"My king! my Jove!" Falstaff had eyes and ears for the monarch alone. "I speak to thee, my heart."

It was no easy matter "to cut" Sir John Falstaff. He would make himself heard ; and nature had provided him with the amplest resources for making himself seen. The future conqueror of Agincourt was for a moment nonplussed. But, with characteristic promptness, he rapidly decided on the part he should play. Taking Sir John's last greeting as his cue to speak, he gave utterance to one of the most remarkable royal speeches on record. The only assumed verbatim report of this oration extant is from the pen of Shakspeare, by whom it was, doubtless, slightly modified, as to verbal construction, in obedience to the rules of versification usually observed by

T 4

writers of his school and epoch.   But there is no reason to believe that any undue advantage of the reporter's prescriptive licence to correct, harmonise, and embellish, was taken on the occasion.   That the substance of the speech was as follows we have the amplest corroborative evidence in the pages of various contemporary historians :—

> " I know thee not, old man !   Fall to thy prayers.
> How ill white hairs become a fool and jester !
> I have long dreamed of such a kind of man,
> So surfeit swell'd, so old, and so profane ;
> But, being awake, I do despise my dream.
> Make less thy body, hence, and more thy grace ;
> Leave gormandising ; know the grave doth gape
> For thee thrice wider than for other men."

As one entertaining an excusable professional jealousy on behalf of the much-maligned and decidedly unprofitable calling of " fool and jester "— (which I was so injudicious as to take up with, very early in life, and have already an "ill-becoming" sprinkling of premature "white hairs" amongst my black ones, to show as a natural consequence of that error) — I dwell with malicious pleasure on the fact that, at this juncture of his homily, his no longer jocular majesty, Henry the Fifth, was suddenly "pulled up" by a reminder, on the countenance of his senior whom he had presumed to lecture, that he, the king, had unconsciously slipped back into his old habits, and, while reprimanding levity, had committed himself by making a joke upon Falstaff's bulk, as in the jolly old days of the Boar's Head fraternisation.   In the words of an able commentator upon this historical passage : — " He saw the rising smile and smothered retort upon Falstaff's lip, and he checks him with — ' Reply not to me with a fool-born jest.' "

The very thing he was afraid of !   He had rashly challenged old Jack with the knight's own weapons, and was fain to plead benefit of royalty to sneak out of the combat in which he knew he must be worsted.   To impose silence on his adversary was his only chance.

He continued : —

> " Presume not that I am the thing I was :
> For Heaven doth know, so shall the world perceive,
> That I have turn'd away my former self,
> So will I those that kept me company.
> When thou dost hear I am as I have been,
> Approach me ; and thou shalt be as thou wast,
> The tutor and the feeder of my riots ;
> Till then, I banish thee on pain of death,
> As I have done the rest of my misleaders,
> *Not to come near our person by ten mile.*
> For competence of life I will allow you,
> That lack of means enforce you not to evil ;
> And as we hear you do reform yourselves,
> We will, according to your strength and qualities,

Drawn & Etched by George Cruikshank

Published by Mssrs Longman & Co.

Sir John Falstaff - on a visit, to his Friend Page, at Windsor —
Merry Wives of Windsor Act 1st Scene 1st —

Give you advancement.—Be it your charge, my lord,
To see perform'd the tenor of our word.
Get on."

And then King Henry the Fifth, with his crown on, followed by his brothers, cousins, nobles, ambassadors, clergy, mace-bearers, sword-bearers, pages, retainers, and what not—by no means forgetting James the First, poet and King of Scotland (who, I am sure, cast a glance of sympathy at the paralysed figure of Sir John Falstaff, kneeling aghast and open-mouthed among the damp rushes of the courtyard), and Master John Lydgate, the laureate monk of Bury (who also, I am willing to believe, was rather distressed at the turn things had unfortunately taken)—took the arm of the triumphant Lord Chief Justice Gascoigne, and proceeded to dinner in the hall of Richard the Second, as though such a person as John Falstaff had never had existence.

Sir John, after a moment's stupefaction, started to his feet. He pressed his hand over his burning eyeballs. A convulsive shudder passed through his entire system; and one brief sob escaped him. It was over. Sir John relieved his oppressed lungs of a long-pent-up breath; wiped his smoking forehead, and looked composedly at Justice Shallow. Justice Shallow looked at Sir John Falstaff. Not composedly though, by any means.

"Master Shallow, I owe you a thousand pounds," said Sir John Falstaff. It was a fact at all events, and, therefore, worthy of mention.

"Ay, marry Sir John," the justice faltered, "which I beseech you to let me have home with me."

"That can hardly be, Master Shallow," was the reply. "Do not you grieve at this; I shall be sent for in private to him! Look you, he must seem thus to the world. Fear not your advancement; I will be the man yet that shall make you great."

"I cannot well perceive how, unless"—imminent pecuniary danger had lent the worthy justice unwonted smartness,—"you should give me your doublet and stuff me out with straw. I beseech you, good Sir John, let me have five hundred of my thousand."

"Sir, I will be as good as my word: this that you heard was but a colour."

"A colour, I fear, that you will die in, Sir John."

"Fear no colours; go with me to dinner. Come, Lieutenant Pistol*; come, Bardolph; I shall be sent for to-night."

Sir John Falstaff had not to wait until nightfall ere he was sent for. Scarcely had he spoken when the Lord Chief Justice Gascoigne, accompanied

---

* A spontaneous promotion of the worthy Ancient, as it would seem, upon the brevet principle.

by Prince John of Lancaster (whose grudge against our knight, for the Gualtree affair, was, if possible, stronger than that of the justice himself), reappeared on the scene with a posse of constables. These men had even quitted a royal dinner table for the gratification of private vengeance. Could the force of malignity go further?

The lord chief justice, not trusting himself to an accusation which might have led to discussion, wherein he would inevitably have been discomfited, ordered Sir John Falstaff and his companions to be conveyed to the Fleet Prison!

Sir John naturally attempted to protest against a persecution so unprecedented.

" My lord, my lord, —— "

" I cannot now speak," said the chief justice. " I will hear you soon. Take them away."

And they *were* taken away — Bardolph, Pistol, and poor little Robin included — aye, and even Master Robert Shallow, of Gloucestershire, in the commission of the peace, *custos rotulorum*, whose only offence was one against the laws of ordinary human judgment; to wit, that he had lent Sir John Falstaff the sum of one thousand pounds under the impression that he would one day get it back again.

Now I should be very much obliged to any individual learned in the antiquities of English law, who will inform me by what then existing statute Sir John Falstaff, with his friend and retainers, were committed to the Fleet Prison? If, after all I have been at the pains of writing in the course of this publication, — since the acknowledged failure of my attempt to make out a case in favour of the Lord Chief Justice Gascoigne — there should remain any apologists for the character and conduct of that eminent justiciary, I should also feel thankful to them if they can inform me how they intend reconciling the behaviour of their *protégé*, on this occasion, with his hitherto established reputation as an upright judge. With regard to Prince John of Lancaster, afterwards Duke of Bedford, I trouble myself but little. History can have left him no friends. No amount of apologetic whitewash would serve to frost over the thick coating of smut from the funeral pyre of Joan of Arc, by which his memory must stand blackened to all eternity.

Apropos des bottes. I am happy to be able to convict Henry the Fifth in a glaring falsehood. He did *not* banish, " on pain of death," the whole of his early associates in debauchery and misdemeanour, nor forbid them all " to come near his person by ten mile." Master Edward Poins, a discreet, time-serving young gentleman, continued in the enjoyment of court favour, and received the dignity of knighthood on the very day of his majesty's coronation.

Drawn & Etched by George Cruikshank

Pub.d by Maj.rs Longman & C.o London

Sir John Falstaff in the Buck-basket — Merry Wives of Windsor. Act 3.rd Scene 3.rd

BOOK THE FIFTH.

1413—1415.

I.

THE accession of Henry the Fifth to the throne of England was not marked by such lavish and prolonged rejoicings as the people of that time were accustomed to on similar occasions. Things, indeed, seem to have been done on rather a niggardly and puritanical scale. For this there were doubtless many sufficient reasons. The royal treasury was impoverished. The nation had not been engaged in a civil war for several months, and the public mind was getting impatient for the recurrence of that indispensable necessary of national life—which indeed was kindly furnished them by certain patriots who (for lack of better excuse) pretended that King Richard the Second was still alive and a claimant to the throne—a contingency which the statesmanlike policy of the late King Henry had most effectually guarded against. Moreover the newly crowned monarch, having so publicly pledged himself to measures of reform, and the adoption of business-like habits, was in common consistency bound to show signs of moral amendment by setting about the invasion of a foreign country, and torturing to death certain dangerous persons who had ventured to differ with him in religious opinions. The body of Richard the Second had to be exhumed and exhibited for public inspection. The conquest of France had to be undertaken. The exacting spirit of the times, moreover, required that a reward of 337*l.* 10*s.* should be offered by the crown for the apprehension of Sir John Oldcastle *, the supposed leader of a Protestant conspiracy, — a circumstance in itself sufficient, (considering that the accused might have been caught and the reward claimed,) in the then existing state of the exchequer, to indispose the monarch for any

---

* Oldcastle was good enough to keep out of the way, in return for which considerate behaviour he was let off with a "grand cursing at St. Paul's Cross." He was captured four years later, and "roasted to death by a fire kindled under him" at Smithfield—the crown being then in better circumstances and able to defray the expenses of his prosecution.

exuberance of mirth or expenditure. But unquestionably the arch reason why the coronation festivities should have gone off flatly and without brilliancy or *éclat* was the absence from court of the man whose gifts and antecedents would naturally have pointed him out as the *arbiter elegantiarum* for the occasion. The master of the revels — which did not take place — was at the time of their non-occurrence a languishing captive, on an illegal warrant, in the Fleet Prison. The idea of any merriment in the court of Henry the Fifth without the assistance of Sir John Falstaff is simply preposterous. But Henry the Fifth had forsworn merriment and Falstaff together, and taken up with invasion and Smithfield bonfires in their stead. The only remarkable public boons consequent upon the coronation were a wholesale creation of Knights of the Bath — from participation in which honour Sir John Falstaff was of course excluded — and a general jail delivery, whereof, equally as a matter of course, our knight took the most prompt and summary advantage. Sir John and his companions were liberated by royal amnesty after a confinement of twenty-four hours.

But of what use was the so-called liberty to Sir John Falstaff? It was, after all, but the liberty which you grant to a gudgeon when you unhook him from the end of your fishing line and toss him contemptuously into the nearest corn-field. Was not Sir John an exile from the court? Had not the idol of his misplaced affections, "his king, his Jove," forbidden him admission to the Olympian circle, where nectar and ambrosia were alone to be found? Had not Henry the Fifth commanded him

"Not to come near our person by ten mile?"

He had indeed! And that cruel radius was a rigid bar at the end of which Sir John was ruthlessly chained ten miles aloof from all that was life, and warmth, and breath to him. It was the very mockery of mercy. It was like saying to a man, "I will only keep your mouth and nostrils ten inches below the surface of the water, but above that altitude you shall never rise." Mighty like drowning after all!

The present book, the last and saddest of our history! will be, of necessity, a short one. The public career of Sir John Falstaff may be said to have terminated with the catastrophe recorded in the last chapter. The remaining months of his existence he passed in retirement — would I could add in prosperity! — as a private gentleman. There is a completeness and consistency in the life of this remarkable man almost without parallel in history. He was born in difficulties; he lived sixty-three years in embarrassed circumstances; and died in hot water. And yet throughout the whole of this trying pilgrimage Sir John was never once tempted to depart from his guiding prin-

Drawn & Etched by George Cruikshank

Pub.d by Me.s.r.s Longman &c.o Paternoster Row.

Sir John Falstaff, thrown into the muddy ditch close by the Thames side — Merry Wives of Windsor — Act 3rd

ciples. What were Sir John Falstaff's guiding principles ? the inconsiderate reader may ask,—yielding to the popularly received opinion that the knight never had any, than which a greater mistake can scarcely be imagined. Who shall accuse of irregularity a man who, for upwards of three-score years, based his every act upon the rigid observance of two rules of life ? These were, firstly, never to let his business interfere with his pleasure ; secondly, on no occasion to suffer his income to exceed his expenditure ; principles which, it will be admitted, Sir John adhered to in the teeth of no common or unfrequent temptations to their abandonment. It must not be supposed that Sir John Falstaff for a moment believed that King Henry the Fifth intended to fulfil his promise of allowing his banished associates a sufficiency for " competence of life ; " still less that his majesty, among his other "startling effects " of reformation, meditated keeping his word upon so delicate a matter. There is reason to believe that a nominal pension of three hundred pounds a year was conferred upon our knight, but not the slightest to suppose that any measures were ever thought of for paying as much as the first quarterly instalment. Henry the Fifth had at least profited by Falstaff's training in this respect, that he managed through life to make his liabilities exceed his resources, and contrived to secure an immense deal of *éclat* and enjoyment without troubling himself to pay for it. He endowed his beautiful young wife, Katherine of Valois, out of the private fortune of his step-mother (whom he had previously incarcerated in Pevensey Castle on a charge of witchcraft). The whole of the young queen's household, with numerous pensioners of her family, were suffered to help themselves out of the same convenient fund. In the year of his marriage Henry drew upon the treasury of the captive dowager for a hundred marks, which he graciously presented to the Abbess of Sion. Soon afterwards he provided for the maintenance of his dearly beloved cousin *Dame Jake*** (otherwise the Princess Jaqueline of Hainault) by the moderate allowance of a hundred pounds a month, also to be paid from the "profits " of the dower of Joanna, late Queen of England. The historic parallel to these liberal disbursements suggested by Sir John Falstaff paying Bardolph arrears of wages, liquidating tavern scores for Ancient Pistol, and bestowing money on new liveries for little Robin (with perhaps a gallant souvenir for old Mistress Ursula, and some pretty toys for the young Whittingtons) out of the unfortunate Master Shallow's thousand pounds, is most striking. A few years later we find Sir William Bardolf, lieutenant-governor of Calais, complaining bitterly in a letter to the king, that his garrison had only received 500*l.* in the two last years, himself having had to make up the deficiency requisite for their

---

* Rymer's Fœdera, vol. x. p. 134.

maintenance.   There is still extant a letter, apparently written by a public scrivener of the time, in the name of one Francis, a drawer at the " Old Boar's Head " tavern, addressed to Sir John Falstaff, at the sign of " 𝔜𝔢 𝔐𝔞𝔨𝔢𝔡 𝔏𝔞𝔡𝔶𝔢 𝔬𝔫 𝔥𝔬𝔯𝔰𝔢𝔟𝔞𝔠𝔨," at Coventry, praying the knight to transmit by carrier the sum of forty-eight marks seven shillings and three-farthings, the price of lodging and entertainment afforded to Corporal Nym and others of " the worshipful knight his following," which the said drawer asserts he has been compelled by his mistress* to pay out of his own earnings.   History delights in these startling coincidences !

With such pressing claims upon his purse (or rather upon the purses of other people at his disposal), as those above alluded to, it would have been unreasonable to suppose that the king would put himself — or even any one else — out of the way to meet his pecuniary engagements with a disgraced favourite.   Sir John Falstaff at once understood that he had little to hope from the royal bounty or good faith.   With his usual philosophy he deter-mined to make the best of his position.   Having nothing to live on but the king's promise he determined to live upon that — and appears to have suc-ceeded in doing so pretty comfortably.   For we find him in the autumn of 1414, with a goodly retinue of followers and a stud of horses, " sitting at ten pounds a week " at the Garter Inn, Windsor — a liberal scale of accom-modation for which Sir John's assumed " expectations " were doubtless accepted as permanent security.

Much idle dissertation has been wasted in Sir John Falstaff's probable motives for making Windsor his residence at this juncture of his career. The motives live on the surface.   The court was in London.   The atmosphere of a kingly residence was, as has been shown, indispensable to Sir John Falstaff.   The neighbourhood of Windsor Castle was the most convenient locality of that description — beyond the prescribed limits of his banishment from the royal person.   Moreover, your true knight errant must be ever wandering in search of new fields for adventure.   The resources of Oxford, Coventry, and other country districts our knight had doubtless long since exhausted.   Windsor was virgin soil to him.   Here he was unknown, and — as we have seen — trusted.

There was an additional inducement for Sir John to visit Windsor.   It must not be supposed that he had relinquished all hope of restoration to court favour — what deposed favourite ever did ?   To the end of his days he was

---

* Fits of splenetic economy of this description were by no means of unfrequent occurrence with good Mrs. Quickly.   For the original of the document here alluded to, (the discovery of any answer to which has hitherto baffled the researches of antiquarians,) *vide* the Potter MSS. vol. viii. p. 397a.

Drawn & Etched by George Cruikshank

Pub⁴ by Mess⁵ Longman, &c. Paternoster Row

Sir John Falstaff, disguised as "Mother Prat," cudgelled and driven out by M⁵ Ford.

— Merry Wives of Windsor. Act 4. Scene 2ⁿᵈ —

constantly occupied in diplomatic schemes for the recovery of his forfeited position. He left no stone unturned in the fruitless endeavour to regain the royal ear. He deluged his courtly acquaintances with unavailing letters on the subject. He intrigued with secretaries, grooms-in-waiting, pages, lacqueys, and even the lords of the bedchamber and equerries. I am afraid he was rapidly becoming a nuisance.

It is to be regretted that the preserved fragments of the Falstaff correspondence, in connection with this most interesting phase of our knight's fortunes, are confined to two specimens.* These, however, consisting of a letter and its answer, it would be difficult to estimate at their adequate value. Their transference to these pages will sufficiently explain the motive for Sir John's visit to Windsor last alluded to.

To the Right (or Wrong) Worshipful Sir Edward Poins, Knight of the Bath and Garter, Comptroller of the Staircases, Groom of the Laundry, &c. &c., dwelling at Windsor Castle, be this delivered.

"NED, and be hanged in thine own garter or drowned in thine own bath, according as thou needest most trussing or washing.

"They told me in London thou hadst grown great at Windsor, and I hastened hither post to witness the marvel with mine own eyes—mistrusting other testimony. Lo, I am convinced! I saw thee this morning strutting on Wykeham's Tower—marshalling the workmen with thy wand of office, and noted that thou hadst become fat. At length, then, I may greet thee as an equal—the more, as it would seem I myself have so dwindled to thy former proportions that thou didst not know me ; but when I sought to catch thine eye, twirledst thy chain and soughtest quarrel with a knave who was miscarrying a hod of mortar. Since, then, thou art so puffed up and I so crushed and flattened—what should be the difference between us ? If there be any, I pri'thee, lessen it. If at length thou hast grown to outweigh me, slice thyself down and throw me the parings. I but claim to compound a debt. I will cry quits for the wit I have lent thee if thou wilt give me the supernbundance of favour and dignity which in truth thou seemest still somewhat too spindle-shanked of spirit to carry with grace. Nay, I will throw thee a good thing into the bargain. Thou lackest humility—a commodity whereof more than I know what to do with hath been of late forced upon me. Thou shalt have it all.

"Indite me to dinner at the Castle by ten o'clock to-morrow. Till then I will be tongue-tied. If thou failest to send for me and to prove over many a pottle-pot that thou hast still the memory of old times and that thou hast but assumed the guise of a strutting feathered jackdaw as formerly thou didst that of a very owl of wisdom — on grounds of policy to be forgiven — then will I make it known by the town-crier of Windsor what an ass thou really art and ever will be. 'Tis a secret worth hushing and known to none better than thine, forgivingly,

"JOHN FALSTAFF.

" [In sober earnest, dear Ned, thou mayest serve me near him thou wottest of. I pri' thee forget not old friends and comrades. Thou couldst not know me this morning—for reasons I guess at. But see me and it shall bring thee to no harm. J. F.]

"At the Garter Inn, Friday, 1414. 2. H. V."

---

* In the Strongate Collection.

ANSWER TO THE FOREGOING.

To Sir John Falstaff, Knight, be this delivered.

"Sir Edward Poins grieves that his many duties as a humble but diligent servant of King Henry (whom Heaven preserve!) may not permit him to enjoy the pleasure of Sir John Falstaff's company at Windsor Castle, whereof his Most Gracious Majesty hath been pleased to appoint Sir Edward for a time custodian. It is not, however, in Sir Edward's nature to refuse a service to any one. If Sir John Falstaff is anxious for himself or friends to obtain the privilege of viewing the improvements in progress as well as the tapestries and pictures of the palace, Sir Edward will give instructions to the wardens and porters of the building to admit Sir John and friends to the same (within the hours allotted to the admission of the public) with the assurance that Sir John and friends will be treated with right due courtesy.

"P.S. It is entreated that no largesse or drink money shall be given to any of the Castle servitors — the same subjecting such servitors to immediate dismissal."

That Sir Edward Poins — always a faithful imitator, to the best of his ability, of King Henry the Fifth — should have thus behaved towards his early friend and patron will surprise no student of human nature. This coolness and ingratitude, however, of a supposed friend had no other effect than to induce Sir John Falstaff during his residence in the neighbourhood to choose his associates exclusively from the middle classes — the lesser landowners, clergy, and even small traders of extra-palatial Windsor. In such unassuming society Sir John passed his time for the most part agreeably enough, and not altogether unprofitably — though with many serious drawbacks to his comfort, dignity, and finances.

On the whole, I confess, I feel no temptation whatever to expatiate upon this portion of my hero's rapidly closing career. The Windsor adventures of Sir John Falstaff, forming as they do the basis of one of the most admirably faithful and picturesque of Shakspeare's historical studies, present, after all, but an exceptional and, in my opinion, most painful episode in the knight's history. They show us the harrowing spectacle of a great man in his decline. Many thoughtless commentators have pronounced the portrait of Sir John Falstaff, as drawn in the "Merry Wives of Windsor," to be wanting in verisimilitude, and have therefore called its authenticity into question. No discerning mind can mistake the likeness. It is the same man whom we have so often seen drawn by the same master-hand under more favourable circumstances — but how changed, how fallen! The features are all unmistakeably there; but the expression, bearing, and complexion, how sadly deteriorated! Age, disappointment, and suffering have done their work. Sir John can no longer hold his ground against the most contemptible adversary. The victor is vanquished — the biter bitten. The more than match for the keen-witted Harry Monmouth — the conqueror of Gascoigne and the terror of Poins — becomes the easy dupe of a couple of practical-

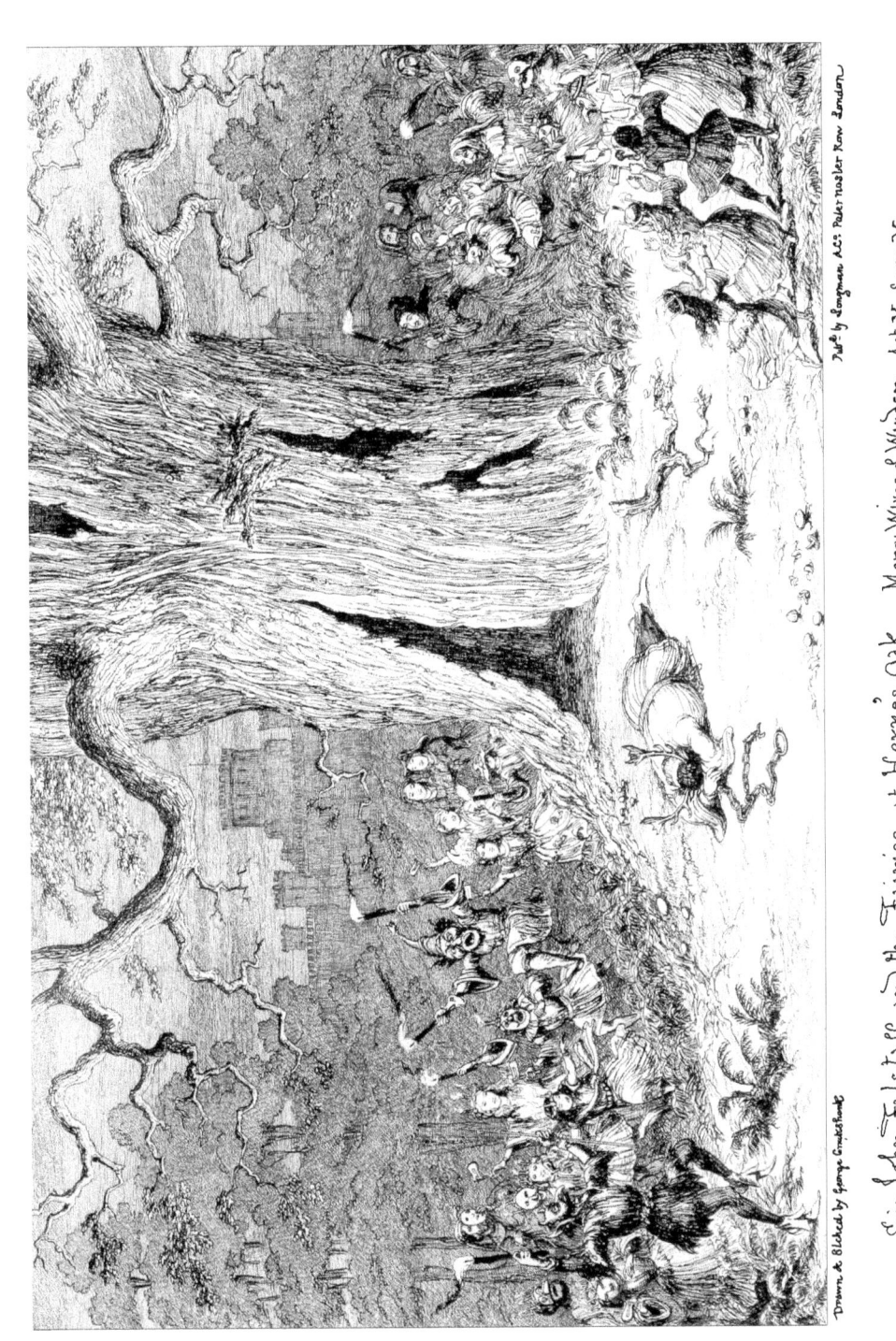

Drawn & Etched by George Cruikshank

Pub^d by Longman &C^o: Pater noster Row London

Sir John Falstaff and the Fairies, at Herne's Oak. Merry Wives of Windsor. Act V. Scene V.

joking Berkshire housewives. It is distressing to contemplate a man —
whom we have seen cross swords with Douglas; capture Colevile of the
Grange; and who, after all (as hath been demonstrated), there is strong
reason to believe, was the actual slayer of the terrible Henry Percy — sunk
so low as to receive without resentment a sound cudgelling administered, in
a fit of insensate jealousy, by a *bourgeois* inhabitant of Peascod Street,
Windsor — who, for aught I can discover to the contrary, may have been a
retired grocer.* It may be urged that Sir John Falstaff, in justice to his
knightly standing, could not challenge an ignoble curmudgeon like Ford to
mortal combat; and that he acted becomingly in preferring the more appropriate vengeance of keeping that citizen's money — intrusted to him for an
avowedly immoral purpose. This was all very well in its way, but did not
wipe out the original outrage. That shameful business of the buck-basket,
also, was an indignity to which Sir John in the heyday of his powers could
never have submitted. " Men of all sorts take a pride to gird at him " with
a vengeance, at this time, and the meanest are permitted to do so with
impunity. His very retainers turn against him (always excepting the
faithful Bardolph, who relieves his master, when under the pressure of
pecuniary difficulties, of the cost of his maintenance, by turning tapster and
waiting on the knight at another person's expense). He is even braved by
Pistol; and that " drawling, affecting rogue," Nym, refuses to carry his
messages. He is cajoled, hoaxed, bamboozled. He suffers himself to be
" made an ass " in Windsor Park, where he exposes himself in a tom-fool
disguise, and gets pinched by all the charity boys and girls in the parish,
believing them to be avenging fairies. He is bound to admit that his wit has
been " made a Jack a Lent of." A Cambrian parson, even, dares to laugh at
him; and he is " not able to answer the Welsh flannel." It is a sad business.

I repeat that I have no heart to dwell upon these painful details. Shakspeare has not scrupled to particularise them, and the curious are referred to
his able but pitiless pages. My good friend George Cruikshank also — an
amiable man in the social relations of life, but who when there is a stern
truth to be recorded pictorially, has no more feeling than the sun peering
through a photographic lens — has added his testimony to the principal
features of the case. Let *my* feelings be spared — for I sympathise with
poor Sir Jack, and, with all his faults, love him.

There is this excuse to be urged for Sir John Falstaff's submitting to all
kinds of temporary inconvenience and degradation at the hands of the contemptible citizens of Windsor. His mind was occupied with more exalted

* For the events here referred to, see the *Merry Wives of Windsor.*

subjects. He still contemplated the possibility of his restoration to Court favour. He was sixty-three, it is true, and prematurely broken in constitution. But a courtier and statesman must be very old and shaken indeed to renounce his hopes of power and advancement. Sir John watched his opportunity, and was willing to abide his time. *You* will be willing to abide your time, reader, at the age of a hundred (Heaven send you may live to it!) and never suspect for a moment that your "time" will be out in the early part of next autumn.

Sir John's opportunity (as he imagined) at length arrived. King Henry the Fifth prepared for his memorable invasion of France, by demanding, from the French king, the hand of the Princess Katherine, and a concession of territory sufficiently unreasonable to ensure the refusal desired by the English crown. The Dauphin Louis answered the application by his memorable present of a cask of tennis balls, which he assured King Henry "were fitter playthings for him, according to his former course of life, than the provinces demanded."* The British cabinet was nonplussed, there being nobody in office capable of replying to a joke. This was Sir John Falstaff's opportunity.

Sir John, who had, of course, his agents posted about the Court, heard of the dilemma. He despatched the following private note to His Majesty, having securely arranged for its certain delivery into the royal hands: —

𝕬 timely 𝖂ord to the 𝕶ing from one perchance thought dead.†

"KING HAL: thou hast forgotten me, but not I thee. Thou wilt not relieve me from my difficulty. Lo! I relieve thee of thine.

"Write back to the French fellow, thus: —

"'These balls shall be struck back with such a *racket* as shall force open Paris gates.'

"The thought is thine, for I give it to thee. Pay me for it by remembrance that I still live and can bear armour, or not, as thou listest.

"JOHN FALSTAFF.

"NOTE.—Observe well the clench upon *racket*‡, which meaneth both hurly-burly noise and tennis bat.

"*At the Garter, Windsor,*
"30 *March,* 1415, 3 *H. V.*"

In the course of a few days Sir John learnt that his witticism (unacknowledged) had been made use of as a rejoinder to the insolent message of the dauphin. He accepted this as a recognition of renewed friendly dispositions towards him on the king's part. He hastily raised such funds as his

---

* *Hollinshed. Vide* also *White Kennet's History;* and an inedited MS. in the British Museum, first published in Sir H. Nicolas's *History of the Battle of Agincourt.*
† In the Potter MSS.
‡ Caxton has recorded this pun.

Drawn & Etched by George Cruikshank

Pub.d by Longman & Comp.y London

Sir John Falstaff discovering that Mrs Ford, and Mrs Page...have been making a fool of him. !!!!

— Merry Wives of Windsor – Act V. Scene V.

powers of persuasion could induce his Windsor acquaintances to supply him with, and struck his tent. In defiance of the royal edict he presented himself at the Court of Westminster in the thick of the active preparations for the coming French campaign and solicite a command.

<hr>

II.

THE END OF THE LIFE OF SIR JOHN FALSTAFF.

"The king has killed his heart, good husband, come home presently."

The speaker was Mrs. Pistol, late Quickly. Her husband was disputing about nothing particular with Corporal Nym. The heart that had been killed by the king (dear Mrs. Quickly! she always spoke truly upon vital questions) was that of Sir John Falstaff. He had presented himself, clad in all the panoply of war, at the palace of Westminster, just as the galleys for the French invasion were getting under weigh. The king had refused him an audience. The Lord Chief Justice Gascoigne, acting ostensibly under the directions of the Dowager Queen Regent Joanna, had threatened him with constables. Sir John came home to his old quarters, the Old Boar's Head in Eastcheap — to die!

And Sir John Falstaff died on the 5th of August, 1415, at the Old Boar's Head Tavern, Eastcheap. His eyes were closed by poor Dame Quickly, and the only mourners round his death bed were the blackguards whom he had fed, and who were humanised and softened by his death. Pistol and Nym forgot their quarrel about nothing, sheathed their unmeaning swords and glared blood-shot condolence one at the other. Bardolph had come up from Windsor, resigning his tapstership to attend on the master whom he had loved and served consistently — long ere he knew how to speak. Our rubicund friend never acquired the art of speech to anything like perfection; but when he learnt that Falstaff was dead he somehow managed to give utterance to a poem.

"Would I were with him, wheresom'er he is, either in heaven, or in hell!"

I cannot describe Sir John Falstaff's death half as well as it has been described by Mrs. Quickly. Take her words:—

"He's in Arthur's bosom, if ever man went to Arthur's bosom. 'A made a finer end, and went away, an it had been any christom child; 'a parted even just between twelve and one, e'en at turning of the tide: for after I saw him fumble with the sheets, and play with the flowers, and smile upon his fingers' ends, I knew there was but one way; for his nose was as sharp as a pen, and 'a babbled of green fields. How now, Sir John? quoth I: what, man! be of good cheer. So 'a cried out, God, God, God! three or four times: now I, to comfort him, bid him, 'a should not think of God; I hoped, there was no need to trouble himself with any such thoughts yet: so 'a bade me lay more clothes on his feet: I put my hand into the bed, and felt them, and they were as cold as any stone; then I felt to his knees, and so upward, and upward, and all was as cold as any stone."

I will not comment upon this. I bow my head as one at a dear friend's funeral and hold my tongue — loving and thanking those whom I hear weeping and sobbing around me.

Sir John Falstaff was buried in the church of St. Michael Paternoster in the Royal, at the expense of Sir Richard Whittington, founder of that edifice, and Sir John's faithful friend throughout his eventful life — more than ever towards its close. It is recorded that Sir Richard wept bitterly the loss of his ever dear but often estranged friend, and was given to chide severely those who spoke slightingly of Sir John Falstaff's memory — saying that none knew Sir John Falstaff but himself; and that the waste of such a heart and brain as Sir John's to humanity was a loss deplorable. All who had been kind or faithful to Sir John in his lifetime were well cared for by Sir Richard. He subsidised Bardolph, Nym, and Pistol. But it was destined they should not prosper. They were bound for the French wars. They wasted Sir Richard's bounty before starting. Nym and Bardolph were hanged for the pettiest larceny on the field of Agincourt. Heaven knows what became of Pistol, and Earth does not care.

Sir Richard erected a simple tomb over the remains of Sir John Falstaff in the crypt of St. Michael Paternoster. King Henry the Fifth, on his return from France, in a remorseful fit, took his fair bride to see his old friend's last resting-place. It is whispered that he left the church with reddened eyes. It is certain that he caused to be inlaid, at his own expense, on the marble tomb, the following inscription in brass:—

"𝔚e could habe better spared a better 𝔐an."

This might have been seen up to the year 1666, when the church of St. Michael Paternoster was burnt to the ground — and the last material traces of Sir John Falstaff's existence faded from the memory of man, even as fades the recollection of having read a foolish book.

FINIS.

LONDON: PRINTED BY SPOTTISWOODE AND CO., NEW-STREET SQUARE.

Drawn & Etched by George Cruikshank.

Pub.d by Messrs Longman & Co London.

The last Scene, in the life of S.r John Falstaff — Henry V. Act 2.d Scene 2.d

For EU product safety concerns, contact us at Calle de José Abascal, 56–1°,
28003 Madrid, Spain or eugpsr@cambridge.org.

www.ingramcontent.com/pod-product-compliance
Ingram Content Group UK Ltd.
Pitfield, Milton Keynes, MK11 3LW, UK
UKHW051009240426
470322UK00018B/570